D1175206

The Golden Treasury of Puritan Quotations

199 2359

NCMC
Ref
PN
6084
.R3
G6

The Golden Treasury of Puritan Quotations

*Compiled
By*

I. D. E. Thomas

MOODY PRESS
CHICAGO

© 1975 by

THE MOODY BIBLE INSTITUTE
OF CHICAGO

ISBN: 0-8024-3080-5

Printed in the United States of America

Books may preach when the author cannot, when the author may not, when the author dares not, yea, and which is more, when the author is not.

THOMAS BROOKS

ACKNOWLEDGMENTS

It is a privilege to express my indebtedness to many people who, at different times and in different places, have introduced me to some of the less-known and unsung Puritan authors. In particular I would mention Mr. Ian Murray of the Banner of Truth Trust, Edinburgh; Mr. Micklewright of the Evangelical Library, London; Mr. Palmer G. Brown of the Los Angeles County Library, Los Angeles; and Dr. Leighton H. James, Swansea. And, for first igniting this interest, I remain a debtor to Dr. Martyn Lloyd-Jones, who by his preaching and lecturing, has made a whole generation of preachers aware of their great Puritan heritage. My gratitude I extend also to my secretary, Miss Carolyn Bobango, for her painstaking typing of the manuscript, and to Mr. Leslie H. Stobbe of Moody Press for his courteous cooperation and counsel throughout the various processes of publication.

PREFACE

It is probably true that the vast majority of Christian people have never read a single book of Puritan literature, apart from *Pilgim's Progress*, by John Bunyan. Of these people, many would not be aware that a Puritan literature existed.

One of the purposes of this book is to introduce this incomparable library, and to acquaint the Christian believer with the great Puritan authors. These divines of the sixteenth and seventeenth centuries were men of one consuming passion: the communication of God's Word to man. It is true that in the process of time their Puritanism evolved into political action, and Cromwell became Lord Protector of England. But the Puritans themselves were first and foremost men of religion. Just as it has been said of modern democracy that it is the child of the Reformation rather than of the Reformers, the same could be said of the political revolution of the 1650's—it was more the child of Puritanism than of the Puritans.

For most people, the image of the Puritan is not an attractive one. He has been cast as a sort of rigid, sour, dour kill-joy. This, however, is a one-sided judgment, and in many instances, a caricature. The tendency of modern, specialized research is to rehabilitate the Puritan, and to underscore the nobler traits of his makeup. Foremost among these would be the massive intellectual capacity of the Puritan, equalled only by the profundity of his spiritual comprehension. No men ever were more conversant with the whole sweep of biblical revelation, or more specialized in the probing and discerning of spiritual behavior. As seers of Divine truth, and as surgeons of human souls, the Puritans remain peerless.

These men brought to their work a manliness and a thoroughness that one meets all too rarely in current evangelical theology. They were men of the stamp of Samuel Rutherford, who

7

in order to spend his time in prayer and study, would commonly rise about three in the morning. Or John Preston, who was so indulgent in study that he begrudged the very hours he had to sleep! To counteract this, "he would let the bed clothes hang down, that in the night they might fall off, and so the cold awaken him."

During the hundred years or so of Puritanism in England, it is not always easy to trace a common, consistent tradition. Often, and at many points, their beliefs overlapped with those of their antagonists. However, there were some distinctives that characterized the Puritan movement and spirit throughout this whole period. Foremost among these were:

1. A thorough adherence to Calvinistic theology, underscoring the absolute sovereignty of Almighty God;
2. A recognition of the supreme authority of Scripture;
3. A passionate belief in the importance of preaching as a means of grace;
4. An overwhelming desire for church purity;
5. A strict and stringent morality;
6. A fervent advocacy of civil liberty.

From the almost inexhaustible placer of Puritan literature I have been able to retrieve some rare, spiritual nuggets, and here in this book they are on display. Needless to say, many more such nuggets await the discovery of future miners.

The nuggets have been chosen from a variety of deposits; and for a variety of reasons:

1. Their brevity: geared to a generation that reads very little, and often that little "on the run."
2. Their proverbial qualities: shortness, sense, and salt!
3. Their intrinsic value: although lifted from their native habitat, they possess a value of their own. They embody truths that can stand by themselves, quite apart from the particular context in which originally found.
4. Their thought-provoking quality: one "teasing" phrase may sometimes trigger thought into a prolonged pursuit of a particular truth. In the process, the pursuer may stumble

upon another truth, and yet another. He may soon find himself engaged in a sort of spiritual serendipity, acquiring much wisdom and illumination as he travels on.

5. Their stimulating effect: these nuggets may so affect our intellectual and spiritual curiosity, that we shall not rest satisfied until we have discovered the whole field where they were mined. We will want to know the books, and the masters who wrote them.

Above all, it is my prayer that we may not stop with the masters—important though they be—but proceed to know the masters' own Master, the Lord Jesus Christ. Without that discovery, these nuggets will be of academic value at best.

ADOPTION

More than a name:

A man adopts one for his son and heir that does not at all resemble him; but whosoever God adopts for His child is like Him; he not only bears His heavenly Father's name, but His image. Col 3:10.

THOMAS WATSON

The sign:

The least degree of sincere sanctification, being an effect of regeneration, is a certain sign of adoption, and may minister a sure argument to him that has it, that he is the adopted child of God.

THOMAS GATAKER

ADVERSITY

Adversity is the diamond dust Heaven polishes its jewels with.

ROBERT LEIGHTON

AFFLICTION

Universal:

One son God hath without sin, but none without sorrow.

JOHN TRAPP

AFFLICTION

"Man is born to trouble;" he is heir apparent to it; he comes into the world with a cry, and goes out with a groan.
THOMAS WATSON

Transitory:

Affliction may be lasting, but it is not everlasting.
THOMAS WATSON

If the darkness which a man be under be such, that there are some openings of light withal, then it is the darkness of a cloud, and not of the night.... Now thus it is always with the people of God. They never are in any affliction, temptation, or desertion, but before their great deliverance comes, they have some special providence, some reviving in the midst of their trouble, some interim of light, some openings of the cloud; and therefore, in the midst of all, they may say, Surely this my darkness is not the darkness of the night, but of a cloud. I say, there is no discouragement befalls the saints, but the matter thereof is a cloud, and they may say, It is but a cloud, it will pass over.
WILLIAM BRIDGE

Affliction has a sting, but withal a wing: sorrow shall fly away.
THOMAS WATSON

Not necessarily evil:

There is more evil in a drop of sin than in a sea of affliction.
THOMAS WATSON

A recognition of strength:

Not to be afflicted is a sign of weakness; for, therefore God imposeth no more on me, because He sees I can bear no more.
JOSEPH HALL

The Lord does not measure out our afflictions according to our faults, but according to our strength, and looks not what we have deserved, but what we are able to bear.
GEORGE DOWNAME

AFFLICTION

Can my affliction be traced to God?

It is one heart-quieting consideration in all the afflictions that befall us, that God has a special hand in them: "The Almighty hath afflicted me." Instruments can no more stir till God gives them a commission, than the axe can cut of itself without a hand. Job eyed God in his affliction: therefore, as Augustine observes, he does not say, "The Lord gave, and the devil took away," but "The Lord hath taken away."

THOMAS WATSON

Whoever brings an affliction, it is God that sends it.

THOMAS WATSON

He is not drowning His sheep when He washeth them, nor killing them when He is shearing them. But by this He showeth that they are His own; and the newborn sheep do most visibly bear His name or mark, when it is almost worn out and scarce discernible on them that have the longest fleece.

RICHARD BAXTER

If a sheep stray from his fellows, the shepherd sets his dog after it, not to devour it, but to bring it in again; even so our Heavenly Shepherd.

DANIEL CAWDRAY

There is no cross or misery that befalls the church of God or any of His children, but it is related to God.

SAMUEL RUTHERFORD

Whatsoever is upon you is from the Lord, and whatsoever is from the Lord, to you it is in mercy; and whatsoever comes in mercy ought not to be grievous to you. What loss is it when the losing of earthly things is the gaining of spiritual things? All shall be for your good, if you make your use of all.

RICHARD GREENHAM

AFFLICTION

Can my afflictions be justified?

Take note that when men oppress and persecute most unjustly,
yet there is cause to justify God in suffering it to be so. God's
justice is executed upon us by their injustice; if men falsely
accuse us, yet God can truly charge us. When Job has to deal
with men, he maintains his integrity against their accusations,
Job 27:4-6, but when he has to deal with God, he acknowledges
his sin, and will not stand upon his own justification; he will
not plead but supplicate.

JOHN OLDFIELD

The whole creation groans, and God's children bear a part in the
concert. They have their share in the world's miseries; and
domestical crosses are common to them with other men in the
world; yea, their condition is worse than others'. Chaff and corn
are threshed in the same floor, but the corn is grinded in the mill
and baked in the oven. Jeremiah was in the dungeon when the
city was besieged. The world hates them more than others, and
God loves them more than others. The world hates them because they are so good, and God corrects them because they are
no better.

THOMAS MANTON

Do not even such things as are most bitter to the flesh, tend to
awaken Christians to faith and prayer, to a sight of the emptiness of this world, and the fadingness of the best it yield? Doth
not God by these things (ofttimes) call our sins to remembrance,
and provoke us to amendment of life? How then can we be
offended at things by which we reap so much good?. . . .
Therefore if mine enemy hunger, let me feed him; if he thirst, let
me give him drink. Now in order to do this, (i) We must see good
in that, in which other men can see none. (ii) We must pass by
those injuries that other men would revenge. (iii) We must
show we have grace, and that we are made to bear what other
men are not acquainted with. (iv) Many of our graces are kept
alive, by those very things that are the death of other men's
souls. . . . The devil, (they say) is good when he is pleased; but
Christ and His saints, when displeased.

JOHN BUNYAN

(Some say) "I am grieved that I am thus dealt with because I never deserved it; had I done anything worthy of punishment it would not have grieved me. . . ." Thou speakest like a foolish man. . . . Whether is it better to suffer, when thy conscience is free and suffereth not, or when with thy outward affliction thou art afflicted also of thine own heart? And is it not a glorious thing to suffer for well doing wherein thy cause of grief is the less. . . .? For if the cause of affliction rather than affliction itself should grieve thee, then affliction without cause of affliction—being for God, His cause—should rather comfort thee.

RICHARD GREENHAM

Can my afflictions issue in blessing?

The vessels of mercy are first seasoned with affliction, and then the wine of glory is poured in. Thus we see afflictions are not prejudicial, but beneficial, to the saints.

THOMAS WATSON

A sanctified person, like a silver bell, the harder he is smitten, the better he sounds.

GEORGE SWINNOCK

We often learn more of God under the rod that strikes us, than under the staff that comforts us.

STEPHEN CHARNOCK

God's house of correction is His school of instruction.

THOMAS BROOKS

God does by affliction magnify us three ways. (i) In that He will condescend so low as to take notice of us . . . It is a magnifying of us, that God thinks us worthy to be smitten. God's not striking is a slighting: "Why should ye be stricken any more?" Isaiah 1:5. (ii) Afflictions also magnify us, as they are ensigns of glory, signs of sonship. "If you endure chastening, God dealeth with you as with sons." Hebrews 12:7. Every print of the rod is a badge of honour. (iii) Afflictions tend to the magnifying of the saints, as they make them renowned in the world. Soldiers have

AFFLICTION

never been so admired for their victories, as the saints have been for their sufferings.

THOMAS WATSON

The thorn is one of the most cursed and angry and crabbed weeds that the earth yields, and yet out of it springs the rose, one of the sweetest smelled flowers, and most delightful to the eye.

SAMUEL RUTHERFORD

The flowers smell sweetest after a shower; vines bear the better for bleeding; the walnut-tree is most fruitful when most beaten; saints spring and thrive most internally, when they are most externally afflicted. Afflictions are the mother of virtue. Manasseh's chain was more profitable to him than his crown. . . . All the stones that came about Stephen's ears did but knock him closer to Christ, the corner-stone.

THOMAS BROOKS

Such is the condition of grace, that it shines the brighter for scouring, and is most glorious when it is most clouded.

WILLIAM JENKYN

God's corrections are instructions, His lashes our lessons, His scourges our schoolmasters, His chastisements our admonitions! And to note this, the Hebrews and Greeks both do express chastening and teaching by one and the same word, because the latter is the true end of the former.

THOMAS BROOKS

It was a noble and zealous speech of Ignatius, "Let me be ground with the teeth of wild beasts, if I may be God's pure wheat."

THOMAS WATSON

As the wicked are hurt by the best things, so the godly are bettered by the worst.

WILLIAM JENKYN

Poverty and affliction take away the fuel that feeds pride.

RICHARD SIBBES

AFFLICTION

He gives gifts that we may love Him, and stripes that we may fear Him. Yea, oftentimes He mixes frowns with His favours.

GEORGE DOWNAME

It is said that in some countries trees will grow, but will bear no fruit, because there is no winter there.

JOHN BUNYAN

I am mended by my sickness, enriched by my poverty, and strengthened by my weakness. . . . Thus was it with. . . . Manasseh, when he was in affliction, "He besought the Lord his God": even that king's iron was more precious to him than his gold, his jail a more happy lodging than his palace, Babylon a better school than Jerusalem. What fools are we, then, to frown upon our afflictions! These, how crabbed soever, are our best friends. They are not indeed for our pleasure, they are for our profit.

ABRAHAM WRIGHT

N.B.:*

Labour to grow better under all your afflictions, lest your afflictions grow worse, lest God mingle them with more darkness, bitterness and terror.

JOHN OWEN

The secret formula of the saints:

When I am in the cellar of affliction, I look for the Lord's choicest wines.

SAMUEL RUTHERFORD

Let us learn like Christians to kiss the rod, and love it.

JOHN BUNYAN

An obedient child doth not only kiss the hand which giveth, but the rod which beateth.

HENRY SMITH

*Nota bene—"note well"

17

AFFLICTION

When God lays men upon their backs, then they look up to heaven.

THOMAS WATSON

If in our affliction we would pour forth to God such acceptable prayers as may obtain comfort in our crosses and deliverance from our calamities, we must confess our sins, and humbly acknowledge that we have not deserved God's smallest benefits, but are worthy to be overwhelmed with much more heavy plagues and punishments. And so the Lord will excuse us, when we accuse ourselves.

GEORGE DOWNAME

The way to be eased is not struggling with it, but meekly to bear it.

There is a fable, but it has its moral for this purpose. A certain ass, laded with salt, fell into a river, and after he had risen, found his burden lighter, for the moisture had made it melt away; whereupon he would ever after lie down in the water as he travelled with his burden, and so ease himself. His owner perceiving this craft, after laded him with wool. The ass purposing to ease himself, as before, laid himself down in the water, and thinking to have ease, rising again to feel his weight, found it heavier.

RICHARD STOCK

When you meet with crosses and calamities, say, "Now I see God's justice and God's truth; now I see the hatefulness and hurtfulness of sin; and therefore now I will mourn, not because I am crossed, but because I have deserved this cross, and a worse too."

WILLIAM WHATELY

Well's them who are under crosses, and Christ says to them, "Half Mine."

SAMUEL RUTHERFORD

Look how fears have presented themselves, so have supports and encouragements; yea, when I have started, even as it were at nothing else but my shadow, yet God, as being very tender of me, hath not suffered me to be molested, but would with one Scripture or another, strengthen me against all; insomuch that I have often said, Were it lawful, I could pray for greater trouble, for the greater comfort's sake.

JOHN BUNYAN

N.B.:

He that rides to be crowned, will not think much of a rainy day.

JOHN TRAPP

ANGER

Its issue:

It is the great duty of all Christians to put off anger. It unfits for duty . . . A man cannot wrestle with God and wrangle with his neighbour at the same time. Short sins often cost us long and sad sorrows.

PHILIP HENRY

It is the base and vile bramble, the fruit of the earth's curse, that tears and rends what is next to it.

THOMAS ADAMS

He that is inebriated with passion is unfit for an action.

THOMAS ADAMS

The angry man, like the two hot disciples that called fire from heaven, ordains himself the judge, and would have God turn his executioner.

THOMAS ADAMS

N.B.:

Plato said to his servant, "I would have killed thee, but that I am angry."

JOHN KING

Can it be ever justified?

He that will be angry, and not sin, must not be angry but for sin.

JOHN TRAPP

Be soonest angry with thyself.

THOMAS FULLER

Can it be gainfully employed?

Anger should not be destroyed but sanctified.

WILLIAM JENKYN

APOSTASY

Apostasy is a perversion to evil after a seeming conversion from it.

TIMOTHY CRUSO

Indifference in religion, is the first step to apostasy from religion.

WILLIAM SECKER

None sink so far into hell as those that come nearest heaven, because they fall from the greatest height.

WILLIAM GURNALL

N.B.:

It were far easier to write a book of apostates in this age than a book of martyrs.

JOHN TRAPP

ASSURANCE OF LIFE ETERNAL

What is assurance?

It is a new conversion; it will make a man differ from himself in what he was before in that manner almost as conversion doth before he was converted. There is a new edition of all a man's graces.

THOMAS GOODWIN

Assurance is the fruit that grows out of the root of faith.

STEPHEN CHARNOCK

Assurance is glory in the bud, it is the suburbs of paradise.

THOMAS BROOKS

Faith is our seal; assurance of faith is God's seal.

CHRISTOPHER NESSE

I am wholly His; I am peculiarly His; I am universally His; I am eternally His.

THOMAS BROOKS

Can I have eternal life and not know it?

A child of God may have the Kingdom of grace in his heart, yet not know it. The cup was in Benjamin's sack, though he did not know it was there.

THOMAS WATSON

As an infant hath life before he knoweth it; and as he hath misapprehensions of himself, and most other things for certain years together; yet it will not follow that, therefore, he hath no life or reason.

RICHARD BAXTER

ASSURANCE OF LIFE ETERNAL

Assurance is a fruit that grows out of the root of faith; the fruits in Winter appear not upon the tree. Because I see not a flourishing top, shall I deny the existence and sappiness of the root? Mary, when she wept at Christ's feet, had no assurance of His love, yet Christ sends her away with the encomium of her faith, acted before the comfort dropped from His lips.

STEPHEN CHARNOCK

We have peace with God as soon as we believe, but not always with ourselves. The pardon may be past the prince's hand and seal, and yet not put into the prisoner's hand.

WILLIAM GURNALL

Assurance is not of the essence of a Christian. It is required to the *bene esse* (the well-being), to the comfortable and joyful being of a Christian; but it is not required to the *esse*, to the being of a Christian. A man may be a true believer, and yet would give all the world, were it in his power, to know that he is a believer. To have grace, and to be sure that we have grace, is glory upon the throne, it is heaven on this side of heaven.

THOMAS BROOKS

None have assurance at all times. As in a walk that is shaded with trees and chequered with light and shadow, some tracks and paths in it are dark and others are sunshine. Such is usually the life of the most assured Christian.

EZEKIEL HOPKINS

Does assurance remain when comforts are gone?

Take heed thou thinkest not grace decays because thy comfort withdraws. . . . Did ever faith triumph more in our Saviour crying "My God, my God!" Here faith was at its meridian when it was midnight in respect of joy.

WILLIAM GURNALL

A man's assurance may be as good, as true, when he lies on the earth with a sense of sin, as when he is carried up to the third heaven with a sense of love and foretaste of glory.

JOHN OWEN

22

ASSURANCE OF LIFE ETERNAL

Sense of sin may be often great, and more felt than grace; yet not be more than grace. A man feels the ache of his finger more sensibly than the health of his whole body; yet he knows that the ache of a finger is nothing so much as the health of the whole body.

THOMAS ADAMS

God dwells as glorious in a saint when he is in the dark, as when he is in light, for darkness is His secret place, and His pavilion round about Him are dark waters.

WILLIAM ERBERY

Great comforts do, indeed, bear witness to the truth of thy grace, but not to the degree of it; the weak child is oftener in the lap than the strong one.

WILLIAM GURNALL

It is natural to the soul to rest upon everything below Christ; to rest upon creatures, to rest upon graces, to rest upon duties, to rest upon divine manifestations, to rest upon celestial consolations, to rest upon gracious evidences, and to rest upon sweet assurances. Now the Lord, to cure His people of this weakness, and to bring them to live wholly and solely upon Jesus Christ, denies comfort, and denies assurance, etc., and for a time leaves His children of light to walk in darkness. Christians, this you are always to remember, that though the enjoyment of assurance makes most for your consolation, yet the living purely upon Christ in the absence of assurance, makes most for Christ's exaltation. He is happy that believes upon seeing, upon feeling, but thrice happy are those souls that believe when they do not see; that love when they do not know that they are beloved; and that in the want of all comfort and assurance, can live upon Christ as their only all. He that hath learned this holy art, cannot be miserable; he that is ignorant of this art cannot be happy.

THOMAS BROOKS

The Christian must trust in a withdrawing God.

WILLIAM GURNALL

ASSURANCE OF LIFE ETERNAL

Steps to awareness:

He that wants assurance of the truth of his grace, and the comfort of assurance, must not stand still and say, "I am so doubtful and uncomfortable that I have no mind to duty," but ply his duty, and exercise his grace, till he find his doubts and discomforts to vanish.

RICHARD BAXTER

It is the very drift and design of the whole Scripture, to bring souls first to an acquaintance with Christ, and then to an acceptance of Christ, and then to build them in a sweet assurance of their actual interest in Christ.

THOMAS BROOKS

To make sense and feeling the judges of our spiritual conditions, what is it but to make ourselves happy and miserable, righteous and unrighteous, saved and damned in one day, ay, in one hour.... What is this but to toss the soul to and fro, and to expose it to a labyrinth of fears and scruples? What is this but to cast a reproach upon Christ, to gratify Satan, and to keep yourselves upon the rack? Well, doubting souls, the counsel that I shall give you is this, be much in believing, and make only the Scripture the judge of your condition; maintain the judgement of the Word against the judgement of sense and feeling.... If you resolve to make sense and feeling the judge of your conditions, you must resolve to live in fears, and lie down in tears.

THOMAS BROOKS

If a physician that feels not what you feel, shall yet, upon your speeches and other evidences, tell you that he is confident your disease is not mortal, nor containeth any cause of fear, you may rationally be much encouraged by his judgement. . . . (your faithful pastor) is able to pass a far sounder judgement of your life or death than yourselves can do, for all your feeling; for he knows better what those symptoms signify. . . .

RICHARD BAXTER

Whenever God pardons sin, He subdues it. Micah 7:19. Then is the condemning power of sin taken away, when the commanding power of it is taken away. If a malefactor be in prison, how shall he know that his prince hath pardoned him? If a jailer come and knock off his chains and fetters, and lets him out of prison, then he may know he is pardoned; so, how shall we know God hath pardoned us? If the fetters of sin be broken off, and we walk at liberty in the ways of God, this is a blessed sign we are pardoned.

THOMAS WATSON

Motion is the most perfect discoverer of life. He that can stir his limbs, is surely not dead. The feet of the soul are the affections. Hast thou not found in thyself a hate and detestation of that sin whereinto thou hast been miscarried? Hast thou not found in thyself a true grief of heart, for thy wretched indisposition to all good things? Without a true life of grace, these things could never have been.

JOSEPH HALL

Another sure mark of sensible faith and comfort, is this; that they that have tasted of it, CAN NEVER BE SATISFIED, but still hunger and labour for more.

EZEKIEL CULVERWELL

I have sought but not found?

It may be you have been more earnest and vehement for assurance, and the effects of it, viz., joy, comfort, and peace, than you have been for grace and holiness, for communion with God, and conformity to God. It may be your requests for assurance have been full of life and spirits, when your requests for grace and holiness, for communion with God, and conformity to God, have been lifeless and spiritless. If so, no wonder that assurance is denied you. Assurance makes most for your comfort, but holiness makes most for God's honour. Man's holiness is now his greatest happiness, and in heaven man's greatest happiness will be his perfect holiness.

THOMAS BROOKS

ASSURANCE OF LIFE ETERNAL

By-products of assurance:

The being in a state of grace will yield a man a heaven hereafter, but the seeing of himself in this estate will yield him both a heaven here and a heaven hereafter; it will render him doubly blest, blest in heaven, and blest in his own conscience.

THOMAS BROOKS

Assurance of better things makes the soul sing care away, as that martyr said, "My soul is turned to her rest; I have taken a sweet nap in Christ's lap, and therefore I will now sing care away, and will be careless according to my name."

THOMAS BROOKS

If a loving heart is without fear of the day of judgement, he is without fear of falling away.

JOHN COTTON

A soul under assurance is unwilling to go to heaven without company.

THOMAS BROOKS

There is a reward not only in keeping, but also for keeping of His commands, Psalm 19:11. Joseph, for his thirteen years' imprisonment, had the honour to reign fourscore years like a king; David, for his seven years' banishment, had a glorious reign of forty years' continuance; Daniel, for his lying a few hours among the lions, is made chief president over a hundred and twenty princes. . . . Ah! doubting souls, pray hard, work hard for assurance; the pay will answer the pains.

THOMAS BROOKS

The assured Christian is more motion than notion, more work than word, more life than lip, more hand than tongue.

THOMAS BROOKS

Assurance and comforts are desirable, but fruitfulness is absolutely necessary. . . . The end why the Lord offers us comfort and assurance of His love, is to make us cheerful in His service, and to encourage us in His work, and engage our hearts in it thoroughly.

DAVID CLARKSON

N.B.:

Assurance made David divinely fearless, and divinely careless.

THOMAS BROOKS

The greatest thing that we can desire, next to the glory of God, is our own salvation; and the sweetest thing we can desire is the assurance of our salvation. . . . All saints shall enjoy a heaven when they leave this earth; some saints enjoy a heaven while they are here on earth.

JOSEPH CARYL

Assurance will assist us in all duties; it will arm us against all temptations; it will answer all objections; it will sustain us in all conditions. . . .

EDWARD REYNOLDS

ATHEISM

Unless the being of a God be presupposed, no tolerable account can be given of the being of any thing.

EZEKIEL HOPKINS

Now, if according to the impiety of atheists, there is no God, why do they invoke Him in their adversities? If there be, why do they deny Him in their prosperity?

WILLIAM BATES

There is a conscience in man; therefore there is a God in heaven.

EZEKIEL HOPKINS

When we see wicked ones prosper in the world, and godly men crushed and destroyed in the way of righteousness and integrity, it may tempt us to think there is no advantage by religion, and all our self-denial and holiness to be little better than lost labour. . . . "Verily I have cleansed my heart in vain, and washed my hands in innocency." This irreligious inference carnal

27

reason was ready to draw from the dispensations of outward prosperity to wicked men; but now, if we would heedfully observe, either the signal retributions of Providence to *many* of them *in this world*, or to *all* of them in the *world to come*, O what a full confirmation is this to our faith!

JOHN FLAVEL

N.B.:

Men may have atheistical hearts without atheistical heads.

STEPHEN CHARNOCK

He that doth not believe that there is a God, is more vile then a devil. To deny there is a God, is a sort of atheism that is not to be found in hell.

THOMAS BROOKS

ATONEMENT

All sufficient:

If the Lord Jesus Christ made full satisfaction unto God the Father, how is it that believers, many of them have their consciences so perplexed in regard of sin, as if there were no satisfaction at all made? The reason is, because that men do not study this truth, but are ignorant of it. As, suppose that a man do owe three or four hundred pounds to a shopkeeper for wares that he hath taken up there; a friend comes, pays the debt, and crosses the book; but the debtor when he comes and looks upon the book is able to read all the particulars; and not being acquainted with the nature of crossing the book, he is able to read all the particulars, and he charges it still upon himself, because he does not understand the nature of crossing the book. . . . So now it is here: the Lord Jesus Christ hath come and crossed our book with His own blood; the sins are to be read in your own consciences, but we, being not acquainted with the nature of Christ's satisfaction, we charge ourselves, as if no sin at all were satisfied for us.

WILLIAM BRIDGE

If He hides the sin, or lesseneth it, He is faulty; if He leaves it still upon us, we die. He must then take our iniquity to Himself, make it His own, and so deliver us; for thus having taken the sin upon Himself, as lawfully He may, and lovingly He doth, it followeth that we live if He lives; and who can desire more?

JOHN BUNYAN

When the Lord Jesus Christ offered up Himself a sacrifice unto God the Father, and had our sins laid upon Him, He did give more perfect satisfaction unto Divine justice for our sins than if you, and I, and all of us had been damned in hell unto all eternity.

For a creditor is more satisfied if his debt be paid him all down at once, than if it be paid by the week.

WILLIAM BRIDGE

Sufficient for all:

All are not saved by Christ's death, but all which are saved, are saved by Christ's death; His death is sufficient to save all, as the sun is sufficient to lighten all; but if any man wink, the sun will not give him light.

HENRY SMITH

As the sun is the general giver of light to the whole world, although there be many who do receive no light at all of it . . . even so the redemption of mankind by Christ is available for all, although reprobate and wicked men, for want of the grace of God, do not receive the same; yet there is no reason that it should lose its title and glory of universal redemption because of the children of perdition, seeing that it is ready for all men and all be called unto it.

DANIEL CAWDRAY

ATONEMENT

That mystical Sun of Righteousness (saith St. Ambrose) is risen to all, come to all, did suffer and rise again for all—but if any one doth not believe in Christ, he defrauds himself of the general benefit. As if one shutting the windows should exclude the beams of the sun, the sun is not therefore not risen to all.

ISAAC BARROW

Human virtue no substitute:

Obedience will not make amends for past crimes; for obedience is a debt due of itself, and what is a debt of itself cannot be a compensation for another. . . . Obedience was due from man if he had not sinned, and therefore is a debt as much due after sin as before it; but a new debt cannot be satisfied by paying an old. . . . So obedience to the law in our whole course was a debt upon us by our creation . . . but upon sin a new debt of punishment was contracted, and the penalty of the law was to be satisfied by suffering, as well as the precepts of the law satisfied by observing them.

STEPHEN CHARNOCK

There is no death of sin without the death of Christ.

JOHN OWEN

The wrong that man had done to the Divine Majesty, *should* be expiated by none but man, and *could* be by none but God.

JOHN HOWE

Human sin notwithstanding:

"He hath not dealt with us after our sins." Why is it that God hath not dealt with us after our sins? Is it not because He hath dealt with another after our sins? Another who took our sins upon Him; of whom it is said, that "God chastened Him in His fierce wrath"? and why did He chasten Him, but for our sins? O gracious God, thou art too just to take revenge twice for the same faults; and therefore, having turned Thy fierce wrath upon Him, Thou wilt not turn it upon us too; but having rewarded Him according to our iniquities, Thou wilt now reward us according to His merits.

SIR RICHARD BAKER

Ultimate goal:

Christ was offered twice; first in the temple, which is called His *morning sacrifice*; then on the cross, which is termed *His evening sacrifice*. In the one He was redeemed, in the other He did redeem.

JOHN BOYS

If Christ had not died, sin had never died in any sinner unto eternity.

JOHN OWEN

Christ did not die for any upon condition, *if they do believe*; but He died for all God's elect, *that they should believe*.

JOHN OWEN

N.B.:

This precious Lamb of God gave up His golden fleece for us.

CHRISTOPHER NESSE

Oh, look upon the *wounds* of Thine hands, and forget not the *work* of Thine hands: so Queen Elizabeth prayed.

JOHN TRAPP

BACKSLIDING

He falls deepest into hell who falls backward.

THOMAS WATSON

None will have such a sad parting from Christ, as those who went half-way with Him and then left Him.

WILLIAM GURNALL

Weariness maketh way for wandering.

THOMAS MANTON

N.B.:

The best way never to fall is ever to fear.

WILLIAM JENKYN

BIBLE, THE

The Bible is the statute-book of God's Kingdom, wherein is comprised the whole body of the heavenly law, the perfect rules of a holy life, and the sure promises of a glorious one.

EZEKIEL HOPKINS

The Scripture is the library of the Holy Ghost; it is a pandect of divine knowledge, an exact model and platform of religion. The Scripture contains in it the *credenda*, "the things which we are to believe," and the *agenda*, "the things which we are to practice."

THOMAS WATSON

Good for saint and sinner:

O ye saints, how you should love the Word, for by this you have been converted. . . . Tie it about your neck, write it upon your hand, lay it in your bosom. When you go let it lead you, when you sleep let it keep you, when you wake let it talk with you. (Proverbs 6:21-22). You that are unconverted, read the Word with diligence; flock to where it is powerfully preached. Pray for the coming of the Spirit in the Word. Come from your knees to the sermon, and come from the sermon to your knees.

JOSEPH ALLEINE

The Christian is bred by the Word, and he must be fed by it.

WILLIAM GURNALL

The Word generates faith and regenerates us.

JOSEPH ALLEINE

The godly man will read the Word *by day*, that men, seeing his good works, may glorify his Father who is in heaven; he will do it in the *night*, that he may not be seen of men; by *day*, to show that he is not one of those who dread the light; by *night*, to show that he is one who can shine in the shade; by *day*, for that is the time for working—work whilst it is day; by *night*, lest his Master should come as a thief, and find him idle.

SIR RICHARD BAKER

The Scriptures teach us the best way of living, the noblest way of suffering, and the most comfortable way of dying.

JOHN FLAVEL

Conversion turns us to the Word of God, as our touchstone, to examine ourselves . . . as our glass, to dress by (James 1); as our rule to walk and work by (Galatians 6:16); as our water, to wash us (Psalm 119:9); as our fire to warm us (Luke 24); as our food to nourish us (Job 23:12); as our sword to fight with (Ephesians 6); as our counsellor, in all our doubts (Psalm 119:24); as our cordial, to comfort us; as our heritage, to enrich us.

PHILIP HENRY

The Scripture is both the breeder and feeder of grace. How is the convert born, but by "the word of truth"? (James 1:18). How doth he grow, but by "the sincere milk of the Word."? (1 Peter 2:2)

THOMAS WATSON

Danger in adding or detracting:

I will give you this as a most certain observation, that there never was anything of false doctrine brought into the church, or anything of false worship imposed upon the church, but either it was by neglecting the Scripture, or by introducing something above the Scripture.

JOHN COLLINS

We hold that neither man nor angel is any wise to add or detract any thing, to change or to alter any thing from that which the Lord hath set down in His Word.

JOHN PENRY

BIBLE

Its supremacy:

I know there is nothing in the Word or in the works of God that is repugnant to sound reason, but there are some things in both which are opposite to carnal reason, as well as above right reason; and therefore our reason never shows itself more unreasonable than in summoning those things to its bar which transcend its sphere and capacity.

JOHN FLAVEL

In brief, where the Scripture is silent, the church is my text; where that speaks, 'tis but my comment; where there is a joint silence of both, I borrow not the rules of my religion from Rome or Geneva, but the dictates of my own reason.

SIR THOMAS BROWNE

Its inspiration:

We say not that the Spirit ever speaks to us *of* the Word, but *by* the Word. . . .

JOHN OWEN

The Spirit of God rides most triumphantly in his own chariot.

THOMAS MANTON

The two Testaments are the two lips by which God hath spoken to us.

THOMAS WATSON

The same Testator made both Testaments.

THOMAS TAYLOR

Among the many arguments to prove the penmen of the Scripture inspired by the Spirit of God, this is not the last and least—that the penmen of Holy Writ do record their own faults and the faults of their dearest and nearest relatives. For instance hereof, how coarsely doth David speak of himself: "So foolish was I, and ignorant; I was as a beast before Thee." And do you think that the face of St. Paul did look the more foul by being drawn with his own pencil, when he says, "I was a murderer, a persecuter, the greatest of sinners," etc.? . . . . Moses sets down the sin and punishment of his own sister, the idolatry and superstition of Aaron his brother, and his own fault in his preposterous striking the rock.

THOMAS FULLER

Its revelation:

If all the light of the heavenly luminaries had been contracted into one, it would have been destructive, not useful, to our sight. . . . So, if the whole revelation of the glory of Christ, and all that belongs to it, had been committed into one series and contexture of words, it would have overwhelmed our minds rather than enlightened us. Wherefore God has distributed the light of it through the whole firmament of the books of the Old and New Testaments. . . .

JOHN OWEN

One great object of revelation was to show us God as our Father.

SIDRACH SIMPSON

Its translation:

Bless God for the translation of the Scriptures. The Word is our sword; by being translated, the sword is drawn out of its scabbard.

WILLIAM GURNALL

As the title set over the head of Christ crucified, was the same in Hebrew, Greek, and Latin, so are the Scriptures the same, whether in the original, or other language into which they are faithfully translated. Yet, as the waters are most pure, and sweet in the fountain, so are all writings, Divine and human, in their original tongues.

JOHN ROBINSON

Its application:

Read the Scripture, not only as a history, but as a love-letter sent to you from God.

THOMAS WATSON

BIBLE

When you hear the Word, say, "There God spoke to my soul."
Men forget truths because they are apt to put them off to others,
and not to look on themselves as concerned in them.

JOHN WHITLOCK

He that would comprehend all things, apprehends nothing. As
he that comes to a corn heap, the more he opens his hand to
take, the less he graspeth, the less he holdeth. Where the
Scripture hath no tongue, we should have no ear.

THOMAS ADAMS

He doth not bid us take a taste of all sins and vanities, as
Solomon did, to try them: for they are tried already; but that we
should set the Word of God alway before us like a rule, and
believe nothing but that which it teacheth, love nothing but that
which it prescribeth, hate nothing but that which it forbideth,
do nothing but that which it commandeth, and then we try all
things by the Word.

HENRY SMITH

Leave not off reading the Bible till you find your hearts warmed.
. . . Let it not only inform you, but inflame you.

THOMAS WATSON

When Satan borrows sense to speak one thing, let faith borrow
Scripture to speak the contrary.

DAVID DICKSON

N.B.:

The Word of life may be so distorted from the life of the Word,
till it becomes the food of death.

THOMAS ADAMS

Its interpretation:

Compare Scripture with Scripture. False doctrines, like false
witnesses, agree not among themselves.

WILLIAM GURNALL

BIBLE

The Scripture is to be its own interpreter, or rather the Spirit speaking in it; nothing can cut the diamond but the diamond; nothing can interpret Scripture but Scripture.

THOMAS WATSON

God's truth always agrees with itself.

RICHARD SIBBES

There is in Scripture but one proper, and immediate sense; others are rather collections from it, relations unto it, or illustrations of it.

JOHN ROBINSON

It is a safe rule in interpreting Scripture, that in places mentioning the love and grace of God to us, the words are to be taken in their utmost significance.

JOHN OWEN

In the waters of life, the Divine Scriptures, there are shallows, and there are deeps; shallows where the lamb may wade; and deeps where the elephant may swim. If we be not wise to distinguish, we may easily miscarry; he that can wade over the ford, cannot swim through the deep.... What infinite mischief hath arisen to the church of God from the presumption of ignorant and unlettered men, that have taken upon them to interpret the most obscure Scriptures, and pertinaciously defend their own sense!

JOSEPH HALL

As there is a foolish wisdom, so there is a wise ignorance; in not prying into God's ark, not inquiring into things not revealed. I would fain know all that I need, and all that I may: I leave God's secrets to Himself. It is happy for me that God makes me of His court though not of His council.

JOSEPH HALL

Common reason tells us that we must first have a general proof that Scripture is God's Word, and argue thence to the verity of the parts, and not begin with a particular proof of each part. It seems that you would argue thus: This and that text of Scripture

BIBLE

are true, therefore they are God's Word. But reason telleth you that you should argue thus: This is God's Word, therefore it is true.

RICHARD BAXTER

Remember that greatest misery to an honest heart is this, a misdrawing of rules out of the Word of God: you take a word and do not compare it with other Scriptures, and see whether it be temporary and doth absolutely bind.

WALTER CRADOCK

You know how it was with Moses, when he saw two men fighting, one an Egyptian, and another an Israelite, he killed the Egyptian; but, when he saw two Hebrews fighting, Now, saith he, I will go and reconcile them, for they are brethren; why so, but because he was a good man, and gracious? So also it is with a gracious heart; when he sees the Scripture fighting with an Egyptian, an heathen author, or apocrypal, he comes and kills the heathen. . . . but when he sees two Scriptures at variance (in view, though in truth not), Oh, saith he, these are brethren, and they may be reconciled, I will labour all I can to reconcile them; but when a man shall take every advantage of seeming difference in Scripture, to say, Do ye see what contradictions there are in this book, and not labour to reconcile them; what doth this argue, but that the corruption of a man's nature, is boiled up to an unknown malice against the word of the Lord.

THOMAS BRIDGE

Its priority:

For it is not what a church practices, but what it is warranted to practice: not what it holds for a truth, but what it is warranted to hold as the word of truth. The Word was written after the church; but as it is the Word of God, it is before it.

JOHN COLLINS

The Scripture is the sun; the church is the clock, whose hands point us to and whose sound tells us the hours of the day. The sun we know to be sure, and regularly constant in his motion; the clock, as it may fall out, may go too fast or too slow. We are

38

wont to look at, and listen to the clock, we know the time of the day; but, where we find the variation sensible, we believe the sun against the clock, not the clock against the sun.

JOSEPH HALL

Self-authenticating:

Let the sun arise in the firmament, and there is no need of witnesses to prove and confirm unto a seeing man that it is day. . . . It is all one, by what means, by what hand, whether of a child, or a church. . . . the Scripture comes to us; come how it will, it hath its authority in itself. . . . and hath its power of manifesting itself. . . . from its own innate light.

JOHN OWEN

N.B.:

The Lord has more truth yet to break forth out of His holy Word.

JOHN ROBINSON

BLESSINGS

Exceeding abundant:

Did you never run for shelter in a storm, and find fruit which you expected not? Did you never go to God for safeguard, driven by outward storms, and there find unexpected fruit?

JOHN OWEN

Beyond price:

He (God) gives them three jewels more worth than heaven—the blood of His Son, the grace of His Spirit, and the light of His countenance.

THOMAS WATSON

BLESSINGS, BONDAGE, CHASTISEMENT

Compounded interest:

To bless God for mercies is the way to increase them; to bless Him for miseries is the way to remove them.

WILLIAM DYER

Those blessings are sweetest that are won with prayers and worn with thanks.

THOMAS GOODWIN

To qualify?

God forgives, then He gives; till He be merciful to pardon our sins through Christ, He cannot bless or look kindly on us sinners. All our enjoyments are but blessings in bullion, till Gospel grace and pardoning mercy stamp and make them current.

WILLIAM GURNALL

BONDAGE

There is no real bondage, but what is either *from*, or *for* sin.

VAVASOR POWELL

CHASTISEMENT

A proof of sonship:

None but the godly are capable of desertion. Wicked men know not what God's love means, nor what it is to want it. . . . You fear you are not God's child because you are deserted.

The Lord cannot be said to withdraw His love from the wicked, because they never had it. The being deserted, evidences you to be a child of God. How could you complain that God has estranged Himself, if you had not sometimes received smiles and tokens of love from Him?

THOMAS WATSON

We may feel God's hand as a Father upon us when He strikes us as well as when He strokes us.

ABRAHAM WRIGHT

The underlying reason:

Whatsoever we have over-loved, idolized, and leaned upon, God has from time to time broken it, and made us to see the vanity of it; so that we find the readiest course to be rid of our comforts is to set our hearts inordinately upon them.

JOHN FLAVEL

God's wounds cure, sin's kisses kill.

WILLIAM GURNALL

Better be pruned to grow than cut up to burn.

JOHN TRAPP

Thou art beaten that thou mayest be better.

JOHN BUNYAN

Learning the lesson:

Especially look to those sins to which your crosses have some reference and respect. Are you crossed in your goods? Think if you did not over-love them and get them unjustly, or if in your children, see if you did not over-love them and cocker them, and so in all things of like kind. In what God smites you, see if you have not in that sinned against Him, and so frame to lament your sins and to seek help against them.

WILLIAM WHATELY

N.B.:

It is in mercy and in measure that God chastiseth His children.

JOHN TRAPP

CHILDREN

Christian education vital:

There is little hope of children who are educated wickedly. If the dye have been in the wool, it is hard to get it out of the cloth.

JEREMIAH BURROUGHS

This is the difference between religion and atheism, religion doth not grow without planting, but will die even where it is planted without watering. Atheism, irreligion, and profaneness are weeds that will grow without setting, but they will not die without plucking up.

WILLIAM GURNALL

It is common sense to put the seal to the wax while it is soft.

ARTHUR JACKSON

In spite of disappointments:

What if some prove naught that are well brought up? It is not the generality of them. Will you say that Noah's family was no better than the drowned world, because there was one Ham in it; nor David's because there was one Absalom; nor Christ's because there was one Judas?

RICHARD BAXTER

A motive for parental solicitude:

Children are their parents' heirs; the mercies of God are not the least part of the parents' treasure, nor the least of children's inheritance, being helps for their faith, matter for their praise, and spurs to their obedience. "Our fathers have told us what work Thou didst in their days, in the days of old." Indeed, as children are their parents' heirs, so they become in justice liable to pay their parents' debts. The great debt of the saint at death is that which he owes God for His mercies. Therefore it is but reason that parent should tie his children to the payment thereof.

WILLIAM GURNALL

CHILDREN

A motive for filial regard:

So must the son please him that begot him, that he displease not Him that created him.

THOMAS FULLER

Let others boast their blood and their parentage, and reckon up a long row of monuments and ancestors: if they have been wicked, lewd and ungodly, but thine virtuous and the sincere servants of God, they possibly may be the last of their family, and thou the first of thine: howsoever know that it is far more noble to be born of those that have been born of God, than to be the grandchildren of the devil. Thou hast better blood running in thy veins, even the blood of them whom Christ hath judged worthy to be redeemed and washed with His own blood, whose name are written in heaven in the Lamb's book of life: a greater honour and dignity than if they were written in the worm-eaten pages of idle heraldry. And if thou followest their good examples, thy relations and portion too are greater and richer, for thou hast God for thy father, Christ for thy brother, and the whole heaven of stars for thine inheritance.

EZEKIEL HOPKINS

What a mercy was it to us to have parents that prayed for us before they had us, as well as in our infancy when we could not pray for ourselves!

JOHN FLAVEL

N.B.:

It is easy to observe that none are so gripple and hard-fisted as the childless; whereas those, who, for the maintenance of large families, are inured to frequent disbursements, find such experience of Divine providence in the faithful management of their affairs, as that they lay out with more cheerfulness what they receive.

JOSEPH HALL

CHRIST

His all-sufficiency:

When Christ reveals Himself there is satisfaction in the slenderest portion, and without Christ there is emptiness in the greatest fulness.

ALEXANDER GROSSE

They lose nothing who gain Christ.

SAMUEL RUTHERFORD

The Lord Jesus has provided a common dole of grace and salvation for every poor soul that stands in need of it, only He will have men come and receive it; they shall have it for carrying away.

PAUL BAYNE

The lawyer can deliver his client but from strife, the physician can deliver his patient but from sickness, the master can deliver his servant but from bondage, but the Lord delivereth us from all.

HENRY SMITH

His example:

His cry not Forward, but Follow.

WILLIAM GUTHRIE

"Know that the Lord has set apart him that is godly for Himself." Therefore, it is no excuse for him to say, "I do but as others do." He is to reckon his hours by the sun, not the town clock.

THOMAS MANTON

His glory:

There are three things to be considered concerning the glory of Christ, three degrees of its manifestation, the shadow, the perfect image, and the substance itself. Those under the law had only the shadow of it and of the things that belong to it. . . . Under the Gospel we have the perfect image, which they had not. . . . But the enjoyment of these things in their substance is reserved for heaven; we must be "where He is, that we may behold His glory."

JOHN OWEN

Should the Lord Jesus appear now to any of us in His majesty and glory, it would not be to our edification nor consolation. For we are not meet nor able, by the power of any light or grace that we have received, or can receive, to bear the immediate appearance and representation of them. His beloved apostle John had leaned on His bosom probably many a time in his life, in the intimate familiarities of love; but when He afterward appeared to him in His glory, "he fell at His feet as dead."

JOHN OWEN

Though Christ's coat was once divided, He will never suffer His crown to be divided.

THOMAS BROOKS

His manifestation of God:

God is best known in Christ; the sun is not seen but by the light of the sun.

WILLIAM BRIDGE

In the Scriptures there is a draught of God, but in Christ there is God Himself. A coin bears the image of Caesar, but Caesar's son is his own lively resemblance. Christ is the living Bible.

THOMAS MANTON

No men can know the Father any farther than it pleaseth the Son to reveal Him.

JOHN PENRY

In nature, we see God, as it were, like the sun in a picture; in the law, as the sun in a cloud; in Christ we see Him in His beams; He being "the brightness of His glory, and the exact image of His person."

STEPHEN CHARNOCK

45

CHRIST

His sacrifice:

As a sacrifice, our sins were laid upon Him, (Isaiah 53); as a Priest, He beareth them, (Exodus 28:38); and as an Advocate, He acknowledges them to be His own. (Psalm 69:5).

JOHN BUNYAN

He suffered not as God, but He suffered who was God.

JOHN OWEN

As the burgess of a town or corporation, sitting in the parliament house, beareth the person of that whole town or place, and what he saith the whole town saith, and what is done to him is done to the whole town, even so Christ upon the cross stood in our place, and bare our persons, and whatsoever He suffered we suffered, and when He died all died with Him—all the faithful died in Him, and, as He is risen again, so the faithful are risen in Him.

JOHN BOYS

Sin could not die, unless Christ died; Christ could not die, without being made sin; nor could He die, but sin must die with Him.

ELISHA COLES

All in all:

Cast thine eyes which way thou wilt and thou shalt hardly look upon anything but Christ. Jesus hath taken the name of that thing upon Himself. Is it day? and dost thou behold the sun? He is called the Sun of Righteousness. Or is it night? and dost thou behold the stars? He is called a Star, "There shall come a Star out of Jacob." Or is it morning?. . . . He is called "the bright Morning Star." Or is it noon? and dost thou behold clear light all the world over? He is "that light that lighteth every man that cometh into the world." Come nearer; if thou lookest upon the earth, and takest a view of the creatures about thee, dost thou see the sheep? "As a sheep before her shearer is dumb." Or seest thou a lamb? "Behold the Lamb of God." Seest thou a shepherd watching over his flock? "I am the Good Shepherd." Or seest thou a fountain, waters, rivers. . . .?

ISAAC AMBROSE

The best way to reconcile two disagreeing families is to make some marriage between them: even so, the Word became flesh, and dwelt among us in the world that He might hereby make our peace, reconciling God to man and man to God. By this happy match the Son of God is become the Son of Man, even flesh of our flesh, and bone of our bones; and the sons of men are made the sons of God.

JOHN BOYS

Jesus Christ is a threefold King. First, His enemies' King; secondly, His saints' King; thirdly, His Father's King. . . . Well may He be our King, when He is God's King. But you may say, how is Christ the Father's King? Because He rules for His Father.

WILLIAM DYER

It is a destructive addition to add anything to Christ.

RICHARD SIBBES

To forsake Christ for the world, is to leave a treasure for a trifle. . . . eternity for a moment, reality for a shadow.

WILLIAM JENKYN

The light of the law shone only on the Jews; but this Light spread itself wider, even over all the world.

JOHN LIGHTFOOT

The Sun of Righteousness appeared in three signs especially; Leo, Virgo, Libra. (1) In Leo, roaring as a lion, in the law . . . (2) In Virgo, born of a pure virgin in the Gospel . . . (3) In Libra, weighing our works in His balance at the Day of Judgement.

JOHN BOYS

N.B.:

Since He looked upon me my heart is not my own, He hath run away to heaven with it.

SAMUEL RUTHERFORD

CHRIST

His coming Kingdom:

There will come a time when in this world holiness shall be more general, and more eminent, than ever it hath been since Adam fell in paradise.

THOMAS BROOKS

As Adam had a world made for him, so shall Jesus Christ, the second Adam have a world made for Him. This world was not good enough for Him; He had a better appointed than that which Adam had, a new heaven and a new earth, according to the promise of Isaiah 66:22, where the saints shall reign.... And this world He hath not subjected unto angels.

THOMAS GOODWIN

Be not too curious in searching where God has not discovered or revealed. For example, there are great thoughts of hearts as to when God will deliver His people, and set His churches at liberty; and many men talk much of the year 1666. Some say that shall be the year in which Antichrist shall be destroyed.... Some go to the year 1669, and others pitch upon other times.... But, truly, if you will have my judgement, and I am glad of this opportunity to tell you, this is to pry too much into the ark. Remember the text, "It is not for you to know the times or the seasons which the Father hath put in His own power."

EDMUND CALAMY

Christ hath told us He will come, but not when, that we might never put off our clothes, or put out the candle.

WILLIAM GURNALL

(He) that.... rose from the clods, we expect from the clouds.

THOMAS ADAMS

N.B.:

In the Gospel history, we find that Christ had a fourfold entertainment among men. Some received Him into house, not into heart, as Simon the Pharisee....; some into heart, but not into house, as the faithful centurion....; some neither into house

nor heart, as the graceless Gergesites. . . . ; some both into house
and heart, as Lazarus, Mary, Martha.

JOHN BOYS

CHRISTIANS

Their many designations:

You are those worthies "of whom the world is not worthy,"
Hebrews 11:38. You are the princes "that prevail with God,"
Genesis 32:28. You are those "excellent ones" in whom is all
Christ's delight, Psalm 16:3. You are His glory. You are His
picked, culled, prime instruments which He will make use of to
carry on His best and greatest work against His worst and
greatest enemies in these latter days.

THOMAS BROOKS

The saints of God are called His hidden ones, Psalm 83:3. Why
so? Not only because they are hid in God's decree, and hid in
Christ's wounds, but oftentimes God hides them in a time of
danger and calamity. He reserved to Himself seven thousand
that had not bowed the knee to Baal. The prophet knew not
where there was one, but God knew there were seven thousand.

THOMAS WATSON

"Saints." A title not to be restricted to the godly of the first
times, but common to all that are saved in all after-times also, as
Ephesians 4:12. This name putteth mere morality and formal
profession out of countenance, as the sun doth a glow-worm.
Saintship is a matter of Divine workmanship, and therefore it is
far more remarkable than human excellence. We should keep
up the name of "saints," that the reality of the true religion be
not lowered by avoiding this title; for in these times it is to be
feared that the name is out of use, because holiness itself is out
of fashion.

THOMAS GOODWIN

49

CHRISTIANS

Their privileges:

See the privilege of believers. They have both a spiritual and a civil right to what they possess. They who can say, "Our Father," can say, "our bread." Wicked men that have a legal right to what they possess, but not a covenant-right; they have it by providence, not by promise; with God's leave, not with God's love.

THOMAS WATSON

God has made His children, by adoption, nearer to Himself than the angels. The angels are the friends of Christ; believers are His members.

THOMAS WATSON

Their distinctives:

He is not half a saint who is but a negative saint. . . . The tree that is barren and without good fruit is for the fire, as well as the tree that brings forth evil fruit.

GEORGE SWINNOCK

'Tis strange that the saints, who dare not judge any man, yet are said to judge all things, and to be judged of no man; that they who hurt no man should be said to destroy all men; that those who have nothing, should be said to be heirs of all, and inherit all things.

WILLIAM ERBERY

Christians must be thrown to the lions because they are Christians.

NEHEMIAH ROGERS

That which the saints scarce take notice of in themselves, God in a special manner observes. "I was an hungered, and ye gave me meat; I was thirsty, and ye gave me drink. Then shall the righteous say, Lord, when saw we Thee an hungered and fed Thee?" (Matthew 25:35). They as it were overlooked and disclaimed their own works of charity, but Christ takes notice of them.

THOMAS WATSON

CHRISTIANS

It argues more grace to grieve for the sins of others than for our own. We may grieve for our own sins out of fear of hell, but to grieve for the sins of others is from a principle of love to God.

THOMAS WATSON

He who is godly is both a diamond and a loadstone; a diamond for the sparkling of his grace; and a loadstone, for his attractive virtue in drawing others to the love of God's precepts.

THOMAS WATSON

As there is need of no law to compel the body to eat or drink, to digest, to sleep. . . . or to do the works of nature, for it is ready to do them of itself when the case so requireth, without respect either of reward or punishment. . . . even so, after the same sort altogether, doth the godly man behave himself concerning the works of godliness. He is carried to the doing of them by his new nature, which is of the Spirit.

DANIEL CAWDRAY

Gospel duties are to be performed with a Gospel temper.

STEPHEN CHARNOCK

We are to receive our reward not according to our success, but according to our sincerity.

JOHN OLDFIELD

Visibility and universality are Popish marks of a true church, and Protestant marks of a true Christian.

GEORGE SWINNOCK

The world does not know, nor is able to make a right judgement of believers. . . . Their infirmities are visible to all — their graces invisible; the King's daughter is glorious within.

JOHN OWEN

Be as holy as you can, as if there were no gospel to save you. Yet when you are as holy as you can, you must believe in Christ as if there were no law at all to condemn you.

THOMAS LYE

CHRISTIANS

A hypocrite knows more than he is willing to do; but a true saint desires to do what he knows, and to know more that he may do more, and better.

VAVASOR POWELL

Everything betters a saint. Not only ordinances, word, sacraments, holy society, but even sinners and their very sinning. Even these draw forth their graces into exercise, and put them upon godly, broken-hearted mourning. A saint sails with every wind. As the wicked are hurt by the best things, so the godly are bettered by the worst.

WILLIAM JENKYN

Their limitations:

You are to follow no man further than he follows Christ.

JOHN COLLINS

It was a charge long ago laid upon Christianity, that it was better known in leaves of books, than in the lives of Christians.

WILLIAM GURNALL

He is like the man that has many kin and few friends. Many now are with Christ, and few for Christ.

SAMUEL RUTHERFORD

The weak Christian is willing to live and patient to die; but the strong, patient to live and willing to die.

JOHN BOYS

Their persecution:

Wicked men seem to bear great reverence to the saints departed; they canonize dead saints, but persecute living.

THOMAS WATSON

Martyrdom came into the world early; the first man that died, died for religion.

WILLIAM JENKYN

Saints must be best in worst times.

JOHN TRAPP

Their perseverance:

In spite of all devils there shall be saints.

JOSEPH HALL

Their rewards:

Piety shall have riches without rust, wealth without want, store without sore, beauty without blemish, mirth without mixture.

JOHN TRAPP

They that side with the saints shall thrive with the saints.

JOHN TRAPP

Though our reward be not for our good works, yet we shall have our good works rewarded, and have a good reward for our works. Though the best of men deserve nothing at the hands of God, yet they may deserve much at the hands of men; and if they have not the recompense they deserve, yet it is a kind of recompense to have deserved. As he said, and nobly, "I had rather it should be said, Why doth not Cato's image stand here? than that it should be said, Why doth it stand here?"

RALPH VENNING

If there be glory laid up for them that die in the Lord; much more shall they be glorified that die for the Lord.

SIR RICHARD BAKER

CHURCH, THE

Origin:

The church comes out of Christ's side in the sleep of His death.

WILLIAM JENKYN

CHURCH

Designations:

His *tabernacles* did but serve to shew His power, His *courts* but to shew His majesty; His *altars* but to shew His deity, His *house* serves to shew them all; for in His *house* there will still be praising Him, and His praise and glory is the sum of all.

SIR RICHARD BAKER

Unity but not uniformity:

For one sect then to say, Ours is the true Church, and another to say, Nay, but ours is the true Church, is as mad as to dispute whether your hall, or kitchen, or parlour, or coal-house is your house; and or one to say, This is the house, and another, Nay, but it is that; when a child can tell them, that the best is but a part, and the house containeth them all.

RICHARD BAXTER

For as a kingdom, divided into many shires, and more towns and villages, is called one, because it hath one and the same king, one and the same law; so the church is one, because it liveth by one and the same Spirit, and is ruled by one and the same Lord, and professeth one and the same faith; hath one and the same hope, and hath been baptized with one and the same baptism.

NEHEMIAH ROGERS

Holy, in spite of unholy members:

As a heap of wheat, though it have chaff in it, is yet called wheat; or as a tun of wine, though it have lees in it, is yet called wine; or as a field wherein tares appear with the wheat is called a cornfield; even so the visible Church is the Church. Though it consisteth of good and bad, and be mixed of the elect and reprobate, yet are they called God's Church for the elect's sake, and have their denomination from the better, not the bigger part.

DANIEL CAWDRAY

CHURCH

Though we have sins too many, yet the better part gives the name. Corn-fields we see have many weeds, yet we call them corn-fields, not fields of weeds. . . .

PAUL BAYNE

The church hath more professing than regenerate members, and will have to the end of the world, and none must expect that they be commensurate.

RICHARD BAXTER

Salvian observeth that the church, like a river, loseth in depth, what it gaineth in breadth.

THOMAS MANTON

Many crowd to get into the church, but make no room for the sermon to get into them.

THOMAS ADAMS

Every one that hangs about the court does not speak with the king.

THOMAS WATSON

As Christ hath His saints in Nero's court; so the devil his servants in the outer court of the visible church.

WILLIAM GURNALL

A program for discipline:

After proof and trial made of their fidelity, we are to trust our brethren without any further suspicion. Not to try before we trust is want of wisdom, not to trust after we have tried is want of charity. The goldsmith must purify the dross and ore from the gold, but he must be wary lest he make waste of good metal if over anxious in too often refining.

THOMAS FULLER

As a corn-field, — (i) corn, (ii) straw and chaff, and (iii) weeds and stricken ears — is denominated from the corn, which is the chief part; but the straw must not be cast out because it is necessary for the corn; but the weeds must be pulled up, except when doing it may hurt the wheat; even so the Church hath (i) sincere Christians from whom it is denominated; (ii) Close hypocrites, whose gifts are for the good of the sincere, and must not be cast out by the pastors; (iii) Heretics and notorious wicked men, who are impenitent after due admonition; and these must be cast out, except when it may hazard the Church.

RICHARD BAXTER

There is no place for any loose stone in God's edifice.

JOSEPH HALL

God cannot endure that in His fields which He suffers in the wilderness.

JOHN FLAVEL

It is better for a bramble to be in the wilderness than in an orchard; for a weed to be abroad, than in a garden, where it is sure to be weeded out, as the other to be cut down. If a man will be unprofitable, let him be unprofitable out of the Church. But to be so where he has the dew of grace falling on him, in the means of salvation, where are all God's sweet favours. . . . will God, the great Husbandman, endure this? Whatsoever is not for fruit is for the fire.

RICHARD SIBBES

We read not that Christ ever exercised force but once, and that was to drive profane ones out of His Temple, and not to force them in.

JOHN MILTON

Subservient to the Bible:

God speaks in the Scriptures, and by it teaches the Church herself; and therefore His authority in the Scriptures is greater, the authority of Him that teaches, than of those by whom He teaches as the authority of a king in his laws is greater than that of an officer that proclaims them.

UNKNOWN

God speaks by the Church (the true Church we mean); but He speaks nothing by her but what He speaks in the Scriptures, which she does only ministerially declare to us; and therefore the authority of God and His law is above hers, who, though she publish, yet did not make it, but is herself subject to it.

JOHN OWEN

Is church attendance necessary?

Objection: I can profit as much by staying at home and reading the Scripture or some good book; it is the word of God which they preach, and it is that which I read at home. The books that are written by learned men are better than the sermons that are preached by our ministers.

Answer: What foolish pretences are these against the plain command of God and our own necessary duty! When God hath appointed you your duty, will He allow you to forsake it upon your own reason, as if you were wiser than God, and knew what will profit you better than He? . . . . Is it not horrible pride in you to think that you are able to understand the word of God as well without a teacher as with one? . . . . as if your children that go to school should say, "We have the same books at home, and therefore we will not go to school; our master doth but teach us grammar, and other books, and these we can read at home."

RICHARD BAXTER

What church should I attend?

Those who have found the presence and power of the spirit of Christ breathing in their ministers, either to their conversion, or edification, will be slow to change such a ministry of faith, and holiness, for the liberty of church order.

JOHN COTTON

Where God does not find a mouth to speak, you must not find an ear to hear, nor a heart to believe.

THOMAS LYE

Her survival guaranteed:

The whole course of affairs in the world is steered by Providence in reference to the good of Salem.

JOHN OWEN

CHURCH

Joseph said to his brethren, "You did intend me hurt, but God did intend me good." So it may be said concerning all ungodly, wicked men; they do intend evil against the Church and people of God, but God intends His people's good, and, in conclusion, effects it.

JEREMIAH WHITAKER

God's love for the church:

All the glory that He (God) looks for to eternity must arise out of this one work of building Zion; this one work shall be the only monument of His glory to eternity; this goodly world, this heaven and earth, that you see and enjoy the use of, is set up only as a ship, as a workshop, to stand only for a week, for six or seven thousand years; and when His work is done He will throw this piece of clay down again, and out of this He looks for no other glory than from a cabul, a land of dirt, or a shepherd's cottage, or a gourd which springs up in a night and withers in a day; but this piece He sets up for a higher end, to be the eternal mansion of His holiness and honour; this is His metropolis, His temple, His house.

STEPHEN MARSHALL

The saints' love for the church:

Seeing they prosper that love and bear affection to Jerusalem, let men learn to show good will unto Christ's church, though as yet they be no ripe scholars themselves in Christ's school; though they be not grown to perfection let them express a good affection.

ANDREW WILLET

Either our beds are soft, or our hearts hard, that can rest when the church is at unrest, that feel not our brethren's hard cords through our soft beds.

JOHN TRAPP

N.B.:

O be not too quick to bury the Church before she is dead.

JOHN FLAVEL

CONFESSION

Confession is verbal humiliation.

RICHARD SIBBES

Many blush to confess their faults, who never blush to commit them.

WILLIAM SECKER

God puts away many in anger for their supposed goodness, but not any at all for their confessed badness.

JOHN TRAPP

CONSCIENCE

Conscience is God's spy and man's overseer.

JOHN TRAPP

Conscience, the domestic chaplain.

JOHN TRAPP

Its excellency:

A quiet conscience never produced an unquiet conversation.

JOHN FLAVEL

A good conscience and a good confidence go together.

THOMAS BROOKS

No flattery can heal a bad conscience, so no slander can hurt a good one.

THOMAS WATSON

Strive greatly to have and to exercise a good conscience towards God, and men; to commit thy soul, life, and cause to the Lord; and then expect the worst of men, and the best of Christ.

VAVASOR POWELL

59

CONSCIENCE

Peace of conscience is nothing but the echo of pardoning mercy.

WILLIAM GURNALL

Its ministry:

If conscience speaketh not, it writeth; for it is not only a witness, but a register, and a book of record: "The sin of Judah, is written with a pen of iron, and the point of a diamond."

THOMAS MANTON

Even as he who is troubled with a burning fever is hotter than he who is parched with the sun; so is that man more troubled who hath a guilty conscience than a good man by all outward afflictions.

DANIEL CAWDRAY

The Lord God hath set it as His deputy in the breast of man, which, though it be oftentime a neuter when the act is doing and while sin is a committing, yet afterwards it will prove a friend and faithful witness for the Lord, but an adversary against man.

NEHEMIAH ROGERS

As a lamp near expiring, shines more clearly, so conscience, that burned dimly for a time, gives a dying blaze, and discovers Him who is alone able to save or to destroy.

WILLIAM BATES

Its limitations:

Conscience is God's sergeant He employs to arrest the sinner. Now the sergeant hath no power to release his prisoner upon any private composition between him and the prisoner; but listens, whether the debt be fully paid, or the creditor be fully satisfied; then, and not till then, he is discharged of his prisoner.

WILLIAM GURNALL

Oh, it is to be feared that there are many that give themselves to lusts, and carnal pleasures, that so they may put a foggy mist between their conscience and themselves. Others dig into the world, labouring to become senseless, that so there may be an eclipse of this light by the interposition of the earth. Others run to damnable heresies, denying Scriptures, God, heaven, hell. . . . What are these but refuges of guilty consciences? We must distinguish between our carnal concupiscence, and conscience; between deluded imaginations, and conscience; between an erroneous and scrupulous conscience, and a well-grounded and truly informed conscience; and when we have done so, we must follow conscience as far as that follows the Word.

ANTHONY BURGESS

Why it often fails to function?

Conscience is a check to beginners in sin, reclaiming them from it and rating them for it; but this in longstanders becometh useless; either failing to discharge its office, or assaying it to no purpose: having often been slighted, it will be weary of chiding; or, if it be not wholly dumb, we shall be deaf to its reproof: as those who live by cataracts or downfalls of water, are, by continual noise, so deafened as not to hear or mind it.

ISAAC BARROW

N.B.:

The conscience is not to be healed if it be not wounded.

WILLIAM PERKINS

CONTROVERSY

Often foolish and unprofitable:

As in the burning of some wet fuel, we cannot see the fire for smoke; so the light of the Scriptures is dusked by the vapours of controversies.

THOMAS ADAMS

CONTROVERSY

Were it not a piece of strange madness, when the enemy is at the walls, and the town every moment in danger of being stormed, the bullets flying thick about the streets, for the people within to be sitting still and consulting, whether a musket would carry further than a trunk. Truly, such folly, such madness, is it to employ ourselves about needless discourse about the world or superficial things, when our inestimable souls are continually in danger of being surprised and slain.

GEORGE SWINNOCK

Many controversies of these times grow up about religion, as suckers from the root and limbs of a fruit tree, which spend the vital sap that should make fruit.

JOHN FLAVEL

The devil loves to fish in troubled waters.

JOHN TRAPP

There are some controversies prickly like brambles, and apt to scratch those that handle them, but yielding no savoury or wholesome fruit.

ISAAC BARROW

I have other things to do than to be a contentious man.

JOHN PENRY

Occasionally justified:

The servants of God do mind the matter of religion more seriously than others do; and therefore their differences are made more observable to the world. They cannot make light of the smallest truth of God; and this may be some occasion of their indifference; whereas the ungodly differ not about religion, because they have heartily no religion to differ about. Is this a unity and peace to be desired? I had rather have the discord of the saints than such a concord of the wicked.

RICHARD BAXTER

There is no learned man but will confess that he hath much profited by reading controversies—his senses awakened, his judgement sharpened, and the truth which he holds more firmly established. All controversy being permitted, falsehood will appear more false, and truth the more true.

JOHN MILTON

It is not controversy we have to dread as much as the spirit of controversy.

RICHARD TREFFREY, JR.

N.B.:

The differences among Christians are nothing in comparison of the differences among heathens.

RICHARD BAXTER

When we have a controversy with the wicked we should take heed that private spleen do not rule us, but that only our interest in God's quarrel with them doth move us.

DAVID DICKSON

CONVERSION

Is it always sudden and traumatic?

We have known those who having misspent their younger times in notoriously lewd and debauched courses, who after long and deep humiliation, have been raised up, through God's mercy, to a comfortable sense of the Divine favour; and have proceeded to a very high degree of regeneration, and lived and died saints. But this is not every man's cause. . . . Those, who, having from their infancy been brought up in the nurture and fear of the Lord, and from their youth have been trained up under a godly and conscionable ministry, and have, by an insensible conveyance, received the gracious inoperations of the Spirit of God, framing them to a holy obedience; these cannot expect to find so sensible alterations in themselves. As well may the child know when he was naturally born, as these know the instant of their spiritual regeneration.

JOSEPH HALL

CONVERSION

He that is locked up in a dungeon. . . . may easily discover the very moment of time when either the least beam of the sun shall break in upon him; whereas he that is in the open air is very sensible that the day is broke, that the sun is up, but cannot make out any certain account of the springing of the one or rising of the other. Thus it is in the matter of our spiritual calling.

JOHN BOYS

Whether sincere conversion began now, or before, or after, I was never able to this day to know. . . . God breaketh not all men's hearts alike.

RICHARD BAXTER

The wind bloweth where it listeth, even so the Spirit, both time and place uncertain. . . . so that, if a man can but make out unto his soul that he is certainly called, it matters not much for the time when nor the place where, both of them being so uncertain.

JOHN BOYS

Can a man be converted and not know it?

Can Christ be in thy heart, and thou not know it? Can one king be dethroned and another crowned in thy soul, and thou hear no scuffle?

WILLIAM GURNALL

The pragmatic test?

There is a difference between fencing and fighting for life. So it is with a hypocrite in his seeming reformation; when he makes the greatest stir against his sin in confessing and prayer, and other means, yet he will not resolvedly cast it away, but he secretly useth it as his friend, while he openly abuseth it as his enemy. But it is clean contrary with a man that is converted. Though the remnants of sin will remain in him while he liveth, yet as to the reign of it, he presently casteth it off, and biddeth defiance to it. He fighteth against it in good earnest, as knowing that either he or it must die.

RICHARD BAXTER

CONVERSION

All believers do grow in grace. And this ye know is the difference between a painted child and a living child, and though he
be but little and very weak, yet he grows bigger. But a child that
is painted upon a wall grows not.

WILLIAM BRIDGE

When the wheels of a clock move within, the hands on the dial
will move without. When the heart of a man is sound in
conversion, then the life will be fair in profession.

WILLIAM SECKER

Delay means danger compounded:

All the while thou delayest, God is more provoked, the wicked
one more encouraged, thy heart more hardened, thy debts
more increased, thy soul more endangered, and all the difficulties of conversion daily more and more multiplied upon thee,
having a day more to repent of, and a day less to repent in.

GEORGE SWINNOCK

And the longer you delay, the more your sin gets strength and
rooting. If you cannot bend a twig, how will you be able to bend
it when it is a tree?

RICHARD BAXTER

Many think not of living any holier, till they can live no longer.

WILLIAM SECKER

He that saith he will be good tomorrow, he saith he will be
wicked today.

JAMES JANEWAY

Delays be dangerous, our hearts will cool, and our affections
will fall down.... Satan hath little hope to prevail unless he can
persuade us to omit our duties when the clock strikes, and
therefore his skill is to urge us to put off till another time as fitter
or better. Do it anon, next hour, next day, next week (saith he);
and why not next year?

RICHARD CAPEL

CONVERSION, COVETOUSNESS

Delay is a kind of denial.

TIMOTHY CRUSO

Take heed Professors, lest you be always wooing Christ, and yet never married to Him.

VAVASOR POWELL

Are death-bed conversions genuine?

Some are called at the first hour—that is, in their infancy or childhood, as Samuel, Jeremiah, and John the Baptist; some in the third hour—that is, in their youth, as Daniel the prophet and John the evangelist; others at the sixth hour—in their middle age, as Peter and Andrew; others at the eleventh hour—in their old age, as Gamaliel and Joseph of Arimathea; and some again, not only in the last hour of the day, but even in the last minute of that hour, as the thief upon the cross.

JOHN BOYS

The Bible, which ranges over a period of four thousand years, records but one instance of a death-bed conversion—one that none may despair, and but one that none may presume.

WILLIAM GUTHRIE

There be few at all saved. . . . and fewest saved this way.

WILLIAM GUTHRIE

COVETOUSNESS

Covetousness is dry drunkenness.

THOMAS WATSON

He is not a covetous man, who lays up something *providentially*; but he is a covetous man, who gives out nothing *willingly*.

WILLIAM SECKER

COVETOUSNESS

Non-satisfying!

A ship may be overladen with silver, even unto sinking, and yet
space enough be left to hold ten times more. So a covetous man,
though he have enough to sink him, yet never hath he enough to
satisfy him. . . . a circle cannot fill a triangle, so neither can the
whole world the heart of man; a man may as easily fill a chest
with grace, as the heart with gold.

JOHN TRAPP

A poor man doth want many things, a rich miser wants everything.

JOHN BOYS

It is the *love*, not the lack of money, that makes men churls.

JOHN TRAPP

Non-profitable:

It is a common saying that a hog is good for nothing whilst he is
alive: not good to bear or carry, as the horse; nor to draw, as the
ox; nor to clothe, as the sheep; nor to give milk, as the cow; nor
to keep the house, as the dog; but fed only to the slaughter.

So a covetous, rich man, just like a hog, doth no good with his
riches whilst he liveth, but when he is dead his riches come to
be disposed of. "The riches of a sinner are laid up for the just."

ANDREW WILLET

The ultimate folly:

The miser deprives himself of this world and God will deprive
him of the next.

THOMAS ADAMS

They are fools that fear to lose their wealth by giving, but fear
not to lose themselves by keeping it.

JOHN TRAPP.

COVETOUSNESS

Covetousness is called idolatry, which is worse than infidelity, Colossians 3:5; for it is less rebellion not to honour the king, than to set up another king against him . . .

HENRY SMITH

Antichrist is Mammon's son.

JOHN MILTON

The Christian answer:

Christianity teacheth me that what I charitably give alive, I carry with me dead; and experience teacheth me that what I leave behind, I lose. I will carry that treasure with me by giving it, which the worldling loseth by keeping it; so, while his corpse shall carry nothing but a winding cloth to his grave, I shall be richer under the earth than I was above it.

JOSEPH HALL

To dispense our wealth liberally, is the best way to preserve it.

ISAAC BARROW

We must be convinced that covetousness, I mean that our covetousness, is a vice; for it holds something of a virtue, of frugality, which is not to waste that which one hath; and this makes us entertain thoughts that it is no vice; and we often say that it is good to be a little worldly; a little covetousness we like well; which shows that we do not indeed and in heart, hold it to be a sin. For if sin be naught, a little of sin cannot be good. As good say, a little poison were good, so it be not too much.

RICHARD CAPEL

N.B.:

It is commonly said that covetousness is one of the reigning sins of old age. How strange that it should be so! Especially considering what they have seen, and known, and it may be, *felt* of the emptiness and uncertainty of riches. They have witnessed how often they make themselves wings. What! and not yet convinced! What! almost at the end of thy journey, and yet loading thyself with thick clay! Think of the time of day. It is almost night; even sun-set. And art thou unmindful of the grave? The body is bending downwards, let the heart be upwards.

PHILIP HENRY

This is the great foolishness and disease especially of old age, that the less way a man has to go, he makes the greater provision for it. When the hands are stiff, and fit for no other labour, they are fitted and composed for scraping together.

ROBERT LEIGHTON

DEATH

Its inevitability:

God, to prevent all escape, hath sown the seeds of death in our very constitution and nature, so that we can as soon run from ourselves, as run from death. We need no feller to come with a hand of violence and hew us down; there is in the tree a worm, which grows out of its own substance, that will destroy it; so in us, those infirmities of nature that will bring us down to the dust.

WILLIAM GURNALL

Against this arrest there is no bail.

GEORGE SWINNOCK

All are like actors on a stage, some have one part and some another, death is still busy amongst us; here drops one of the players, we bury him with sorrow, and to our scene again: then falls another, yea all, one after another, till death be left upon the stage. Death is that damp which puts out all the dim lights of vanity. Yet man is easier to believe that all the world shall die, than to suspect himself.

THOMAS ADAMS

69

DEATH

Time ? Anytime:

Death takes not men in seniority, but sometimes sends them first to the burial that came last from the birth.

THOMAS FULLER

There is none so old but thinks he may live one year longer; and though, in the general, he say, "All must die," yet, in the false numbering of his own particular days, he thinks to live for ever.

NEHEMIAH ROGERS

The ministry it performs:

Rebirth brings us into the Kingdom of grace, and death into the Kingdom of glory.

RICHARD BAXTER

Death is only a grim porter to let us into a stately palace.

RICHARD SIBBES

We spend our years with sighing; it is a valley of tears; but death is the funeral of all our sorrows.

THOMAS WATSON

Mighty and gracious lords, I will tell you to what your honour shall come; first, ye shall wax old like others, then ye shall fall sick like others, then ye shall die like others, then ye shall be buried like others, then ye shall be consumed like others, then ye shall be judged like others, even like the beggars which cry at your gates: one sickens, the other sickens; one dies, the other dies; one rots, the other rots: look in the grave, and show me which was Dives and which was Lazarus. This is some comfort to the poor, that once he shall be like the rich; one day he shall be as wealthy, and as glorious as a king; one hour of death will make all alike.

HENRY SMITH

Should death be desired?

I account this body nothing but a close prison to my soul; and the earth a larger prison to my body. I may not break prison, till I be loosed by death; but I will leave it, not unwillingly, when I am loosed.

JOSEPH HALL

Should death be feared?

If a man that is desperately sick today, did believe he should arise sound the next morning; or a man today, in despicable poverty, had assurance that he should tomorrow arise a prince; would they be afraid to go to bed. . . . ?

RICHARD BAXTER

The fear of death is ingrafted in the common nature of all men, but faith works it out of Christians.

VAVASOR POWELL

Let them fear death who do not fear sin.

THOMAS WATSON

Let thy hope of heaven master thy fear of death. Why shouldst thou be afraid to die, who hopest to live by dying!

WILLIAM GURNALL

The way of victory:

Death is half disarmed when the pleasures and interests of the flesh are first denied.

RICHARD BAXTER

He may look on death with joy, who can look on forgiveness with faith.

THOMAS WATSON

Familiarize the thoughts of the evil day to thy soul; handle this serpent often, walk daily in the serious meditations of it, do not run from them because they are unpleasing to flesh, that is the way to increase the terror of it. Do with your souls, when shy of,

DEATH

and scared with the thoughts of affliction or death, as you use to
do with your beast that is given to boggle and start as you ride
on him; when he flies back and starts at a thing, you do not yield
to his fear and go back, that will make him worse another time,
but you ride him up close to that which he is afraid of, and in
time you break him of that quality. The evil day is not such a
fearful thing to thee that art a Christian, as thou shouldst start
for it. Bring up thy heart close to it, show thy soul what Christ
hath done to take the sting out of it. . . .

WILLIAM GURNALL

A godly man is free from the sting, but not from the stroke, from
the curse, but not from the cross of death.

GEORGE SWINNOCK

Pray that thy last *days*, and last *works* may be the best; and that
when thou comest to *die*, thou mayest have nothing else to do
but *die*.

VAVASOR POWELL

It is well known that when a jailer knocks off a prisoner's fetters,
that the constant wearing them hath put him to a great deal less
pain than the knocking of them off doth at the present; yet,
though every blow go to the very heart of him, he never mur-
murs at it. . . . because he knows that the pain will be compen-
sated by the ease that he shall afterwards enjoy.

NEHEMIAH ROGERS

Two things are to be set in order—the house and the heart. The
house—by settling our worldly estate. We shall die none the
sooner, but we shall certainly be readier for death (Isaiah 38:1).
The heart, by settling our spiritual estate; that is, making our
calling and election sure; repenting of sin, receiving Christ
Jesus the Lord, walking in all His commandments blameless.
He who hath done this, is ready for death.

PHILIP HENRY

Death is never sudden to a saint; no guest comes unawares to
him who keeps a constant table.

GEORGE SWINNOCK

72

N.B.:

Lord, be pleased to shake my clay cottage before Thou throwest it down. Make it totter awhile before it doth tumble. Let me be summoned before I am surprised.

THOMAS FULLER

DESERTION

(See *also* Chastisement)

God's desertion of the believer - never complete:

A man sometimes goes from home, and sometimes he does not quite leave his house. There is much difference between those two. If a man leaves his house and comes no more, then he carries away all his goods. . . . But though a man ride a great journey, yet he may come again; and ye say, "Surely he will come again." Why? Because still his goods, wife and children are in his house. So if Christ rejects a man and go away finally, He carries away all His goods, spiritual gifts, graces and principles. But though He be long absent, yet if His household stuff abide in the heart,—if there be the same desires after Him, and delight in Him, and admiring of Him,—ye may say, "Surely, He will come again." Why? Because His household stuff is here still. When did Christ ever forsake a man in whose heart He left this spiritual furniture?

WILLIAM BRIDGE

He who hath engaged to be our God for ever, cannot depart for ever.

TIMOTHY CRUSO

73

DESERTION

Desertion - a discipline:

God being a Father, if He hide His face from His child, it is in love. Desertion is sad in itself, a short hell. (Job 6:9). When the light is withdrawn, dew falls. Yet we may see a rainbow in the cloud, the love of a Father in all this.

THOMAS WATSON

I know that, as night and shadows are good for flowers, and moonlight and dews are better than a continual sun, so is Christ's absence of special use, and that it hath some nourishing virtue in it, and giveth sap to humility, and putteth an edge on hunger, and furnisheth a fair field to faith to put forth itself, and to exercise its fingers in gripping it seeth not what.

SAMUEL RUTHERFORD

Desertion - a safeguard:

Though He leaves us for a time, yet doth He not forsake us for ever, no more than a nurse doth the weakling child. She maketh use of one fall to keep the child from many, and God doth make use of our sinning to make us see how prone we are to sin, and so prevent us for the future.

JOHN LIGHTFOOT

Desertion - a chastisement:

The wounds of conscience which are in God's people are of the quality that none but God can cure them; for the chief thing that wounds them is the loss of God's favour, not simply His wrath. . . . Nothing gives peace but the restoring of His favour and the light of His countenance; the same dart that wounded must heal again. "I smote him, and I will heal him."

THOMAS GOODWIN

N.B.:

Did God really forsake Jesus Christ upon the cross? Then from the desertion of Christ singular consolation springs up to the people of God. . . . (1) Christ's desertion is *preventive* of your final desertion. Because He was forsaken for a time you shall not be forsaken for ever. For He was forsaken for you. . . . (2) . . . . Though God deserted Christ, yet at the same time He powerfully supported Him. His omnipotent arms were under Him, though His pleased face was hid from Him. He had not indeed His smiles, but He had His supportations. So, Christian, just so shall it be with thee. Thy God may turn away His face, He will not pluck away His arm.

JOHN FLAVEL

DEVIL, THE

The devil, that great peripatetic.

JOHN TRAPP

Our greatest adversary:

Let us watch Satan, for he watcheth us. There is no corporeal enemy, but a man naturally fears; the spiritual foe appears less terrible, because we are less sensible of him. Great conquerors have been chronicled for victories and extension of their kingdoms; Satan is beyond them all. Saul has slain his thousands, and David his ten thousands; but Satan his millions. He that fights with an enemy, whom nothing but blood can pacify, will give him no advantage.

THOMAS ADAMS

He sometimes slanders God to men; as to Eve. . . . sometimes men to God; as Job. . . . and continually, man to man.

JOHN ROBINSON

Satan has three titles given in the Scriptures, setting forth his malignity against the church of God; a dragon, to note his malice; a serpent, to note his subtlety; and a lion, to note his strength.

EDWARD REYNOLDS

DEVIL

Our foil:

Satan is only God's master fencer to teach us to use our weapons.

SAMUEL RUTHERFORD

His tactics:

The devil shapes himself to the fashions of all men. If he meet with a proud man, or a prodigal man, then he makes himself a flatterer; if a covetous man, then he comes with a reward in his hand. He hath an apple for Eve, a grape for Noah, a change of raiment for Gehazi, a bag for Judas. He can dish out his meat for all palates; he hath a last to fit every shoe; he hath something to please all conditions.

WILLIAM JENKYN

The devil pieceth the fox's skin of seducers with the lion's skin of persecutors.

WILLIAM GURNALL

Till we sin Satan is a parasite; but when once we are in the devil's hands he turns tyrant.

THOMAS MANTON

It is an old policy the devil hath, to jostle out a greater good by a less.

NEHEMIAH ROGERS

Satan doth not like God, warn before he strikes.

VAVASOR POWELL

The devil has three ways by which he makes men seek after him. First, commonly he covers holiness with other names. Secondly, he persuades men that sins are but little. Thirdly, that they may be repented of hereafter.

JOHN COLLINS

Satan can afflict the body by the mind—for these two are so closely bound together that their good and bad estate is shared between them. If the heart be merry the countenance is cheerful, the strength is renewed, the bones do flourish like an herb. If the heart be troubled, the health is impaired, the strength is dried up, the marrow of the bones wasted, etc. Grief in the heart is like a moth in the garment, it insensibly consumeth the body and disordereth it.

RICHARD GILPIN

The devil's war is better than the devil's peace. Suspect dumb holiness. When the dog is kept out of doors he howls to be let in again.

SAMUEL RUTHERFORD

The devil is called "the prince of the power of the air." Infected air is drawn into the lungs without pain, and we get a disease before we feel it.

THOMAS MANTON

Satan is God's ape.

STEPHEN CHARNOCK

Satan watcheth for those vessels that sail without a convoy.

GEORGE SWINNOCK

N.B.:

The devil is a great student in divinity.

WILLIAM GURNALL

His limitations:

The first limit is his nature, for he is not able to do anything than that which his natural disposition will permit and suffer. The second limit is the Will of God, for he can do nothing against the Will of God.

ARTHUR DENT

Certain it is, and we are to believe it by faith, that the power of Satan is not equal to the power of God. It is not so strong, so large, and so wide. It is every way infinitely less. There is no comparison between that which is infinite and that which is finite. If we compare it with good angels, it will be less than some and greater than other some. . . . But if we compare it with the power of man, it is far greater every way, but yet, we must know, that is a finite and natural power, not supernatural, for then none could be saved. It is mighty, but yet not almighty.

ARTHUR DENT

His ally within:

Our corrupted hearts are the factories of the devil, which may be at work without his presence; for when that circumventing spirit has drawn malice, envy, and all unrighteousness unto well-rooted habits in his disciples, iniquity then goes upon its own legs; and if the gates of hell were shut up for a time, vice would still be fertile and produce the fruits of hell. Thus, when God forsakes us, Satan also leaves us; for such offenders he looks upon as sure and sealed up, and his temptations then needless unto them.

SIR THOMAS BROWNE

N.B.:

God sets the devil to catch himself.

WILLIAM GURNALL

DISCIPLINE

Administer with care:

There must be great care taken, that when we seek to pluck up the tares, we pluck not up the wheat also; this may be understood of things, of truths and falsehoods, as well as of persons. . . . in respect of things good or evil, there are some things apparently evil, they are rather thistles and briars, than tares; we may freely pluck them up; but other things, though perhaps they may prove evil, yet they have some likeness to good, so as you can hardly discern whether they be good or evil; Now, saith

DISCIPLINE

Christ, take heed what you do then, do not out of eagerness to oppose all evil, to get out every tare, pluck out some wheat too; what if that you oppose with violence as evil, prove to be good? You had better let forty tares stand, than pluck up one wheat.

JEREMIAH BURROUGHS

There is more confidence needful in a thing that we impose upon others, than in what we practice ourselves. If a thing be to us rather true than otherwise, we may lawfully do it, but this is not enough to be a ground for the imposing it upon others, who cannot see it to be a truth; in such a case we need to be very sure.

JEREMIAH BURROUGHS

The nature and end of judgement or sentence must be corrective, not vindictive; for healing, not destruction.

JOHN OWEN

Prudence must be exercised in the proceeding, lest we do more hurt than good. . . . we should deal humbly even when we deal sharply.

RICHARD BAXTER

Excommunication:

The proper inward effect that accompanies this ordinance (excommunication) is inward affliction and distress of conscience by Satan, which of all afflictions is the greatest punishment. . . . This we see in the excommunication of the Corinthian; whose excommunication is said to be a delivering up unto Satan in the name of the Lord Jesus (1 Corinthians 5:4f). He was to be cast out by a commission from Christ, which going forth in His name, when they published it on earth, He signed it in heaven.

THOMAS GOODWIN

Self-discipline:

By fasting, the body learns to obey the soul; by praying, the soul learns to command the body.

WILLIAM SECKER

DIVISIONS

Can they be justified?

Would Christ not have His coat rent, and can He endure to have His body rent?

THOMAS WATSON

God makes account, that He brings a heavy judgement upon a people when He Himself leaves them. If the Master leaves the ship, it is near sinking indeed; and truly, no readier way to send Him going than by strifes among brethren; these smoke Him out of His own house.

WILLIAM GURNALL

Better to be like such heretics as do nothing else but pray, than to be such schismatics as do nothing else but prate.

JOHN BOYS

What! at peace with the Father, and at war with His Children? It cannot be.

JOHN FLAVEL

I will never join with them that will have but one Form in Christ's School. I would have the ABC there taught as well as the profoundest mysteries. 'Tis no sign of the family of God to have no children in it, but strong men only; nor of the hospital of Christ, to have none sick; nor of His net to have no fish but good; nor of His field, to have no tares; flesh and blood hath ticed me oft to separation and ease; but it's too easy a way to be of God.

RICHARD BAXTER

Fractions always breed factions.

RICHARD SIBBES

Is it not to be bitterly lamented, that in a reformed and orthodox church there should be such schisms, rents and divisions; altar against altar, pulpit against pulpit, and one congregation against another? And what is all this contention and separation for? Oh, they will tell you it is for the purity of religion; for the true and sincere worship of God; that they may serve Him purely without human additions or inventions. . . . Alas, my brethren, was there ever any schism in the world that did not plead the same? Do not others separate from their communion upon the same pretences on which they now separate from ours? And may not the same arguments serve to crumble them into infinite fractions and subdivisions; till, at last, we come to have almost as many churches as men?

EZEKIEL HOPKINS

It is a fearful sin to make a rent and a hole in Christ's mystical body because there is a spot in it.

SAMUEL RUTHERFORD

It is better to have divisions than an evil uniformity.

WALTER CRADOCK

Simeon and Levi never did worse than when they agreed best.

JOHN OWEN

Division is better than agreement in evil.

GEORGE HUTCHESON

Better a holy discord than a profane concord.

THOMAS ADAMS

There is a due in a penny, as well as in a pound; therefore we must be faithful in the least truth, when season calleth for it.

RICHARD SIBBES

The hidden hand of Satan:

Yet this I know to be the usual badge of the truth, to be called after the names of men, to be accounted schismatical, but thereby the hearts of the simple may be alienated from the same. And Satan in this latter age hath been a marvellous cunning rhetorician this way, there hath been no truth brought to light, but he hath taken pains to paint it out for Zwinglianism, Lutheranism, Calvinism, Brownism, etc.

JOHN PENRY

A program of healing:

If we saw God, and heaven, and hell before us, do you not think it would effectually reconcile our differences and heal our unbrotherly exasperations and divisions? Would it not hold the hands that itch to be using violence against those that are not in all things of their minds. What abundance of vain controversies would it reconcile! As the coming in of the master doth part the fray among the school boys; so the sight of God would frighten us from contentions or uncharitable violence.

RICHARD BAXTER

DRUNKENNESS

It is worse to live like a beast than to be a beast.

WILLIAM GURNALL

While the wine is in thy hand, thou art a man; when it is in thine head, thou art become a beast.

THOMAS ADAMS

He that will never drink less than he may, sometimes will drink more than he should.

THOMAS FULLER

I had rather be a sober heathen than a drunken Christian.

WILLIAM GURNALL

There is no medicinal cup to the body, that is poisonous to the conscience.

THOMAS ADAMS

And as for drunkenness, whereas in the apostle's days, even among the heathen themselves, shame so far prevailed upon vice and debauchery, that it left sobriety the day, and took only the night to itself, 1 Thess. 5:7; yet now among us Christians, wickedness is grown so profligate that we meet the drunkard reeling and staggering even at noon-day.

EZEKIEL HOPKINS

Drunken porters keep open gates.

HENRY SMITH

ELECTION

Based on God's decree:

A king, consulting with himself and purposing to declare his honour and authority, enacteth such laws and statutes as the best industry of his subjects shall not be able to observe, pretending nevertheless, of his own especial grace, to be favourable or merciful to some and upon the remnant of transgressors to execute justice. From this spring (to wit, the honour of the king) do distill two streams, the one for his beloved subjects to drink at and live, the other for the malignant to drown in.

ARTHUR DENT

Moreover, as God respects no persons, so He respects no conditions upon which He gives salvation to us.

THOMAS GOODWIN

It is absurd to think that anything in us could have the least influence upon our election. Some say that God did foresee that such persons would believe, and therefore did choose them; so they would make the business of salvation to depend upon something in us. Whereas God does not choose us FOR faith, but TO faith. "He hath chosen us, that we should be holy," (Ephesians 1:4), not because we would be holy, but that we might be holy. We are elected to holiness, not for it.

THOMAS WATSON

83

ELECTION

Let us then ascribe the whole work of grace to the pleasure of God's Will. God did not choose us because we were worthy, but by choosing us He makes us worthy.

THOMAS WATSON

The purpose of God is the sovereign cause of all that good that is in man, and of all that external, internal and eternal good that comes to man. Not works past, for men are chosen from everlasting; not works present, for Jacob was loved and chosen before he was born; nor works forseen, for men were all corrupt in Adam. All a believer's present happiness, and all his future happiness springs from the eternal purpose of God.

THOMAS BROOKS

This doctrine affords comfort: thy unworthiness may dismay thee, but remember that thy election depends not upon thy worthiness but upon the will of God.

ELNATHAN PARR

Election is ascribed to God the Father, sanctification to the Spirit, and reconciliation to Jesus Christ. . . . This is the chain of salvation and never a link of this chain must be broken. The Son cannot die for them whom the Father never elected, and the Spirit will never sanctify them whom the Father hath not elected nor the Son redeemed.

THOMAS MANTON

If so be that free-will were our tutor, and we had our heaven in our own keeping, then we would lose all. But because we have Christ for our tutor, and He has our heaven in His hand, therefore the covenant it must be perpetual.

SAMUEL RUTHERFORD

Immutable:

Election having once pitched upon a man, it will find him out and call him home, wherever he be. It called Zaccheus out of accursed Jericho; Abraham out of idolatrous Ur of the Chaldees; Nicodemus and Paul, from the College of the Pharisees, Christ's sworn enemies; Dionysius and Damaris, out of superstitious

84

Athens. In whatsoever dunghills God's elect are hid, election will find them out and bring them home.

JOHN ARROWSMITH

Whom He chooseth, shall be created, called, justified, sanctified, glorified; because His purpose cannot be altered, His promise revoked. Let Manasseh repair the high places, rear altars for Baal; the Prodigal run from his Father, drink and swill, consume his portion; Saul make havoc of the saints, put them in prison, do many things against Jesus of Nazareth; yet shall they come to themselves, mourn for their sins, and be saved. For they are elected, beloved of Him who is the same for ever. Were it not thus, what hope could the faithful have to see Babel ruined, the Roman whore burned, the Jew called, the Devil's kingdom destroyed and Christ's perfected?

JOHN BARLOW

Christ is to be answerable for all those that are given to Him, at the last day, and therefore we need not doubt but that He will certainly employ all the power of His Godhead to secure and save all those that He must be accountable for. Christ's charge and care of these that are given to Him, extends even to the very day of their resurrection, that He may not so much as lose their dust, but gather it together again, and raise it up in glory to be a proof of His fidelity; for, saith He, "I shall lose nothing, but raise it up again at the last day."

THOMAS BROOKS

If the elect could perish then Jesus Christ should be very unfaithful to His Father because God the Father hath given this charge to Christ, that whomsoever He elected, Christ should preserve them safe, to bring them to heaven. John 6:39.

CHRISTOPHER LOVE

Our spiritual estate standeth upon a sure bottom: the beginning is from God the Father, the dispensation from the Son, and the application from the Holy Ghost. . . . It is free in the Father, sure in the Son, ours in the Spirit.

THOMAS MANTON

ELECTION

Oh despise not election! therein lies all your hope, that there is a remnant who shall infallibly be saved.

THOMAS GOODWIN

The right procedure:

You begin at the wrong end if you first dispute about your election. Prove your conversion, and then never doubt your election. If you cannot yet prove it, set upon a present and thorough turning. Whatever God's purposes be, which are secret, I am sure His promises are plain. How desperately do rebels argue! "If I am elected I shall be saved, do what I will. If not, I shall be damned, do what I can." Perverse sinner, will you begin where you should end?

JOSEPH ALLEINE

Do not stand still disputing about your election, but set to repenting and believing. Cry to God for converting grace. Revealed things belong to you; in these busy yourself. . . . Whatever God's purposes may be, I am sure His promises are true. Whatever the decrees of heaven may be, I am sure if I repent and believe I shall be saved.

JOSEPH ALLEINE

Paradise had four rivers that watered the earth. . . . and howsoever neglected by many, they make glad the city of God. So Bernard sweetly: Eternal life is granted to us in election, promised in our vocation, sealed in our justification, possessed in our glorification. Conclude then, faithfully to thy own soul. I believe, therefore I am justified; I am justified, therefore I am sanctified; I am sanctified, therefore I am called; I am called, therefore I am elected; I am elected, therefore I shall be saved. Oh! settled comfort of joy, which ten thousand devils shall never make void.

THOMAS ADAMS

I tell you again, God hath not ordinarily decreed the end without the means; and if you will neglect the means of salvation, it is a certain mark that God hath not decreed you to salvation. But you shall find that He hath left you no excuse, because He hath not thus predestinated you.

RICHARD BAXTER

Predestination is pleaded. If I be written to life, I may do this; for many are saved that have done worse. If not, were my life never so strict, hell appointed is not to be avoided. These men look to the top of the ladder, but not to the foot. God ordains not men to jump to heaven, but to climb thither by prescribed degrees. He that decreed the end, decreed also the means that conduce to it. If thou take liberty to sin, this is none of the way. Peter describes the rounds of this ladder: "Faith, virtue, knowledge, temperance, patience, godliness, charity." Thou runnest a contrary course, in the wild paths of unbelief, profaneness, ignorance, riot, impatience, impiety, malice; this is none of the way. These are the rounds of a ladder that goes downward to hell. God's predestination helps many to stand, pusheth none down. Look thou to the way, let God alone with the end.

THOMAS ADAMS

Some are much troubled because they proceed by a false method and order in judging of their estates. They will begin with election, which is the highest step of the ladder; whereas they should begin from a work of grace wrought within their hearts, from God's calling by His Spirit, and their answer to His call, and so raise themselves upwards to know their election by their answer to God's calling. "Give all diligence," says Peter, "to make your calling and election sure," your election by your calling. God descends unto us from election to calling, and so to sanctification; we must ascend to Him beginning where He ends.

RICHARD SIBBES

Mark in what order: first, our calling; then, our election; not beginning with our election first. By our calling, arguing our election.

JOSEPH HALL

ELECTION

We know there is a sun in heaven, yet we cannot see what matter it is made of, but perceive it only by the beams, light and heat. Election is a sun, the eyes of eagles cannot see it; yet we may find it in the heat of vocation, in the light of illumination, in the beams of good works.

THOMAS ADAMS

When you are dangerously sick, and the physician tells you unless you take such a course of physic, your case is desperate, do you use to reason thus: If I knew that God had decreed my recovery, I would take that course that is so like to restore me; but till I know that God has decreed my recovery I'll take nothing? Surely we should think such a reasoner not only sick, but distracted.... Even so are the arms of Christ always open to receive a perishing sinner fleeing to Him for refuge. And wilt thou destroy thyself by suffering Satan to entangle thee with a needless, impertinent, and unreasonable scruple? If there be no way but one.... then fly into it without delay, never perplexing (yourself) with the decrees and secrets of God.

DAVID CLARKSON

This truth may be handled either sinfully or profitably; sinfully as when it is treated on only to satisfy curiosity, and to keep up a mere barren speculative dispute.... This point of election.... is not to be agitated in a verbal and contentious way, but in a saving way, to make us tremble and to set us upon a more diligent and close striving with God in prayer, and all other duties.

ANTHONY BURGESS

For no man is damned precisely because God hath not chosen him, because he is not elected, but because he is a sinner, and doth wilfully refuse the means of grace offered.

ANTHONY BURGESS

Caution:

A man may be so bold of his predestination, that he forget his conversation.

THOMAS ADAMS

EMOTION

Never a complete assessor:

Measure not God's love and favour by your own feeling. The sun shines as clearly in the darkest day as it does in the brightest. The difference is not in the sun, but in some clouds which hinder the manifestation of the light thereof.

RICHARD SIBBES

As we feel the calamities of war more than the pleasures of peace, and diseases more than the quietness of health, and the hardness of poverty more than the commodities of abundance; even so we ought not to marvel if we feel the stingings and pricks of sin a great deal more than the consolations of the righteousness of Jesus Christ.

DANIEL CAWDRAY

Its use and misuse:

It is weakness to be hot in a cold matter, but worse to be cold in a hot matter.

JOHN TRAPP

A man must first love that he would be, before he can be that which he loveth.

ANDREW WILLET

Zeal is like fire; in the chimney it is one of the best servants; but out of the chimney it is one of the worst masters.

THOMAS BROOKS

Faith and feeling:

Grace comes not to take away a man's affections, but to take them up.

WILLIAM FENNER

Christianity doth not abrogate affections, but regulates them.

THOMAS MANTON

ENVY

Envy is sin, and it punisheth itself like gluttony; for it fretteth the heart, shorteneth the life, and eateth the flesh.

HENRY SMITH

The beasts of the field are armed with horns, with hoofs, with tusks and such like, to take revenge; but nature hath left nothing for man to put him in mind of revenge.... therefore it is against nature to envy.

HENRY SMITH

'Tis very hard to behold our own gifts without pride, and the gifts of others without envy.

VAVASOR POWELL

We must not envy them that have greater gifts, for if we have any it is more than (our) due or than we have deserved; and this will teach us to be contented with that which we have had. Let us then look on what we have and give God thanks for it, and know that if we should have more, He would give more; yea if we consider that they that have much must make the greater account, and that we are unfit to do so, we will thank God that we have no more than we have.

RICHARD GREENHAM

ETERNAL SECURITY

Based on God's decree:

God's decree is the very pillar and basis on which the saints' perseverance depends. That decree ties the knot of adoption so fast, that neither sin, death, nor hell, can break it asunder.

THOMAS WATSON

90

ETERNAL SECURITY, ETERNITY

When God calls a man, He does not repent of it. God does not, as many friends do, love one day, and hate another; or as princes, who make their subjects favourites, and afterwards throw them into prison. This is the blessedness of a saint; his condition admits of no alteration. God's call is founded upon His decree, and His decree is immutable. Acts of grace cannot be reversed. God blots out His people's sins, but not their names.

THOMAS WATSON

In our first paradise in Eden there was a way to go *out* but no way to go *in again*. But as for the heavenly paradise, there is a way to go in, but not way to go out.

RICHARD BAXTER

He (God) may for a time desert His children, but He will not disinherit them.

THOMAS WATSON

Even in spite of our sins?

It may be that we are sinful; but God did not love us for our goodness, neither will He cast us off for our wickedness. Yet this is no encouragement to licentiousness, for God knows how to put us to anguishes and straits and crosses, and yet to reserve everlasting life for us.

JOHN COTTON

Though Christians be not kept altogether from falling, yet they are kept from falling altogether.

WILLIAM SECKER

ETERNITY

Eternity to the godly is a day that has no sunset; eternity to the wicked is a night that has no sunrise.

THOMAS WATSON

ETERNITY, EVANGELISM

A man's greatest care should be for that place where he lives longest; therefore eternity should be his scope.

THOMAS MANTON

O my brother! your opinion about "for ever" can have no manner of effect upon the reality of that "for ever!" A party of boatmen on the Niagara river may have a very strong opinion when they are caught by the rapids that it is very pleasant rowing; but neither their shouts nor their merriment will alter the fact that the world's cataract is close at hand.

EDWARD REYNOLDS

He (God) approaches them while gazing on the near prospectus of time, and by raising and extending the point of sight He adds eternity to the view, and leaves them lost in the contemplation of a boundless eternity.

ROBERT HARRIS

Eternity is an everlasting *Now*.

CHRISTOPHER NESSE

There is no wrinkle on the brow of eternity.

THOMAS MANTON

Men that believe not another world, are the ready actors of any imaginable mischiefs and tragedies in this.

JOHN HOWE

EVANGELISM

Oh, if you have the hearts of Christians or of men in you, let them yearn towards your poor ignorant, ungodly neighbours. Alas, there is but a step betwixt them and death and hell; many hundred diseases are waiting ready to seize on them, and if they die unregenerate, they are lost for ever. Have you hearts of rock,

that cannot pity men in such a case as this? If you believe not the
Word of God, and the danger of sinners, why are you Christians
yourselves? If you do believe it, why do you not bestir yourself
to the helping of others? Do you not care who is damned, so you
be saved? If so, you have sufficient cause to pity yourselves, for
it is a frame of spirit utterly inconsistent with grace. . . . Dost
thou live close by them, or meet them in the streets, or labour
with them, or travel with them, or sit and talk with them, and
say nothing to them of their souls, or the life to come? If their
houses were on fire, thou wouldst run and help them; and wilt
thou not help them when their souls are almost at the fire of
hell?

RICHARD BAXTER

We have greater work to do here than merely securing our own
salvation. We are members of the world and Church, and we
must labour to do good to many. We are trusted with our
Master's talents for His service, in our places to do our best to
propagate His truth, and grace, and Church, and to bring home
souls, and honour His cause, and edify His flock, and further
the salvation of as many as we can. All this is to be done on
earth, if we will secure the end of all in heaven.

RICHARD BAXTER

Methinks if by faith we did indeed look upon them as within a
step of hell, it would more effectually untie our tongues, than
Croesus' danger, as they tell us, did his son's.

RICHARD BAXTER

An evangelist:

A man, who had his eyes up to heaven, the best of books was in
his hand, the law of truth was written upon his lips, and he
stood as if he pleaded with men.

JOHN BUNYAN

EVIL THOUGHTS

Their entertainment:

Our hearts are of that colour which our most constant thoughts dye into it. Transient fleeting thoughts, whether of one kind or another, do not alter the temper of the soul. Neither poison kills nor food nourishes, unless they stay in the body; nor does good or evil benefit or harm the mind unless they abide in it.

WILLIAM GURNALL

We cannot keep thieves from looking in at our windows, but we need not give them entertainment with open doors. "Wash thy heart from iniquity, that thou mayest be saved: how long shall thy vain thoughts lodge within thee?" They may be passengers, but they must not be sojourners.

THOMAS ADAMS

Vain thoughts defile the heart as well as vile thoughts.

WILLIAM SECKER

Their chain reaction:

They that are accustomed to evil thoughts can seldom bring forth good words, never good deeds. As the corn is, so will the flour be.

THOMAS ADAMS

(Some) though they cannot sin outwardly, for want of strength of body or a fit opportunity, yet they act sin inwardly with great love and complacency. As players in a comedy, they act their parts in private, in order to a more exact performance of them in public.

GEORGE SWINNOCK

The remedy:

The mighty streams of the evil thoughts of men will admit of no bounds or dams to put a stop unto them. There are but two ways of relief from them, the one respecting their moral evil, the other their natural abundance. The first is by throwing salt into the spring, as Elisha cured the waters of Jericho—that is, to get the heart and mind seasoned with grace. . . . The other is, to turn their streams into new channels, putting new aims and ends upon them, fixing them on new objects: so shall we abound in spiritual thoughts; for abound in thoughts we shall, whether we will or no.

JOHN OWEN

EXAMPLE

Better than precept:

Though "the words of the wise be as nails fastened by the masters of the assemblies," yet their examples are the hammer to drive them in, to take the deeper hold. A father that whipped his son for swearing, and swore himself whilst he whipped him, did more harm by his example than good by his correction.

THOMAS FULLER

Man is a creature that is led more by patterns than by precepts.

GEORGE SWINNOCK

Precepts instruct us what things are our duty, but examples assure us that they are possible. . . . When we see men like ourselves, who are united to frail flesh and in the same condition with us, to command their passions, to overcome the most glorious and glittering temptations, we are encouraged in our spiritual warfare.

WILLIAM BATES

EXAMPLE

Old Testament examples are New Testament instructions.

JOHN OWEN

Example is the most powerful rhetoric.

THOMAS BROOKS

Enduring and expanding influence:

There is little we touch, but we leave the print of our fingers behind.

RICHARD BAXTER

We may occasion other men's sins by example, and the more eminent the example, the more infectious it is. Great men cannot sin at a low rate because they are examples; the sins of commanders are commanding sins; the sins of rulers ruling sins; the sins of teachers teaching sins.

RALPH VENNING

Great men's *vices* are more imitated than poor men's *graces*.

WILLIAM SECKER

We easily catch an infectious disease from one another, but no man receiveth health from another's company.

THOMAS MANTON

Example of Christ:

But instead of all virtues he commendeth the example of Christ for every virtue, and opposeth it to every vice; as if he should say, He which thinketh only to follow Christ, needeth not to be led by the hand from virtue to virtue, but His example will teach him what he shall follow, and what he shall fly, better than all the precepts in the world.

HENRY SMITH

EXCESS

Excess in meat and drink clouds the mind, chokes good affections, and provokes lust. Many a man digs his own grave with his teeth.

THOMAS MANTON

Those who eat too much are just as guilty of sin as those who drink too much. . . . Men oftentimes complain that they have spent too much money in feasting, but it is rare that any have admitted that he has spent too much time in feasting.

JOSEPH CARYL

To the Christian in duty the body is as the beast to the traveller; he cannot go his journey without it, and much ado to go with it. If the flesh be kept high and lusty, then 'tis wanton, and will not obey; if low, then it's weak, and soon tires.

WILLIAM GURNALL

Those that are too merry when pleased are commonly too angry when crossed.

PHILIP HENRY

More are hurt by lawful things than unlawful, as more are killed with wine than poison. Gross sins affright, but how many take a surfeit and die, in using lawful things inordinately. Recreation is lawful, eating and drinking are lawful, but many offend by excess, and their table is a snare. Relations are lawful, but how often does Satan tempt to overlove! How often is the wife and child laid in God's room! Excess makes things lawful become sinful.

THOMAS WATSON

Overdoing is the ordinary way of undoing.

RICHARD BAXTER

The physician saith, nothing better for the body than abstinence; the divine saith, nothing better for the soul than abstinence; the lawyer saith, nothing better for the wits than abstinence; but because there is no law for this vice, therefore it breaketh out so mightily. Whoredom hath a law, theft hath a law, murder hath a law, but this sin is without a law.

HENRY SMITH

Simplicity is the ordinary attendant of sincerity.

RICHARD BAXTER

N.B.:

To rot and to riot, differ but one small letter.

THOMAS ADAMS

EXCUSES

It seems that there were some among the Thessalonians, as there must be amongst us, which did forsake all religion, because the preachers did not agree, or because the lives of professors gave some offence; therefore Paul sheweth, that there is no cause why they should mislike the word for the preacher, or why they should despise religion for the professor, because the word and the religion are not theirs which teach it, and profess it, but God's.

HENRY SMITH

But I have only one sin:

By allowing one sin, we disarm and deprive ourselves of having a conscientious argument to defend ourselves against any other sin. He that can go against his conscience in one, cannot plead conscience against any other; for if the authority of God awes him from one, it will from all. "How can I do this, and sin against God?" said Joseph. I doubt not but his answer would have been the same if his mistress had bid him to lie for her, as now when she enticed him to lie with her. The ninth commandment would have bound him as well as the seventh.

WILLIAM GURNALL

"But," saith the tempter, "it is but one sin, and the rest of thy life is good and blameless."

Answer: If a man be a murderer, or a traitor, will you excuse him because the rest of his life is good, and it is but one sin that he is charged with? . . . . "Whosoever shall keep the whole law, and yet offend in one point, is guilty of all" (James 2:10). Indeed God doth judge by the bent of thy heart and the main drift and endeavour of thy life. . . . The bent of a man's heart and life may be sinful, earthly, fleshly, though it run but in the channel of one way of gross sinning! As a man may be covetous that hath but one whore; and an idolater that hath but one idol. If thou lovedst God better, thou wouldst let go thy sin; and if thou love any one sin better than God, the whole bent of thy heart and life is wicked.

RICHARD BAXTER

"Whosoever shall keep the whole law, and yet offend in one point, he is guilty of all." Not as though the violation of one precept were actually the violation of another; for many may steal, and yet not actually murder; many again may murder, and yet not actually commit adultery: but this place of the apostle must be understood of violating that authority which passeth through them all, and by which all the commandments have their sanction. For since the authority of the great God is one and the same in all these laws, he shall so far disrespect this authority as willfully to break one of them, evidently declares that he owns it not in any.

EZEKIEL HOPKINS

Never forget this: he that savoureth any one sin, though he foregoeth many, doth but as Benhadad—recover of one disease and die of another.

THOMAS BROOKS

EXCUSES

But my sin is sweet:

Those sins that seem most sweet in life, will prove most bitter in death.

THOMAS BROOKS

Sin is no shrouder but a stripper.

HENRY SMITH

But my sin is small:

The least sin is damnable. The smallest bit of sin is a murdering morsel. "Cursed be he that confirmeth not all the words of this law to do them." . . . . A pistol will kill as dead as a cannon. . . . Some have been eaten up by bears and lions, others by mice and lice. It is spiritual murder to stifle and suppress the conceptions of the Spirit in thy soul, as well as to do open despite to the Holy Ghost.

GEORGE SWINNOCK

As a man may die as well by a fly choking him as by a lion devouring him. . . . so, likewise, little sins will sink a man to hell as soon as great sins.

DANIEL CAWDRAY

Little sins unrepented of will damn thee as well as greater. Not only great rivers fall into the sea, but little brooks; not only greater sins carry men to hell, but lesser; therefore do not think pardon easy because sin is small.

THOMAS WATSON

Consider that no sin against a great God can be strictly a little sin, though compared with a greater one it may be. But however little it is, to account it so makes it greater.

RALPH VENNING

But all do it:

"Follow not a multitude to do evil." Examples are not our warrant, but precepts. Neither will it procure a man a discharge,

EXCUSES

because he had a precedent in his sin. Adam indeed said the woman gave him the apple, but it did not excuse him from paying the reckoning with her; she was indeed first in the transgression, yet both met in the punishment.

THOMAS WATSON

The Word will tell you that it is no more safe to follow a multitude to do evil than it will be sweet to be in hell with a great company.

JOHN COLLINS

Think not the better of sin because it is in fashion. Think not the better of impiety and ungodliness, because many walk in those crooked ways. Multitude is a foolish argument; multitude does not argue the goodness of a thing. The devil's name is Legion. . . . The plea of a multitude will not hold out at God's bar when God shall ask you, "Why did you break your oath?" To say then, "Lord, because most men did so," will be but a poor plea: God will say to you, "Then seeing you have sinned with the multitude, you shall now go to hell with the multitude."

THOMAS WATSON

But I had cause to:

Let them pretend what they please, the true reason why any despise the new birth is because they hate a new life.

JOHN OWEN

A sin is two sins when it is defended.

HENRY SMITH

But if I sin, I can always repent:

To this we must say that He who promised forgiveness to them that repent has not promised repentance to them that sin.

RALPH VENNING

FAITH

Essential above all graces:

Our heavenly King is pleased with all our graces: hot zeal and cool patience pleaseth Him; cheerful thankfulness and weeping repentance pleaseth Him; but none of them are welcome to Him without faith, as nothing can please Him without Christ.

THOMAS ADAMS

Other graces make us like Christ, faith makes us members of Christ.

THOMAS WATSON

All other graces like birds in the nest depend upon what faith brings in to them.

JOHN FLAVEL

Faith is the captain grace.

WILLIAM GURNALL

Till men have faith in Christ, their best services are but glorious sins.

THOMAS BROOKS

A gift of God:

This is the terror of mercy: God requires of a man that he should believe; now mercy doth help to perform the duty commanded. The Lord, as He requires the condition of thee, so He worketh the condition in thee.

THOMAS HOOKER

Involves the understanding and the will:

Faith is seated in the understanding, as well as the will. It has an eye to see Christ, as well as a wing to fly to Christ.

THOMAS WATSON

FAITH

Faith, though it hath sometimes a trembling hand, it must not have a withered hand, but must stretch.

THOMAS WATSON

Judas knew the Scriptures, and without doubt did assent to the truth of them, when he was so zealous a preacher of the gospel; but he never had so much as one drachma of justifying faith in his soul. . . . Yea, Judas' master, the devil himself, one far enough (I suppose) from justifying faith, yet he assents to the truth of the Word. He goes against his conscience when he denies them: when he tempted Christ he did not dispute against the Scripture but from the Scripture, drawing his arrows out of this quiver. . . . Assent to the truth of the Word is but an act of the understanding, which reprobates and devils may exercise. But justifying faith is a compounded habit, and hath its seat both in the understanding and will: and, therefore, called a "believing with the heart" (Romans 10:10) yea, a "believing with all the heart" (Acts 8:37).

WILLIAM GURNALL

The office of faith:

It is the office of faith to believe what we do not see, and it shall be the reward of faith to see what we do believe.

THOMAS ADAMS

Faith is your spiritual optic.

ELISHA COLES

Where reason cannot wade there faith may swim.

THOMAS WATSON

It is the nature of faith to believe God upon His bare word. . . . It will not be, saith sense; it cannot be, saith reason; it both can and will be, saith faith, for I have a promise for it.

JOHN TRAPP

How weak soever the believer finds himself, and how powerful soever he perceives his enemy to be, it is all one to him, he hath no more to do but to put faith on work, and to wait till God works.

DAVID DICKSON

FAITH

The soul is the life of the body, Faith is the life of the soul. Christ is the life of faith.

JOHN FLAVEL

The object of faith:

As the act of healing through the eyes of the Israelites and the brazen serpent went together; so, in the act of justifying, these two, faith and Christ, have a mutual relation, and must always concur—faith as the action which apprehendeth, Christ as the object which is apprehended; so that neither the passion of Christ saveth without faith, nor doth faith help unless it be in Christ, its object.

DANIEL CAWDRAY

We must understand that faith does not justify and save us by itself. . . . but as an instrument, whereby we lay hold of and apply to ourselves Christ with His righteousness and merits, by which only we appear just before God. A small and weak hand, if it be able to reach up the meat to the mouth, as well performs its duty for the nourishment of the body as one of greater strength, because it is not the strength of the hand but the goodness of the meat which nourishes the body.

GEORGE DOWNAME

Evaluating our faith:

How shall I depend on Him for raising my body from the dust; and saving my soul at last; if I distrust Him for a crust of bread, towards my preservation.

JOSEPH HALL

Faith is of Rachel's humour: "Give me children or else I die."

THOMAS ADAMS

We must not prove the faith from the persons, but the persons from the faith.

RICHARD STOCK

FAITH

Growth of faith is seen by doing duties in a more spiritual manner. . . . When an apple hath done growing in bigness, it grows in sweetness.

THOMAS WATSON

Can there be faith without assurance?

If faith were assurance, then a man's sins would be pardoned before he believes, for he must necessarily be pardoned before he can know he is pardoned. The candle must be lighted before I can see it is lighted. The child must be born before I can be assured it is born. The object must be before the act. Assurance is rather the fruit of faith, than faith itself. It is in faith as the flower is in the root; faith in time, after much communion with God, acquaintance with the Word, and experience of His dealings with the soul, may flourish into assurance. But as the root truly lives before the flower appears, and continues when that hath shed its beautiful leaves, and is gone again: so doth true justifying faith live before assurance comes and after it disappears.

WILLIAM GURNALL

Faith is not assurance. If it were, Saint John might have spared his pains, who *wrote to them that believe on the name of the Son of God, that they might know that they have eternal life.* They might then have said, "We do this already."

WILLIAM GURNALL

How many, alas, of the precious saints of God must we shut out from being believers, if there is no faith but what amounts to assurance. . . . shall we say their faith went away in the departure of their assurance? How oft then in a year may a believer be no believer? even as often as God withdraws and leaves the creature in the dark. Assurance is like the sun-flower, which opens with the day and shuts with the night. It follows the motion of God's face; if that looks smilingly on the soul, it lives; if that frowns or hides itself, it dies. But faith is a plant that can grow in the shade, a grace that can find the way to heaven in a dark night. It can "walk in darkness, and yet trust in the name of the Lord."

WILLIAM GURNALL

FAITH, FALSE DOCTRINE

The paradox of faith:

A man cannot have faith without asking, neither can he ask it without faith.

EDWARD MARBURY

N.B.:

There be two signal and remarkable acts of faith, both exceedingly difficult, viz. its first act, and its last. The first is a great venture that it makes of itself upon Christ; and the last is a great venture too, to cast itself into the ocean of eternity upon the credit of a promise.

JOHN FLAVEL

What if my faith is weak?

Weak faith is true faith—as precious, though not so great as strong faith: the same Holy Ghost the author, the same Gospel the instrument. . . . For it is not the strength of our faith that saves, but the truth of our faith—not the weakness of our faith that condemns, but the want—of faith.

JOHN ROGERS

FALSE DOCTRINE

Its peril and poison:

Heresy is the leprosy of the head.

JOHN TRAPP

We should as carefully avoid errors as vices; a blind eye is even worse than a lame foot; yea a blind eye may cause a lame foot.

THOMAS MANTON

Error damns as well as vice; the one pistols, the other poisons.

THOMAS WATSON

FALSE DOCTRINE

By entertaining of strange persons, men sometimes entertain angels unawares: but by entertaining of strange doctrines, many have entertained devils unaware.

JOHN FLAVEL

Persistence in error:

The cynic answered smartly, who coming out of a brothel, was asked whether he was not ashamed to be seen coming out of such a bad house; "No," said he, "the shame was to go in, but honesty to come out." Oh sirs, it is bad enough to fall into an error, but worse to persist in it. The first shows thee a man, *humanum est errare*, but the last makes thee like a devil, that will not repent.

WILLIAM GURNALL

The evolution of error:

There is difference betwixt error, schism, and heresy. Error is when one holds a strong opinion alone; schism, when many consent in their opinion; heresy runs further, and contends to root out the truth. Error offends, but separates not; schism offends and separates; heresy offends, separates, and rageth.... Error is weak, schism strong, heresy obstinate. Error goes out, and often comes in again; schism comes not in, but makes a new church; heresy makes not a new church, but no church.... Error is reproved and pitied, schism is reproved and punished, heresy is reproved and excommunicated. Schism is in the same faith, heresy makes another faith. Though they be thus distinguished, yet without God's preventing grace, one will run into another.

THOMAS ADAMS

Divine strategy:

God suffers desperate opinions to be vented for the purging of His own truth. The truth of God is compared to silver. "The words of the Lord are pure, yea, as silver tried in a furnace of earth, purified seven times." Every corrupt opinion that comes to be vented against any truth of God is a new furnace, it comes out the purer for it.

JOHN ARROWSMITH

N.B.:

I believe that upon search it will appear that error hath not been advanced by anything in the world so much as by usurping a power for its suppression.

JOHN OWEN

FALSEHOOD

It is easy to tell one lie, hard to tell but one lie.

THOMAS FULLER

Those that lie in jest will (without repentance) go to hell in earnest.

JOHN TRAPP

There are three kinds of lies: a lie told, a lie taught, a lie acted out.

JOSEPH CARYL

FEAR

We fear men so much, because we fear God so little. One fear cures another. When man's terror scares you, turn your thoughts to the wrath of God.

WILLIAM GURNALL

FEAR

To use oaths ordinarily and indifferently without being constrained by any cogent necessity, or called to it by any lawful authority, is such a sin as wears off all reverence and dread of the great God; and we have very great cause to suspect that where His name is so much upon the tongue there His fear is but little in the heart.

EZEKIEL HOPKINS

By the fear of the Lord men depart from evil; by the fear of man they run themselves into evil.

JOHN FLAVEL

Our help is in the name of the Lord, but our fears are in the name of man.

WILLIAM GREENHILL

The wicked is a very coward, and is afraid of everything; of God, because He is his enemy; of Satan, because he is his tormentor; of God's creatures, because they, joining with their Maker, fight against him; of himself, because he bears about with him his own accuser and executioner. The godly man contrarily is afraid of nothing; not of God, because he knows Him his best friend, and will not hurt him; not of Satan, because he cannot hurt him; not of afflictions, because he knows they come from a loving God, and end in his good; not of the creatures, since "the very stones in the field are in league with Him;" not of himself, since his conscience is at peace.

JOSEPH HALL

N.B.:

How can you affright him? Bring him word his estate is ruined; "Yet my inheritance is safe," says he. Your wife, or child, or dear friend is dead; "Yet my Father lives." You yourself must die; "Well, then, I go home to my Father, and to my inheritance."

ROBERT LEIGHTON

FLATTERY

Be as much troubled by unjust praises, as by unjust slanders.

PHILIP HENRY

FOLLY

Fools are always futuring.

WILLIAM JENKYN

FORGIVENESS

The common denominator:

Poor souls are apt to think that all those whom they read or hear of to be gone to heaven, went thither because they were so good and so holy. . . . Yet not one of them, not any one that is now in heaven (Jesus Christ alone excepted), did ever come thither any other way but by forgiveness of sins.

JOHN OWEN

A blessed certainty:

Sins are so remitted, as if they had never been committed.

THOMAS ADAMS

No child of God sins to that degree as to make himself incapable of forgiveness.

JOHN BUNYAN

God blots out not only the cloud but the thick cloud, enormities as well as infirmities.

THOMAS WATSON

110

FORGIVENESS

For a poor sinner may be driven to a stand after this manner. . . . "I have therefore committed many sins. God hath sealed up the pardon of them unto me. . . . But what if more sins, if more horror seize upon my heart, how then shall I succour myself?" But now this is the fullness and sufficiency of mercy: it doth not only ease a man in regard of present necessity, but lays provision for all future wants and calamities that can befall the soul.

THOMAS HOOKER

The sin which is not too great to be forsaken, is not too great to be forgiven.

THOMAS HORTON

A man pardoned, and justified by faith in Christ, though he may, and sometimes doth, fall into foul sins, yet they never prevail so far as to reverse pardon, and reduce to a state of non-justification.

WILLIAM GREENHILL

Signs of realized forgiveness:

We need not climb up into heaven to see whether our sins are forgiven: let us look into our hearts, and see if we can forgive others. If we can, we need not doubt but God has forgiven us.

THOMAS WATSON

Our forgiving of others will not procure forgiveness for ourselves; but our not forgiving others proves that we ourselves are not forgiven.

JOHN OWEN

Wherever God pardons sin, He subdues it. "He will have compassion on us, He will subdue our iniquity." (Micah 7:19). Where men's persons are justified, their lusts are mortified. There is in sin a commanding and a condemning power. The condemning power of sin is taken away when the commanding power of sin is taken away. We know our sins are forgiven when they are subdued.

THOMAS WATSON

FORGIVENESS, FRIENDSHIP

You pray for pardon; that is a pleasing thing, yet rightly understand not pleasing to the flesh; it mortifies corruption, breaks the heart, engages to a holy life: every answer from our God to us, one way or the other, first or last, shall tend that way. ... God is terrible to sinful flesh; so far as He appears, it dies.

WILLIAM CARTER

A Christian imperative:

He that demands mercy, and shows none, ruins the bridge over which he himself is to pass.

THOMAS ADAMS

A man may as well go to hell for not forgiving as for not believing.

THOMAS WATSON

By revenge thou canst but satisfy a lust, but by forgiveness thou shalt conquer a lust.

JOHN FLAVEL

Whilst wrongs are remembered they are not remitted. He forgives not that forgets not.

JOHN TRAPP

The perfect example:

He shed tears for those that shed His blood.

THOMAS WATSON

FRIENDSHIP

Friendship is the marriage of affections.

THOMAS WATSON

Cultivate carefully:

Too much friendship makes way for hatred. Yea, in truth there is no enmity so dangerous as that which has its foundations upon the ruins of love. And as in nature, the purest substance is turned into the most loathsome corruption; so the hottest love, which has no other ground but carnal respect, degenerates oftentimes into the most deadly and hurtful enmity. For being privy to all their friends' secrets, counsels, and conditions, they are the more enabled thereby to do them the greater mischief when their love is turned to malice. Even as a traitor is much more dangerous than a professed enemy.

GEORGE DOWNAME

In the choice of a bosom friend, some respect ought to be had to his prudence. Some men, though holy, are indiscreet, and in point of secrets are like sieves—they can keep nothing committed to them, but let all run through. A blab of secrets is a traitor to society, as one that causeth much dissension. It is good to try him whom we intend for a bosom friend before we trust him.... Many complain of the treachery of their friends, and say, as Queen Elizabeth, that in trust they have found treason.

GEORGE SWINNOCK

Our afflictions are profitable, as they pluck from us false-hearted parasites, who, like the ivy, cling about us, to suck our sap, and to make themselves fat with our spoil; and to discover to us our true friends, who are hardly discerned from the other till this time of trial; for as the son of Sirach says, "A friend cannot be known in prosperity, and an enemy cannot be hidden in adversity."

GEORGE DOWNAME

Friendship with the ungodly?

All company with unbelievers or misbelievers is not condemned. We find a Lot in Sodom, Israel with the Egyptians, Abraham and Isaac with their Abimelechs; roses among thorns, and pearls in mud; and Jesus Christ among publicans and sinners. So neither we be infected, nor the name of the Lord wronged, to converse with them, that we may convert them, is a

FRIENDSHIP

holy course. But still we must be among as strangers: to pass through an infected place is one thing, to dwell in it another.

THOMAS ADAMS

Clothes and company do oftentimes tell tales in a mute but significant language.

THOMAS BROOKS

It is thy interest to choose only the godly for thy friends. Others will one time or other prove false. . . . Ungodly men may be about us, as mice in a barn, whilst something is up to be had; but when all the corn is gone, they are gone too; if thou ceasest to give, they will cease to love.

GEORGE SWINNOCK

A Christian should always be giving good or taking good, and that company is not for him that will neither give nor take this. What should a merchant do where there is no buying or selling?

WILLIAM GURNALL

Let not any so much presume upon their own strength, as to imagine that they can retain their sincerity, though they keep wicked company, and rather convert them to good, than be perverted by them to evil, seeing this is a matter of great difficulty. . . . For as he who is running down the hill can sooner pull with him one that is ascending, than he who is going up can cause him to ascend that is running down. . . . And thus it is in our spiritual state, wherein the worse more prevails to corrupt the better, than the better to reform the worse.

GEORGE DOWNAME

Man, being a sociable creature, is mightily encouraged to do as others do, especially in an evil example; for we are more susceptible of evil than we are of good. Sickness is sooner communicated than health; we easily catch a disease off one another, but those that are sound do not communicate health to the diseased. Or rather, to take God's own expression that sets it forth thus—by touching the unclean the man became unclean under the law, but by touching the clean the man was not purified.

THOMAS MANTON

If thou choosest the ungodly for thy friends, thou art in danger of suffering, as well as of sinning with them. The wheat has many a blow for being among the chaff. The gold would not be put into the fire if it were not for the dross with which it is mingled.

GEORGE SWINNOCK

Do not incorporate into the society of the wicked, or be too much familiar with them. The wicked are God haters; and "shouldest thou join with them that hate the Lord?" (2 Chronicles 19:2). A Christian is bound, by virtue of his oath of allegiance to God in baptism, not to have intimate converse with such as are God's sworn enemies. . . . The bad will sooner corrupt the good, than the good will convert the bad. Pharoah taught Joseph to swear, but Joseph did not teach Pharoah to pray.

THOMAS WATSON

N.B.:

It was the saying of a heathen, though no heathenish saying, "That he who would be good, must either have a faithful friend to instruct him, or a watchful enemy to correct him."

WILLIAM SECKER

GIFTS

Gifts are but as *dead graces*; but graces are *living gifts*.

CHRISTOPHER NESSE

Often at a price:

Joseph's coat made him finer than his brethren, but it caused all his trouble; so great gifts lift a saint up a little higher in the eyes of men, but they occasion many trials, from which thou who art low art exempt.

WILLIAM GURNALL

GIFTS, GOD

Often co-existent with evil:

Sin, in the reign and power of it, may cohabit with the most excellent natural gifts under the same roof, I mean in the same heart. A man may have the tongue of an angel, and the heart of a devil. The learned Pharisees were but painted sepulchres. Gifts are but as a fair glove drawn over a foul hand.

JOHN FLAVEL

Though a man have never such parts and gifts, yet if have not grace withal, he'may go to hell and perish to all eternity.... and if a man do go to hell and perish, the more gifts he has the deeper will he sink into hell. As it is with a man that is in the water.... the more he is laden with gold the more he sinks, and as he is sinking, if he have any time to cry out, he says, "Oh take away these bags of gold, these bags of gold will sink me." So I say, these golden parts and golden gifts will undo men.

ISAAC AMBROSE

When gifts are in their eminency, sin may be in its prevalency.

THOMAS ADAMS

N.B.:

The least grace is a better security for heaven than the greatest gifts or privileges whatsoever.

JOHN OWEN

GOD

His being:

Now concerning God, two things are to be known: (i) that He is, (ii) what He is.

JOHN PRESTON

GOD

His name:

God's name, as it is set out in the Word, is both a glorious name, full of majesty; and also a gracious name, full of mercy.

WILLIAM GOUGE

Father:

The word *Father* is personal, the word *God* essential.

STEPHEN CHARNOCK

The name Jehovah carries majesty in it: the name Father carries mercy in it.

THOMAS WATSON

The little word Father, pronounced in faith, has overcome God.

THOMAS WATSON

The titles of God are virtually promises, when He is called a sun, a shield, a strong tower, a hiding place, a portion. The titles of Christ: light of the world, bread of life, the way, the truth, and life; the titles of the Spirit: the Spirit of truth, of holiness, of glory, of grace, of supplication, the sealing, witnessing Spirit—faith may conclude as much out of these as out of promises.

DAVID CLARKSON

One God:

If a ship should have two pilots of equal power, one would be ever crossing the other: when one would sail, the other would cast anchor: here were a confusion, and the ship must needs perish. The order and harmony in the world, the constant and uniform government of all things, is a clear argument that there is but one Omnipotent, one God that rules all.

THOMAS WATSON

There can be but one Infinite.

ELISHA COLES

GOD

Incomprehensible - but not unknown:

You may know God, but not comprehend Him.
RICHARD BAXTER

How should finite comprehend infinite? We shall apprehend Him, but not comprehend Him.
RICHARD SIBBES

We know God but as men born blind know the fire: they know that there is such a thing as fire, for they feel it warm them, but what it is they know not. So, that there is a God we know, but what He is we know little, and indeed we can never search Him out to perfection; a finite creature can never fully comprehend that which is infinite.
THOMAS MANTON

It is visible *that* God is, it is invisible *what* He is.
STEPHEN CHARNOCK

We cannot seek God till we have found Him.
GEORGE SWINNOCK

Thomas acknowledged the divinity he did not see, by the wounds he did see.
JOHN BOYS

No bodily eye hath ever, or can possibly see Him. Neither can the eye of the understanding perfectly reach Him.
THOMAS HODGES

His sovereignty:

His sovereignty is gloriously displayed in His eternal decrees and temporal providences.
JOHN FLAVEL

The Lord's pleasure is the Lord's leisure.
THOMAS FULLER

GOD

God is the cause of causes.

CHRISTOPHER NESSE

God's foreknowledge of what He will do doth not necessitate Him to do.

STEPHEN CHARNOCK

God reveals His glorious majesty in the highest heavens, His fearful justice in the hell of the damned; His wise and powerful providence is manifest throughout the whole world; but His gracious love and mercy in, and unto His church here upon earth.

JOHN ROBINSON

His omnipotence:

All things (but lying, dying, and denying Himself) are possible to God.

CHRISTOPHER NESSE

God can make a straight stroke with a crooked stick.

THOMAS WATSON

One Almighty is more than all mighties.

WILLIAM GURNALL

His omnipresence:

God's center is everywhere, His circumference nowhere.

THOMAS WATSON

God is neither shut up in nor shut out of any place.

GEORGE SWINNOCK

The carnal mind sees God in nothing, not even in spiritual things. The spiritual mind sees Him in everything, even in natural things. . . .

ROBERT LEIGHTON

GOD

We are able to appreciate the continual presence of God as a pure act of abstract reason, just as we are able to know that space must be infinite; and that there must be a never-ending eternity; but we cannot realize any of these truths as hard, tangible facts, in the same way that we realize, by their contact with our senses, the existence of the material objects of the world around us—the trees and rivers. . . . That we cannot in this substantial, matter-of-fact way, feel the continual presence of God, is, I say, a merciful and loving provision of our Maker.

JOHN HOOPER

A heathen philosopher once asked: "Where is God?" The Christian answered: "Let me first ask you, where is He not?"

JOHN ARROWSMITH

His glory:

As the sun, which would shine in its own brightness and glory though all the world were blind, or did wilfully shut their eyes against it, so God will be ever most glorious, let men be ever so obstinate or rebellious. Yea, God will have glory by reprobates, though it be nothing to their ease; and though He be not glorified of them, yet He will glorify Himself in them.

NEHEMIAH ROGERS

His holiness:

God had revealed His holiness to Israel; and He wished them to consider it the "beauty" of His nature. If we take a portrait of a man, we try to represent his face, not his hand, nor his back, nor his foot; we try to delineate his beauty, to refresh our minds with that which is most memorable and distinguishing in his exterior semblance; so, while the hand and finger of God denote His power and skill, and His throne is used for majesty and dominion, He considers His holiness as the true luster of His character, as that by which He will be best known.

EDWARD REYNOLDS

120

GOD

His wisdom:

The wisdom of God is seen in this, that the sins of men shall carry on God's work; yet that He should have no hand in their sin. The Lord permits sin, but doth not approve it. He hath a hand in the action in which sin is, but not in the sin of the action.

THOMAS WATSON

His righteousness:

The righteousness of God, whereby He justifieth sinners, and sanctifieth the justified, and executeth judgement for His reconciled people, is the sweetest object of the church's joy.

DAVID DICKSON

Indeed this is one of the greatest mysteries in the world— namely, that a righteousness that resides with a person in heaven should justify me, a sinner on earth.

JOHN BUNYAN

His patience:

God was but six days in making the whole world, yet seven days in destroying one city.

JOHN TRAPP

God's forbearance is no acquittance.

JOHN TRAPP

Though the patience of God be *lasting*, yet it is not *everlasting*.

WILLIAM SECKER

His faithfulness:

As God did not at first choose you because you were high, so He will not forsake you because you are low.

JOHN FLAVEL

The Lord forbade the Israelites to forget what things He had done; how He had cast out nations, taken them from bondage;

GOD

for this end, that it might be remembered. Hence it is that the name of that converts have been, is continued upon them. Matthew is called the *publican*, though now he was not so; Simon the leper.

PAUL BAYNE

Man's faith may fail him sometimes, but God's faithfulness never fails him.

WILLIAM GREENHILL

His love:

Love in the creature ever presupposeth some good, true or apparent in the thing loved, by which that affection of union is drawn. But the love of God on the contrary, causeth all good to be produced in the creature. He first loveth us in the free purpose of His Will, and thence worketh good for us and in us. And hence come the unchangeableness of God's love towards us, because it is founded in Himself, and in the stableness of the good pleasure of His own Will. And although we may be comforted as we observe our love to Him; yet it is far greater comfort drawn from the consideration of His love to us; as being not only the ground of the other, but in Him also infinite, and unchangeable. And, hereupon, it was that the sisters of Lazarus seeking help for their sick brother sent Christ word, not that he, who loved Him, but that "he whom He loved, was sick."

JOHN ROBINSON

My brethren, when God first began to love you, He gave you all that He ever meant to give you in the lump, and eternity of time is that in which He is retailing of it out.

THOMAS GOODWIN

The only ground of God's love is His love. The ground of God's love is only and wholly in Himself. There is neither portion nor proportion in us to draw His love. There is no love nor loveliness in us that should cause a beam of His love to shine upon us.

THOMAS BROOKS

GOD

His mercy:

He is called the "Father of mercy," as who should say, He begets mercy, even a generation of mercies, from day to day.

THOMAS HOOKER

You now know the reason why God stands so long waiting on sinners, months, years, preaching to them; it is that He may be gracious in pardoning them, and in that act delight Himself. Princes very often pardon traitors to please others more than themselves, or else it would never be done; but God doth it chiefly to delight and glad His own merciful heart. Hence the business Christ came about (which is no other but to reconcile sinners to God) is called "the pleasure of the Lord" (Isaiah 53:10).

WILLIAM GURNALL

God is ever giving to His children, yet hath not the less. His riches are imparted, not impaired.

THOMAS WATSON

God is not wasted by bestowing.

THOMAS MANTON

It is an extreme disvaluing of Christ's righteousness and under-prizing of God's mercies in Christ if any greatness of sin hinder from seeking to God for pardon and trusting to find it.

WILLIAM WHATELY

If the end of one mercy were not the beginning of another, we were undone.

PHILIP HENRY

Impossible it is, that He should reject any poor penitent sinner, merely for the greatness of the sins he hath committed. It is the exaltation of His mercy (saith faith) that God hath in His eye when He promiseth pardon to poor sinners.

WILLIAM GURNALL

If God could not be more glorified in our peace and reconciliation, than in our death and damnation, it were a wicked thing to

GOD

desire it. But God hath cleared this up to us, that He is no loser by acts of mercy. In this lies the greatest revenue of His crown, or else He would not love "mercy rather than sacrifice." God is free to choose what suits His own heart best, and most conduceth to the exalting of His great name: and He delights more in the mercy shown to one than in the blood of all the damned, that are made a sacrifice to His justice.

WILLIAM GURNALL

He is righteous to reward according to deserts; He is gracious to reward above deserts; yea, He is merciful to reward without deserts; and how, then, can I doubt of His will to help me?

SIR RICHARD BAKER

Mercy pleaseth Him. It is no trouble for Him to exercise mercy. It is His delight: we are never weary of receiving, therefore He cannot be of giving; for it is a more blessed thing to give than to receive; so God takes more content in the one than we in the other.

ROBERT HARRIS

My brethren, God's mercies are from everlasting; and it is a treasure that can never be spent, never exhausted, unto eternity. In Isaiah 64:5 we read, "In Thy mercy is continuance." If God will but continue to be merciful to me, will a poor soul say, I have enough. . . . Hath God pardoned thee hitherto? but hast thou sinned again? Can He stretch His goodness and mercy a little further? Why, He will stretch them out unto eternity, unto everlasting; and if one *everlasting* be not enough, there are twenty-six everlastings in this one psalm. (Psalm 136).

THOMAS GOODWIN

A sentence of mercy and absolution (shall) be first pronounced at the last day. And it is a laudable custom of princes, at their first entrance to their kingdoms, to shew mercy, by hearing the mourning of the prisoner, and delivering the children of death, by loosing the bands of wickedness, by taking off the heavy burdens, by letting the oppressed go free, and by breaking every yoke of former extortions.

GEORGE HAKEWILL

124

N.B.:

It is a far happier thing to be pitied of God, than to be envied of men.

SIR RICHARD BAKER

His wrath:

As water is deepest where it is the stillest, so where God is most silent in threatening and patient in sparing, there He is most inflamed with anger and purpose of revenge; and, therefore, the fewer the judgements be that are poured forth upon the wicked in this life, the more are reserved in store for them in the life to come.

DANIEL CAWDRAY

As the displeasure of a king draweth many enemies with it, so the displeasure of God setteth all His creatures against us; therefore He is called the Lord of hosts, as though He came with an army against us, Isaiah 1:24. When He fought with the Aramites, the sun took His part, Joshua 10:13; when He fought against the Sodomites, the fire took His part, Genesis 16; when He fought against the Egyptians, the water took His part, Exodus 14; when He fought against the murmurers, the earth took His part, Numbers 16; when He fought against the idolaters, the lions took His part, Daniel 3; when He fought against the mockers, the bears took His part, 2 Kings 2:24.

HENRY SMITH

As we do not cease to hate a young wolf although that he hath not yet worried any sheep, or a young serpent, notwithstanding that it hath not yet cast forth its venom, but do judge them worthy of death because of the perverse nature that is in them: so ought we to esteem that God hath no less occasion to condemn us, even from our mother's womb, because of our perversity and natural malice engendered within us. And though the Lord should damn us eternally, He should do us no wrong, but only that which our nature deserveth.

DANIEL CAWDRAY

GOD, GOOD WORKS

God's anger, like the house that Samson pulled upon his own head, falls not upon us but when we pull it upon ourselves by sin.

SIR RICHARD BAKER

N.B.:

God hath in Himself all power to defend you, all wisdom to direct you, all mercy to pardon you, all grace to enrich you, all righteousness to clothe you, all goodness to supply you, and all happiness to crown you.

THOMAS BROOKS

GOOD WORKS

Limited to the saints?

All our works before repentance are dead works (Hebrews 6:1). And these works have no true beauty in them, with whatsoever gloss they may appear to a natural eye. A dead body may have something of the features and beauty of a living, but it is but the beauty of a carcase, not of a man. . . . Since man, therefore, is spiritually dead, he cannot perform a living service. As a natural death does incapacitate for natural actions, so a spiritual death must incapacitate for spiritual actions.

STEPHEN CHARNOCK

Their importance:

A naked profession of faith is no better than a verbal charity.

THOMAS MANTON

Naked faith is no faith.

THOMAS ADAMS

The want of good works makes faith sick; evil works kill her outright.

THOMAS ADAMS

GOOD WORKS

Faith is full of good works. It believes as if it did not work, and it works as if it did not believe.

THOMAS WATSON

The course of thy life will speak more for thee than the discourse of thy lips.

GEORGE SWINNOCK

Faith justifies the person, and works justify his faith.

ELISHA COLES

As the apple is not the cause of the apple tree, but a fruit of it: even so good works are not the cause of our salvation, but a sign and a fruit of the same.

DANIEL CAWDRAY

We are not justified by doing good works, but being justified we then do good.

WILLIAM JENKYN

Good deeds are such things that no man is saved for them, nor without them.

THOMAS ADAMS

The saints of God are sealed inwardly with faith, but outwardly with good works.

JOHN BOYS

Let me entreat you to join the first and second tables of the law together, piety to God, and equity to your neighbour. The apostle put these two words together in one verse, Titus 2:12, "That we should live righteously and godly": righteously, that relates to morality; godly, that relates to piety. . . . I would test a moral man by the duties of the first table, and I would test a professing Christian by the duties of the second table. Some pretend to faith, but have no works: others have works, but they have no faith.

THOMAS WATSON

GOOD WORKS, GRACE

God loves adverbs better than nouns; not praying only but praying well; not doing good but doing it well.

THOMAS BROOKS

The object matter of all religion is reduced to *credenda* and *agenda*.

THOMAS GOODWIN

When Christ shall say, "Inasmuch as ye did it not to one of these, ye did it not to Me", it will be a poor excuse to say, Lord I was forbidden by the law.

RICHARD BAXTER

Seek that your last days may be your best days, and so you may die in a good old age, which may be best done when you die good in old age.

RALPH VENNING

Their inadequacy:

There is, indeed, mention made of a mercy-seat in the temple, but there was never heard of any school of merit but in the chapel of Antichrist.

JOHN TRAPP

N.B.:

Thy alms to the poor, thy counsel to the simple, thy inheritance to thy children, thy tribute to Caesar, but thy heart to God.

HENRY SMITH

GRACE

Grace is the freeness of love.

THOMAS GOODWIN

For what is grace but the beams of Christ, the Sun of Righteousness.

RICHARD SIBBES

GRACE

"Grace" is more than mercy and love, it superadds to them. It denotes, not simply love, but the love of a sovereign, transcendly superior, one that may do what he will, that may wholly choose whether he will love or no. There may be love between equals, and an inferior may love a superior; but love in a superior, and so superior as he may do what he will, in such a one love is called grace: and therefore grace is attributed to princes; they are said to be gracious to their subjects, whereas subjects cannot be gracious to princes. Now God, who is an infinite Sovereign, who might have chosen whether ever He would love us or no, for Him to love us, this is grace.

THOMAS GOODWIN

Grace is not native but donative.

WILLIAM JENKYN

Its manifestations:
It argues more grace to grieve for the sins of others than for our own. We may grieve for our own sins out of fear of hell, but to grieve for the sins of others is from a principle of love to God.

THOMAS WATSON

The first step to grace is to see they have no grace; and the first degree of grace is the desire of grace. . . . Canst thou approve by evident and sound arguments that thou hast the true desires of grace? Then know for thy comfort that the Lord's Spirit of grace hath been moving and stirring in thee: "It is God that worketh in you both the will and the deed" (Philippians 2:13).

WILLIAM FENNER

Its operation:

Grace does not pluck up by the roots and wholly destroy the natural passions of the mind, because they are distempered by sin. That were an extreme remedy, to cure by killing, and to heal by cutting off. No; but it corrects the distemper in them. It dries not up the main stream of love, but purifies it from the mud it is full of in its wrong course, or calls it to its right channel, by

GRACE

which it may run into happiness, and empty itself in the ocean of goodness.

ROBERT LEIGHTON

It is a rule in divinity, that *grace takes not away nature*; that is, grace comes not to take away a man's affections, but to take them up.

WILLIAM FENNER

Grace and glory:

Grace is young glory.

ALEXANDER PEDEN

The Kingdom of grace is nothing but. . . . the beginning of the Kingdom of glory; the Kingdom of grace is glory in the seed, and the Kingdom of glory is grace in the flower; the Kingdom of grace is glory in the daybreak, and the Kingdom of glory is grace in the full meridian; the Kingdom of grace is glory militant, and the Kingdom of glory is grace triumphant. . . . the Kingdom of grace leads to the Kingdom of glory.

THOMAS WATSON

Grace and glory differ very little; the one is the seed, the other is the flower; grace is glory militant, glory is grace triumphant.

THOMAS BROOKS

It is a greater work of God to bring men to grace, than being in the state of grace, to bring them to glory; because sin is far more distant from grace than grace is from glory.

JOHN TRAPP

As rivers, the nearer they come to the ocean whither they tend, the more they increase their waters, and speed their streams; so will grace flow more fully and freely in its near approaches to the ocean of glory.

JOHN OWEN

Free-grace and free-will?

The friends of free-will are the enemies of free-grace.

JOHN TRAPP

130

There is no reason to be given for grace but grace.

RALPH VENNING

How to grow in grace?

Growth in grace doth not always consist in doing of other works for the kind, but in doing the same works over and over again better than before.

THOMAS BRIDGE

Young Christians perform more duties, and withal spoil more duties; young carpenters make many chips. (But the more spiritual your performances grow, the more fruit there is to be esteemed.) It is not the bigness of the fruit, or juiciness of them, for then crabs were better than apples, but the relish it is that gives the commendation.

THOMAS GOODWIN

The growth of grace is the best evidence of the truth of it; things that have no life will not grow.

THOMAS WATSON

All grace grows as Love to the Word of God grows.

PHILLIP HENRY

The right manner of growth is to grow less in one's own eyes.

THOMAS WATSON

Weak grace may do for God, but it must be strong grace that will die for God.

WILLIAM SECKER

GUIDANCE

The most signal demonstrations of Providence are not to be accepted against a Scripture-rule.

JOHN FLAVEL

131

GUIDANCE

The manner of God's revealing His will to men is (also) very different. Some have had special, personal, and peculiar discoveries of it made to them. So had Samuel about the choice of the person whom he should annoint king. . . . But now, all are tied up to the ordinary standing rule of the written Word, and must not expect any such extraordinary revelations from God. The way we now have to know the will of God concerning us in difficult cases, is to search and study the Scriptures, and where we find no particular rule to guide us in this or that particular case, there we are to apply general rules.

JOHN FLAVEL

If therefore, in doubtful cases, you would discover God's will, govern yourselves in your search after it by these rules:
1. Get the true fear of God upon your hearts; be really afraid of offending Him.
2. Study the Word more, and the concerns and interests of the world less.
3. Reduce what you know into practice, and you shall know what is your duty to practice.
4. Pray for illumination and direction in the way that you should go.
5. And this being done, follow Providence as far as it agrees with the Word, and no farther.

JOHN FLAVEL

Guidance into full-time service?

Wouldest thou know whether God would have thee go or no? Then thou must ask thy own conscience, and ask the church. Thy conscience must judge of thy willingness, and the church of thy ability: and as thou mayest not trust other men, to judge of thy inclination or affection, so thou mayest not trust thy own judgement, to judge thy worthiness or sufficiency.

WILLIAM PERKINS

N.B.:

Take God into thy counsel. Heaven overlooks hell. God at any time can tell thee what plots are hatching there against thee.

WILLIAM GURNALL

HEAVEN

John Bunyan was once asked a question about heaven which he could not answer, because the matter was not revealed in the Scriptures; and he thereupon advised the inquirer to live a holy life and go and see.

What?

In heaven is no war-fare, but all well-fare.

JOHN BOYS

In heaven they are free from want; they can want nothing there unless it be want itself. They may find the want of evil, but never feel the evil of want.

EWARD WILLAN

Where the unveiled glories of the Deity shall beat full upon us, and we for ever sun ourselves in the smiles of God.

EZEKIEL HOPKINS

Where?

Heaven begins where sin ends.

THOMAS ADAMS

How?

The sea enters into the rivers before the rivers can run into the sea. In like manner, God, comes to us before we go to Him; and heaven enters into our souls before we can enter into heaven.

PETER DRELINCOURT

Love puts a man upon the full use of all means to enjoy the thing

HEAVEN

loved. He that loves the world, how active is he! He will break his peace and sleep for it. He that loves honour, what hazards will he run! He will swim to the throne in blood. . . . Love heaven, and you cannot miss it; love breaks through all opposition—it takes heaven by storm.

THOMAS WATSON

Heaven must be in thee before thou canst be in heaven.

GEORGE SWINNOCK

Heaven is large but the way to heaven must be narrow.

HENRY SMITH

In the way to heaven, there are three narrow and hard passages, the entrance into the *new birth*; herein a man must leave behind him sinful self; the entrance into *assurance*; therein a man must leave and deny religious self; and lastly, the *gate of death*, then a man must part with natural self, religious self, and sinful self. The first two I have experienced, the last I expect.

VAVASOR POWELL

He that keeps earth by wrong, cannot expect heaven by right.

WILLIAM GURNALL

He that will be knighted must kneel for it, and he that will enter in at the strait gate must crowd for it—a gate made so on purpose, narrow and hard in the entrance, yet, after we have entered, wide and glorious, that after our pain our joy may be the sweeter.

THOMAS ADAMS

Nothing is more contrary to a heavenly hope than an earthly heart.

WILLIAM GURNALL

N.B.:

Wherever thou meetest a Christian, he is going to heaven.

WILLIAM GURNALL

HEAVEN

Are there degrees of glory?

Like as sundry vessels, whereof some are bigger and some less, if they all be cast into the sea, some will receive more water and some less, and yet all shall be full and no want in any: so likewise, among the saints of God in heaven, some shall have more glory, some less, and yet all, without exception, full of glory.

DANIEL CAWDRAY

The more we grow in grace, the more we shall flourish in glory. Though every vessel of glory shall be full, yet some vessels hold more.

THOMAS WATSON

Will there be recognition of others?

Some have asked whether we shall know one another in heaven? Surely, our knowledge will not be diminished, but increased. The judgement of Luther and Anselm, and many other divines is, that we shall know one another; yea, the saints of all ages, whose faces we never saw; and, when we shall see the saints in glory without their infirmities of pride and passion, it will be a glorious sight.

THOMAS WATSON

Our dilatory ways:

We are like little children strayed from home, and God is now fetching us home; and we are ready to turn into any house, stay and play with everything in our way, and sit down on every green bank, and much ado there is to get us home.

RICHARD BAXTER

Even the tired horse, when he comes near home, mends his pace: be good always, without weariness, but best at last; that the nearer thou comest to the end of thy days, the nearer thou mayest be to the end of thy hopes, the salvation of thy soul.

THOMAS ADAMS

HEAVEN, HELL

But don't all men desire heaven?

There is a great deal of difference between the desires of heaven in a sanctified man and an unsanctified. The believer prizeth it above earth, and had rather be with God than here (though death that stands in the way, may possibly have harder thoughts from him). But to the ungodly, there is nothing seemeth more desirable than this world; and therefore he only chooseth heaven before hell, but not before earth; and therefore shall not have it upon such a choice.

RICHARD BAXTER

HELL

Definitions:

Heaven is aptly compared to a hill, hell to a hole.

JOHN TRAPP

Hell is the center in which all the lines of sin and of misery meet; the common shoal into which they all disgorge themselves, as rivers do their streams into the vast ocean; and as rivers, when they are fallen into the sea, lose their several names in one that comprehends them all—the ocean;—so all the evils of this life, when resolved into this, forget their private names—sickness, pains, poverty, etc.—and are called HELL.

WILLIAM GURNALL

The Scripture tells us that in hell there are these three things: there is darkness, there is fire, and there are chains.

THOMAS WATSON

Hell is an abiding place, but no resting place.

THOMAS WATSON

Hell is full of purposes, heaven of performances.

JOHN ROGERS

HELL

Is hell everlasting?

The damned shall live as long in hell as God Himself shall live in heaven.

THOMAS BROOKS

Wrath to come implies both the futurity and perpetuity of this wrath. . . . Yea, it is not only certainly future, but when it comes it will be abiding wrath, or wrath still coming. When millions of years and ages are past and gone, this will still be wrath to come. Ever coming as a river ever flowing.

JOHN FLAVEL

Thus it is in hell; they would die, but they cannot. The wicked shall be always dying but never dead; the smoke of the furnace ascends for ever and ever. Oh! who can endure thus to be ever upon the rack? This word "ever" breaks the heart. Wicked men now think the Sabbaths long, and think a prayer long; but oh! how long will it be to lie in hell for ever and ever?

THOMAS WATSON

The torments of hell abide for ever. . . . If all the earth and sea were sand, and every thousandth year a bird should come, and take away one grain of this sand, it would be a long time ere that vast heap of sand were emptied; yet, if after all that time the damned may come out of hell, there were some hope; but this word EVER breaks the heart.

THOMAS WATSON

God being love, how does one account for an everlasting hell, and for the innumerable throng that go there?

I confess it greatly quieteth my mind against this great objection of the numbers that are damned and cast off for ever, to consider how small a part this earth is of God's creation, as well as how sinful and impenitent. Ask any astronomer that hath considered the innumerable numbers of the fixed stars and planets. . . . and the uncertainty that we have whether there be not as many more, or a hundred or thousand times as many. . . . this being so, for aught we know, those glorious parts may have inhabitants without sin or misery; who are filled with their Maker's love and goodness, and so, fitter to be the demonstration of that love and goodness than this sinful molehill or dungeon of ignorance is. . . . why then should it be an offence to us, if God, for their final refusal of His grace, do for ever forsake and punish the far greater part of this little, dark and sinful world, while He glorifieth His benignity and love abundantly upon innumerable angels, and blessed spirits, and inhabitants of those more large and glorious seats? If you would judge the beneficence of a king, will you go to the gaol and the gallows to discern it; or to his palace, and all the rest of his kingdom?

RICHARD BAXTER

Curiosity reproved:

When a curious inquisitor asked Austin what God did before He created the world, Austin told him He was making hell for such busy questionists, for such curious inquirers into God's secrets. Such handsome jerks are the best answers to men of curious minds. It concerns us but little to know where hell is. Certainly they are the best and wisest of men, who spend most thoughts, and time, and pains how to keep out of it, than to exercise themselves with disputes about it.

THOMAS BROOKS

N.B.:

Are there not millions of us who would rather go sleeping to hell, than sweating to heaven?

THOMAS WATSON

HOLINESS

What health is to the heart, that holiness is to the soul.

JOHN FLAVEL

Nothing else but the habitual and predominant devotion and dedication of soul, and body, and life, and all that we have to God; and esteeming, and loving, and serving, and seeking Him, before all the pleasures and prosperity of the flesh.

RICHARD BAXTER

More than religious observances:

I do not mean by holiness the mere performance of outward duties of religion, coldly acted over, as a task; not our habitual prayings, hearings, fastings, multiplied one upon another (though these be all good, as subservient to a higher end); but I mean an inward soul and principle of divine life (Romans 8:1-5), that spiriteth all these.

RALPH CUDWORTH

More than morality:

Some would have moral virtue to be holiness, which (as they suppose) they can understand by their own reason and practice in their own strength. . . . Gospel truth is the only root whereon Gospel holiness will grow.

JOHN OWEN

More than forsaking sin:

Pray not only against the power of sin, but for the power of holiness also. A haughty heart may pray against his sins, not out of any inward enmity to them, or love to holiness, but because they are troublesome guests to his conscience. His zeal is false that seems hot against sin, but is key-cold to holiness. A city is rebellious that keeps their rightful Prince out, though it receives not his enemy in.

WILLIAM GURNALL

An ally, not foe, of well-being:

There is nothing destroyed by sanctification but that which would destroy us.

WILLIAM JENKYN

HOLINESS

Holiness hath in it a natural tendency to life and peace.

ELISHA COLES

Will you say that godliness is unpleasant, because it makes a man sorry for his ungodliness? .... Would you wish a man that hath lived so long in sin and misery, to have no sorrow for it in his return—especially when it is but a healing sorrow, preparing for remission, and not a sorrow joined with despair, as theirs will be that die impenitently?

RICHARD BAXTER

Thou hast an art above God Himself, if thou canst fetch any true pleasure out of unholiness.

WILLIAM GURNALL

There is a beauty in holiness as well as a beauty of holiness.

GEORGE SWINNOCK

Here is the Christian's way and his end. ... His way is holiness, his end happiness.

JOHN WHITLOCK

Its disciplines:

God would not rub so hard if it were not to fetch out the dirt that is ingrained in our natures. God loves purity so well He had rather see a hole than a spot in His child's garments.

WILLIAM GURNALL

It is a weak pretence that, because the consummate measure of sanctification can only be attained in the next life, therefore we should not endeavour after it here. For by sincere and constant endeavours we make nearer approaches to it, and according to the degrees of our progress such are those of our joy. ... Not to arrive at perfection is the weakness of the flesh, not to aspire after it is the fault of the spirit.

WILLIAM BATES

When thou trustest in Christ *within* thee, instead of Christ *without* thee, thou settest Christ against Christ. The bride does well to esteem her husband's picture, but it were ridiculous if she should love it better than himself, much more if she should go to it rather than to him to supply her wants. Yet thou actest thus when thou art more fond of Christ's image in thy soul than of Him who painted it there.

WILLIAM GURNALL

It is absurd to imagine that God should justify a people and not sanctify them, He should justify a people whom He could not glorify.

THOMAS WATSON

O Christians! you must look as well to your spiritual wants as to your spiritual enjoyments; you must look as well to your layings out as to your layings up; you must look as well forward to what you should be, as backward to what you are. Certainly that Christian will never be eminent in holiness that hath many eyes to behold a little holiness, and never an eye to see his further want of holiness.

THOMAS BROOKS

It is no small advantage to the holy life to "begin the day with God." The saints are wont to leave their hearts with Him over night, that they may find them with Him in the morning. Before earthly things break in upon us, and we receive impressions from abroad, it is good to season the heart with thoughts of God, and to consecrate the early and virgin operations of the mind before they are prostituted to baser objects. When the world gets the start of religion in the morning, it can hardly overtake it all the day.

THOMAS CASE

There is no imagination wherewith man is besotted, more foolish, none so pernicious, as this—that persons not purified, not sanctified, not made holy in their life, should afterwards be taken into that state of blessedness which consists in the enjoyment of God. Neither can such persons enjoy God, nor would God be a reward to them. Holiness indeed is perfected in heaven: but the beginning of it is invariably confined to this world.

JOHN OWEN

HOLINESS, HOLY SPIRIT

Say not that thou hast royal blood in thy veins, and art born of God, except thou canst prove thy pedigree by daring to be holy.

WILLIAM GURNALL

He leads none to heaven but whom He sanctifies on the earth. This living Head will not admit of dead members.

JOHN OWEN

Perfect holiness is the aim of the saints on earth, and it is the reward of the saints in Heaven.

JOSEPH CARYL

For every sanctified man being a self-denying and a God-advancing man, his God is his center.

SIMEON ASH

N.B.:

What greater crime than holiness, if the devil may be one of the grand jury!

THOMAS WATSON

HOLY SPIRIT

Essential to spiritual life:

We preach and pray, and you hear; but there is no motion Christ-ward until the Spirit of God blows upon them.

JOHN FLAVEL

O such a one doth great things, he prays, and hears, and reads, and disputes much; Aye but hath he the Spirit, or no? The greatest difference (that I know) in all the Book of God, between saints and sinners is, that the one hath the Spirit, and the other hath not.

WALTER CRADOCK

HOLY SPIRIT

Essential to prayer:

To plead Christ's merits in prayer, and not by the Spirit, is to bring right incense but strange fire, and so our prayers are but smoke, offensive to His pure eyes, not incense, a sweet savour to His nostrils.

WILLIAM GURNALL

Christ is the door that opens into God's presence and lets the soul into His very bosom, faith is the key that unlocks the door; but the Spirit is He that makes this key.

WILLIAM GURNALL

Essential to Bible-study:

God is able to interpret His own Word unto thee. Indeed none can enter into the knowledge thereof but he must be beholden unto His Spirit to unlock the door. . . . He that hath not the right key is as far from entering the house as he that hath none, yea, in some sense further off; for he that hath none will call to him that is within, while the other, trusting to his false key, stands pottering without to little purpose.

WILLIAM GURNALL

The natural man may have excellent notions in divinity, but God must teach us to know the mysteries of the Gospel after a spiritual manner. A man may see the figures upon a dial, but he cannot tell how the day goes unless the sun shines; so we may read many truths in the Bible, but we cannot know them savingly, till God by His Spirit shines upon our soul. . . . He not only informs our mind, but inclines our will.

THOMAS WATSON

But not a substitute for Bible-study:

It is not the work of the Spirit to tell you the meaning of Scripture, and give you the knowledge of divinity, without your own study and labour, but to bless that study, and give you knowledge thereby. . . . To reject study on pretence of the sufficiency of the Spirit, is to reject the Scripture itself.

RICHARD BAXTER

HOLY SPIRIT, HOPE

How the Spirit is quenched?

Fire is quenched by pouring on water or by withdrawing fuel; so the Spirit is quenched by living in sin, which is like pouring water on a fire; or by not improving our gifts and graces, which is like withdrawing fuel from the hearth.

THOMAS MANTON

N.B.:

What a sad difference is there in the same person, as to what he is when the Spirit *leads* him, and as to what he is when the Spirit *leaves* him!

THOMAS JACOMBE

HOPE

Hope is a virgin of a fair and clear countenance; her proper seat is upon earth, her proper object is in heaven. . . . Faith is her attorney-general, prayer her solicitor, patience her physician, charity her almoner, thankfulness her treasurer, confidence her vice-admiral, the promise of God her anchor, peace her chair of state, and eternal glory her crown.

THOMAS ADAMS

Its ministry:

Hope fills the afflicted soul with such inward joy and consolation, that it can laugh while tears are in the eye, sigh and sing all in a breath; it is called "the rejoicing of hope" (Hebrews 3:6).

WILLIAM GURNALL

If a Jew pawned his bed-clothes, God provided mercifully that it should be restored before night: "For," saith He, "that is his covering: wherein shall he sleep?" (Exodus 22:27). Truly, hope is the saint's covering, wherein he wraps himself, when he lays his body down to sleep in the grave: "My flesh," saith David, "shall rest in hope."

WILLIAM GURNALL

Its cultivation:

Hope is never ill when faith is well.

JOHN BUNYAN

Nothing more unbecomes an heavenly hope than an earthly heart.

WILLIAM GURNALL

The saints are oft feeding their hopes on the carcases of their slain fears.

WILLIAM GURNALL

N.B.:

Better God's heirs live upon hope than upon hire.

SAMUEL RUTHERFORD

HOSPITALITY

Hospitality is threefold: for one's family, this of necessity; for strangers, this of courtesy; for the poor, this is charity.

THOMAS FULLER

Great boast and small roast makes unsavoury mouths.

HENRY SMITH

HUMAN NATURE

That which Aesop said to his master, when he came into his garden and saw so many weeds in it, is applicable to the heart. His master asked him what was the reason that the weeds grew up so fast and the herbs thrived not? He answered, The ground is natural mother to the weeds, but a stepmother to the herbs.

THOMAS GOODWIN

Sometimes, indeed, there appears a scuffle between Satan and a carnal heart; but it is a mere cheat, like the fighting of two fencers on a stage. You would think at first they were in earnest; but observing how wary they are where they hit one another, you may soon know they do not mean to kill: and that which puts all out of doubt when the guise is done, you shall see them making merry together with what they have got of their spectators, which was all they fought for. When a carnal heart makes the greatest bustle against sin, by complaining of it, or praying against it, follow him but off the stage of duty and you shall see them sit as friendly in a corner as ever.

WILLIAM GURNALL

The force of gunpowder is not known until some spark light on it; and oftentimes the stillest natures, if crossed, discover the deepest corruptions.

RICHARD SIBBES

Every man, take where you will, and every man in his best estate, or standing in his freshest glory, is not only vanity, but altogether vanity.

JOHN FLAVEL

"What is man?" ... Ask the prophet Isaiah. ... and he answers, man is "grass" ..... Ask David, he answers, man is a "lie", not a liar only, or a deceiver, but "a lie" and a deceit. All the answers the Holy Ghost gives concerning man, are to humble man. ... The sinful nature of man is an enemy to the nature of God, and would pull God out of heaven; yet God even at that time is raising man to heaven; sin would lessen the great God, and yet God greatens sinful man.

JOSEPH CARYL

"Lord, what is man?" Take him in his four elements, of earth, air, fire, and water. In the *earth*, he is as fleeting dust; in the *air*, he is as a disappearing vapour; in the *water*, he is as a breaking bubble; and in the *fire*, he is as consuming smoke.

WILLIAM SECKER

HUMILITY

Humility is the repentance of pride.

NEHEMIAH ROGERS

Humility is both a grace and a vessel to receive grace.

JOHN TRAPP

Pride is a sinner's torment, but humility is a saint's ornament.

WILLIAM SECKER

The best of God's people have abhorred themselves. Like the spire of a steeple, we are least at the highest.

THOMAS MANTON

Many are humbled, but not humble, low, but not lowly.

JOHN TRAPP

When the corn is nearly ripe it bows the head and stoops lower than when it was green. When the people of God are near ripe for heaven, they grow more humble and self-denying. . . . Paul had one foot in heaven when he called himself the chiefest of sinners and least of saints.

JOHN FLAVEL

Humility is a necessary veil to all other graces.

WILLIAM GURNALL

147

HUMILITY

The mean between under-rating and over-rating oneself:

Humility doth no more require that a wise man think his knowledge equal with a fool's, or ignorant man's, than that a sound man take himself to be sick.

RICHARD BAXTER

By humility I mean not the abjectness of a base mind; but a prudent care not to over-value ourselves upon any account.

OBADIAH GREW

To affect obscurity or submission is base and suspicious; but that man, whose modesty presents him mean to his own eyes and lowly to others, is commonly secretly rich in virtue. Give me rather a low fulness than an empty advancement.

JOSEPH HALL

How cultivated?

A sight of God's glory humbles. The stars vanish when the sun appears.

THOMAS WATSON

Humility wrestleth with God, like Jacob, and wins by yielding.

THOMAS ADAMS

In spiritual graces let us study to be great, and not to know it.

THOMAS ADAMS

Let us take care to be and to do as we should, and then *for noise and report*, let it be good or ill as God will send it. . . . *If we seek to be in the mouths of men, to dwell in the talk and speech of men, God will abhor us.* . . . Therefore let us labour to be good in *secret.* Christians should be as minerals, rich in the depth of the earth.

RICHARD SIBBES

Four reasons written in the heart of an humble saint:
(1) When he looks upon another that is a sinner, he considereth that he has been worse than he.
(2) A humble heart thinks himself to be worse still.

148

HUMILITY

(3) It is God that hath made it and not anything in himself.
(4) He considereth that the vilest sinner may be, in God's good time, better than he.

WALTER CRADOCK

Well, Christians, remember this, God hath two strings to His bow; if your hearts will not lie humble and low under the sense of sin and misery, He will make them lie low under the lack of some desired mercy.

THOMAS BROOKS

Humility is a strange flower; it grows best in winter weather, and under storms of affliction.

SAMUEL RUTHERFORD

N.B.:

We were earth, we are flesh, and we shall be worm's meat.

HENRY SMITH

Its rewards:

As Christ ceased not to be a King because He was like a servant, nor to be a lion because He was like a lamb, nor to be God because He was made man, nor to be a judge because He was judged; so a man doth not lose his honour by humility, but he shall be honoured for his humility.

HENRY SMITH

If you lay yourself at Christ's feet He will take you into His arms.

WILLIAM BRIDGE

A humble man hath this advantage of a proud man, for he cannot fall.

EDWARD MARBURY

A humble sinner is in a better condition than a proud angel.

THOMAS WATSON

God's choice acquaintances are humble men.

ROBERT LEIGHTON

HUMILITY, HYPOCRITES

There will be a resurrection of credits, as well as of bodies. We'll have glory enough by and by.

RICHARD SIBBES

N.B.:

Better is the sin which humbles me, than that duty which makes me proud.

THOMAS WATSON

HYPOCRITES

Identification marks:

Hypocrites are like pictures on canvas, they show fairest at farthest.

THOMAS ADAMS

A hypocrite is like the Sicilian Etna, flaming at the mouth when it hath snow at the foot: their mouths talk hotly, but their feet walk coldly.

THOMAS ADAMS

The hypocrite sets his watch, not by the sun, that is, the Bible, but by the town clock; what most do, that he will do. *Vox populi* is his *vox Dei*.

WILLIAM GURNALL

His bellows do but blow out the candle, under pretence of kindling the fire.

RICHARD BAXTER

They are set upon excess of ceremonies, because they are defective in the vital parts, and should have no religion if they had not this. All sober Christians are friends to outward decency and order; but it is the empty self-deceiver that is most for the unwarrantable inventions of man, and useth the worship of God but as a mask or puppet-play, where there is great doings, with little life, and to little purpose. . . . The gaudiness of men's religion is not the best sign that it is sincere. Simplicity is the ordinary attendant of sincerity.

RICHARD BAXTER

It is fearful for a man to bind two sins together, when he is not able to bear the load of one. To act wickedness, and then to cloak it, is for a man to wound himself, and then go to the devil for a plaster. What man doth conceal, God will not cancel.

THOMAS ADAMS

The hypocrite, certainly, is a secret atheist; for if he did believe there was a God, he durst not be so bold as to deceive Him to His face.

THOMAS ADAMS

Take heed also of being hypocritical Christians. Take heed you do not receive the truth without receiving the truth in the love of that truth. . . . It is just with God that they should fall into errors whose hearts did never love real truths. Better never to have received the truth, than to receive it, and not in the love of it.

THOMAS LYE

If thou hast an angel's tongue and a devil's heart, thou art no better than a post in the cross-way, that rots itself to direct others.

THOMAS ADAMS

The hypocrite desires holiness only as a bridge to heaven.

JOSEPH ALLEINE

Feigned equity is double iniquity.

GEORGE DOWNAME

They say of the nightingale, that when she is solitary in the woods, she is careless of her note; but when she conceives that she hath any auditors, or is near houses, then she composes

HYPOCRITES

herself more quaintly and elegantly. Verily, this is the frame and temper of the best of hypocrites.

THOMAS BROOKS

It is a sad thing to be Christians at a supper, heathens in our shops, and devils in our closets.

STEPHEN CHARNOCK

A man may wear Christ's livery and do the devil's drudgery.

GEORGE SWINNOCK

It is no new thing to see a people professing godliness to cast off the thing that is good.

JOHN PENRY

There is no visible difference, as unto light, between the light of the morning and the sunlight of the evening; yea, this latter sometimes, from gleams of the setting sun, seems to be more glorious than the other. But herein they differ: the first goes on gradually unto more light until it comes to perfection; the other gradually gives place unto darkness until it comes to be midnight. So is it as unto the light of the just and of the hypocrite.

JOHN OWEN

When grapes come to the press they come to the proof.

GEORGE SWINNOCK

No hypocrite can bear the cross.

HENRY SMITH

A blurred finger is unfit to wipe away a blot.

JEAN DAILLE

Sin, and heresy, and superstition are hypocrites; that is, sin hath the appearance of virtue, and heresy hath the appearance of truth, and superstition hath the appearance of religion.

HENRY SMITH

An hypocrite may well be termed a religious atheist, an atheist masked with religion.

STEPHEN CHARNOCK

HYPOCRITES

Religion which is begun in hypocrisy will certainly end in apostasy.

WILLIAM SPURSTOWE

The wound religion receives from hypocrites is far more dangerous and incurable than that inflicted on it by the open and scandalous sinner. For religion is never brought into question by the enormous vices of an infamous person; all see and all abhor his sin. But when a man shall have his mouth full of piety and his hands full of wickedness, when he shall speak Scripture and live devilism, profess strictly and walk loosely, this lays a grievous stumbling-block in the way of others; and tempts them to think that all religion is but mockery, and that the professors of it are but hypocrites.

EZEKIEL HOPKINS

An apple, if it be rotten at the core, though it have a fair and shining outside, yet rottenness will not stay long, but will taint the outside also. . . . hypocrisy will discover itself in the end.

JOHN BOND

Sometimes God takes away a barren professor by permitting him to fall into open profaneness. There is one that hath taken up a profession of the worthy name of the Lord Jesus Christ, but this profession is only a cloak; he secretly practiceth wickedness; he is a glutton, or a drunkard, or covetous, or unclean. Well, saith God, I will loose the reins of this professor, I will give him up to his vile affections. I will loose the reins of his sins before him, he shall be entangled with his filthy lusts, he shall be overcome of ungodly company.

JOHN BUNYAN

N.B.:

Hypocrites are certain to miscarry at last; so true is that proverb, "Frost and fraud have dirty ends."

THOMAS ADAMS

153

IDLENESS

Divine disapproval:

Sure I am that the same God who says, "Remember the Sabbath-day to keep it holy," also says, "Six days shalt thou labour." The great God never sealed any warrants for idleness.

THOMAS WATSON

Every man should have a calling to follow, and should follow his calling.... God has given no man a dispensation to be idle. The rule is, and that by commandment, that if any will not work, that is able to work, neither should he eat. (2 Thessalonians 3:10). If this rule were observed, I am afraid that more rich than poor would go with hungry stomachs and empty bellies.

RALPH VENNING

Disastrous consequences:

Sin brought in sweat (Genesis 3:19), but now, not to sweat increases sin.

JOHN FLAVEL

A lazy spirit is always a losing spirit.

THOMAS BROOKS

Ah, doubting Christians! remember this, that the promise of assurance and comfort is made over, not to lazy but laborious Christians; not to idle but to active Christians; not to negligent but to diligent Christians.... The lazy Christian hath his mouth full of complaints, when the active Christian hath his heart full of comforts.

THOMAS BROOKS

Idleness tempts the devil to tempt.

THOMAS WATSON

The *proud* person is Satan's *throne*, and the *idle* man his *pillow*. He sitteth in the former, and sleepeth quietly on the latter.

GEORGE SWINNOCK

Flies settle upon the sweetest perfumes, when they are cold, and corrupt them.

RICHARD STOCK

N.B.:

Deny sloth not only continuance, but countenance.

THOMAS ADAMS

A lazy Christian shall always want four things: viz., comfort, content, confidence, and assurance. God hath made a separation between joy and idleness.

THOMAS BROOKS

He loseth his time, when he is getting a penny when he might get a pound, who is visiting his neighbour, when he should be attending his Prince.

RICHARD BAXTER

O spend your time as you would hear of it in the Judgement!

RICHARD BAXTER

JEWS, THE

Will they return home?

The Jews shall be gathered from all parts of the earth where they now are scattered, and brought home into their homeland.

JOHN OWEN

JEWS

Will they turn to Christ?

The Jews are not yet come in under Christ's banner; but God, that hath persuaded Japheth to come into the tents of Shem, will persuade Shem to come into the tents of Japheth. (Genesis 9:27)

RICHARD SIBBES

The faithful Jews rejoiced to think of the calling of the Gentiles; and why should not we joy to think of the calling of the Jews?

RICHARD SIBBES

By such a miraculous apparition of Christ from heaven was St. Paul converted: and I hope it is no heresy to think, that the whole nation of the Jews, those zealots against Christ, may be converted by as strange a means as was that one zealot of their nation.

JOSEPH MEADE

The Lord saith, "All nations shall be blessed in Abraham." Hence I gather that the nation of the Jews shall be called, and converted to the participation of this blessing: when and how, God knows; but that it shall be done before the end of the world we know.

WILLIAM PERKINS

The end of this world shall not be till the Jews are called, and how long after that none yet can tell.

ELNATHAN PARR

There will come a time when the generality of mankind, both Jew and Gentile, shall come to Jesus Christ.

THOMAS GOODWIN

As at the first coming of Christ, so at the overthrow of Antichrist, the conversion of the Jews, there will be much joy.

RICHARD SIBBES

They forget a main point of the Church's glory, who pray not daily for the conversion of the Jews.

ROBERT LEIGHTON

O to see the sight, next to Christ's coming in the clouds, the most joyful! our elder brethren the Jews and Christ fall upon one another's necks and kiss each other.

SAMUEL RUTHERFORD

Their mission?

There is not any promise anywhere of raising up a kingdom unto the Lord Christ in this world but it is either expressed, or clearly intimated, that the beginning of it must be with the Jews.

JOHN OWEN

Undoubtedly, that people of the Jews shall once more be commanded to *arise* and *shine*, and their return shall be the riches of the Gentiles (Romans 11:12), and that shall be a more glorious time than ever the Church of God did yet behold.

ROBERT LEIGHTON

The casting off of the Jews, was our calling; but the calling of the Jews shall not be our casting off, but our greater enriching in grace, and that two ways: First, in regard of the company of believers, when the thousands of Israel shall come in, which shall doubtless cause many Gentiles which now lie in ignorance, error and doubt, to receive the Gospel and join with them. . . . Secondly, in respect of the graces, which shall then in more abundance be rained down upon the Church.

ELNATHAN PARR

JOY

Why it is absent in many believers:

There are two things, which I have always looked upon as difficult. The one is, to make the wicked sad; the other is, to

JOY

make the godly joyful. Dejection in the godly arises from a double spring; either because their inward comforts are darkened, or their outward comforts are disturbed.

THOMAS WATSON

The reason why many poor souls have so little heat of joy in their hearts, is that they have so little light of Gospel knowledge in their mind. The further a soul stands from the light of truth, the further he must needs be from the heat of comfort.

WILLIAM GURNALL

Those that look to be happy must first look to be holy.

RICHARD SIBBES

God is not otherwise to be enjoyed than as He is obeyed.

JOHN HOWE

Its absence in believers, dishonouring to God:

I desire the dejected Christian to consider, that by his heavy and uncomfortable life, he seemeth to the world to accuse God and His service, as if he openly called Him a rigorous, hard, unacceptable Master, and His work a sad unpleasant thing. I know this is not your thoughts: I know it is yourselves, and not God and His service that offendeth you; and that you walk heavily not because you are holy, but because you fear you are not holy, and because you are no more holy. . . . If you see a servant always sad, that was wont to be merry while he served another master, will you not think that he hath a master that displeaseth him? . . . You are born and new born for God's honour; and will you thus dishonour Him before the world? What do you (in their eyes) but dispraise Him by your very countenance and carriage?

RICHARD BAXTER

To see a wicked man merry, or a Christian sad, is alike uncomely.

WILLIAM GURNALL

Self-denial should not imply loss of joy:

God would have us part with nothing for Him, but that which will damn us if we keep it. He has no design upon us, but to make us happy. He calls us to salvation, He calls us to a Kingdom.

THOMAS WATSON

Religion does not banish all joy. As there is seriousness without sourness, so there is a cheerful liveliness without lightness. When the prodigal was converted "they began to be merry." (Luke 15:24). Who should be cheerful, if not the people of God? They are no sooner born of the Spirit, but they are heirs to a crown.

THOMAS WATSON

Christ takes no more delight to dwell in a sad heart, than we do to live in a dark house.

WILLIAM GURNALL

The apostles went away rejoicing that they were counted worthy to suffer shame for the name of Christ, that they were graced so far as to be disgraced for the name of Christ!

THOMAS WATSON

A distinctive of the saints:

Here joy enters into the saints; in heaven, "they enter into joy."

THOMAS WATSON

In our sufferings for Christ there is joy, not so when we suffer for our sins.

JOHN TRAPP

Take a saint, and put him into any condition, and he knows how to rejoice in the Lord.

WALTER CRADOCK

They have joy and comfort—that joy that angels cannot give, and devils cannot take.

CHRISTOPHER FOWLER

JOY, JUDGEMENT

When joy is interrupted:

No wise man can expect that. . . . God should diet us with a continual feast. It would neither suit with our health, nor the condition of this pilgrimage. Live, therefore, on your peace of conscience as your ordinary diet; when this is wanting, know that God appointeth you a fast for your health; and when you have a feast of high joys, feed on it and be thankful! But when they are taken from you, gape not after them as the disciples did after Christ at His ascension; but return thankfully to your ordinary diet of peace.

RICHARD BAXTER

If a man would lead a happy life, let him but seek a sure object for his trust, and he shall be safe: "He shall not be afraid of evil tidings: his heart is fixed, trusting in the Lord." He hath laid up his confidence in God, therefore his heart is kept in an equal poise.

THOMAS MANTON

JUDGEMENT

Inevitable:

The Day of Judgement is remote, thy day of judgement is at hand, and as thou goest out in particular, so shalt thou be found in the general. Thy passing-bell and the archangel's trumpet have both one sound to thee. In the same condition that thy soul leaves thy body, shall thy body be found of thy soul. Thou canst not pass from thy death-bed a sinner, and appear at the great assizes, a saint.

UNKNOWN

Both in thy private sessions, and the universal assizes, thou shalt be sure of the same Judge, the same jury, the same witnesses, the same verdict. How certain thou art to die, thou knowest; how soon to die, thou knowest not. Measure not thy life with the longest; that were to piece it out with flattery. Thou canst name no living man, not the sickest, which thou art sure shall die before thee.

THOMAS ADAMS

There is a place in hell where the covetous judge sitteth, the greedy lawyer, the griping landlord, the careless bishops, the lusty youth, the wanton dames, the thief, the robbers of the commonwealth. They are punished in this life because they ever sin as long as they could, while mercy was offered unto them; therefore because they would not be washed, they shall be drowned.

HENRY SMITH

Inflexible:

His will is the rule of righteousness, and righteousness is the rule of His will.

ELISHA COLES

That which a man spits against heaven, shall fall back on his own face.

THOMAS ADAMS

Deferred. . . . why?

It is the manner of God, throughout the Scripture, to defer judgements a long while before they come, and when they come He sends them by degrees.

WALTER CRADOCK

N.B.:

Alas! that the farthest end of all our thoughts should be the thought of our ends.

THOMAS ADAMS

JUSTIFICATION

He hideth our unrighteousness with His righteousness, He covereth our disobedience with His obedience, He shadoweth our death with His death, that the wrath of God cannot find us.

HENRY SMITH

God does not justify us because we are worthy, but by justifying us makes us worthy.

THOMAS WATSON

Out of the point of justification works cannot be sufficiently commended; into the cause of justification they must not be admitted.

THOMAS ADAMS

By grace we are what we are in justification, and work what we work in sanctification.

RICHARD SIBBES

If you do not put a difference between justification wrought by the Man Christ without, and sanctification wrought by the Spirit of Christ within. . . . you are not able to divide the word aright; but contrariwise, you corrupt the word of God.

JOHN BUNYAN

KNOWLEDGE

Essential:

We must know God's will before we can do it aright, there is no going to heaven blindfolded.

THOMAS WATSON

162

KNOWLEDGE

In the creation, light was the first thing that was made; so it is in the new creation: knowledge is the pillar of fire that goes before us, and lights us into the heavenly Kingdom. It is light must bring us to the "inheritance of the saints in light."

THOMAS WATSON

Inadequate:

Knowledge without wisdom may be soon discerned; it is usually curious and censorious.

THOMAS MANTON

Many a man's knowledge is a torch to light him to hell. Thou who hast knowledge of God's will, but doth not do it, wherein dost thou excel the devil, "who transforms himself into an angel of light."

THOMAS WATSON

A man may be theologically knowing and spiritually ignorant.

STEPHEN CHARNOCK

The bare knowledge of God's will is inefficacious, it doth not better the heart. Knowledge alone is like a winter sun, which hath no heat or influence; it doth not warm the affections, or purify the conscience. Judas was a great luminary, he knew God's will, but he was a traitor.

THOMAS WATSON

Its cultivation:

Let us not satisfy ourselves with a knowledge of God in the mass; a glance upon a picture never directs you to the discerning the worth and art of it.

STEPHEN CHARNOCK

The end of all arts and sciences is the practice of them. And as this is to be confessed in all other arts, so it cannot be decried in divinity and religion.

GEORGE DOWNAME

KNOWLEDGE, LAW

Seek not so much to have thy ear tickled as thy understanding enlightened. The painful bee passeth by roses and violets, and sits upon thyme; so shouldest thou rather choose to feed on plain and wholesome doctrine, though hot and biting, than on the quirks and flowers of man's invention. In a word, learn evermore to judge that sermon best, though plain, whereby thou understandest.

NEHEMIAH ROGERS

N.B.:

Seldom was ever any knowledge given to keep, but to impart.

JOSEPH HALL

The end of all learning is to know God, and out of that knowledge to love and imitate Him.

JOHN MILTON

LAW

Legal observance:

Laws are better unmade than unkept.

HENRY SMITH

Should we observe unjust laws?

Rulers are tutors to Christ's bairns that are minors. Therefore let rulers get all their own, for pride against them stots (rebounds) off them upon God; and when their laws are unjust we owe to them an upholding of the majesty, dignity, credit, and honour which God has given them. . . . seeing we are willed to honour the king. So all comes to this, that troublers of the peace of the Kirk or commonwealth condemned, and discrediting authority in the very act of refusing obedience to the unjust decrees, is unlawful. Again, the patience of an ass in any man that has a conscience, is unlawful.

SAMUEL RUTHERFORD

A directive for magistrates:

He that does not preserve the law does not observe it.

LAW WILLIAM JENKYN

Above all things, it behooveth you that be the Lord's servants in magistracy to establish, everyone within his charge and jurisdiction, this general law, providing that every man have wherein to occupy himself and his gifts, according to the tenor of this law, in his own standing place and vocation.... For none in the church and house of God must want his office; none must walk inordinately. As, therefore, you know your enemies and how to vanquish them, and also the law of the Lord, how to establish it, take heed unto yourselves and dally not in the Lord's matters. For if you shall not betimes by the sword of justice cut off all that deserve death by the law, not suffering your eye to take pity upon any, and also correct other malefactors according to their desert without partiality, know for certainty that the just God will require their blood at your hands.

LAURENCE CHADERTON

The divine law - its necessity:

Human laws are good to establish converse with man, but too short to establish communion with God; and therefore we must consult with the rule which is the law of the Lord, that we may not come short of true blessedness.

THOMAS MANTON

The law is the light and the commandment the lantern.

WILLIAM AUSTIN

The law, though it have no power to condemn us, hath power to command us.

THOMAS ADAMS

The *Law* by which God *rules* us, is as dear to Him as the *Gospel* by which He *saves* us.

WILLIAM SECKER

LAW

N.B.:

Certainly if the giving of the law were so full of terror, much more terrible shall be our being judged according to that law.

EZEKIEL HOPKINS

The Divine law - its limitations:

As a looking-glass doth neither wash nor make him fair, that looketh therein, but giveth him occasion either to seek for water or else for some other thing that may make him fair and clean: even so the law showeth unto us our sins, and maketh known unto us our miserable estate and wretchedness, and how that there is nothing good in us, and that we are far off from all manner of righteousness, and so driveth us of necessity to seek righteousness in Christ.

DANIEL CAWDRAY

The law may *express* sin but cannot *suppress* sin.

THOMAS ADAMS

The preaching of the law does not make us more sinful, but reveals those sins unto us which before we discerned not; as the sun shining upon some filthy place does not make it so filthy, but only makes it manifest which was not seen in the dark.

GEORGE DOWNAME

Danger in "adding to" or "taking from" God's laws:

Make not laws upon the saints where Christ hath not made any.

WALTER CRADOCK

It is safer and better for a man to break the law of God frequently, than to take away one law that God hath made to make the way larger and wider than God hath made it.

WALTER CRADOCK

The Law and the Gospel:

The Law gives menaces, the Gospel gives promises.

THOMAS ADAMS

The Law is a court of justice, but the Gospel a throne of grace.
GEORGE SWINNOCK

A legally-convinced person would only be freed from the pain, an evangelically-convinced person from the sin, the true cause of it.
STEPHEN CHARNOCK

Such as preach not the Law at all may make dead and loose hearers, and such as preach the Law too far may make desperate hearers. The golden mean is to be observed.
(1) I would not have the Law to be preached alone by itself, without a mixture of some of the promises of the Gospel.
(2) I would have the Law to be preached, as it was published, for evangelical and merciful intentions and purposes; not for destruction and desperation, but for edification.
JOHN SEDGWICK

Never any of God's children were comforted thoroughly, but they were first humbled for their sins.
RICHARD GREENHAM

We find the same rules for our actions, the same duties required, the same sins forbidden in the Gospel as in the law.
EZEKIEL HOPKINS

Conducive to happiness?

All the virtues that God requires us to exercise, which respect ourselves, are not only pleasing to Him, but are profitable and conducive to our present well-being and tranquility; such as temperance, chastity, meekness, contentedness, etc. And all the vices He has forbidden have a direct tendency to our ill-being and disquiet; such as gluttony, drunkenness, anger, envy, etc.
THOMAS FULLER

LIBERTY

I would do a hundred things that Christ hath not commanded, and leave undone a hundred things that Christ hath not forbidden, rather than be tied to one thing by men that Christ hath not commanded.

WALTER CRADOCK

Give me the liberty to know, to think, to believe, and to utter freely, according to conscience, above all other liberties.

JOHN MILTON

Honest liberty is the greatest foe to dishonest license.

JOHN MILTON

Liberty - limited?

Wherefore, though the Christian, as a Christian, is the only man at liberty, as called thereunto of God; yet his liberty is limited to things that are good: he is not licensed thereby to indulge the flesh.

JOHN BUNYAN

Liberty - open to abuse:

To argue from mercy to sin is the devil's logic.

JAMES JANEWAY

How many on account of free tongues have chained feet.

THOMAS ADAMS

LIFE

Life is an excellency added to *being*.

THOMAS GOODWIN

There is a threefold life: (1) life natural, (2) life spiritual, and (3) life eternal.

THOMAS MANTON

Brief at best:

Man's life is so short, that Austin doubteth whether to call it a dying life, or a living death. Man's life is but the shadow of smoke, the dream of a shadow.

THOMAS BROOKS

He that will be old long, must be old while he is young.

THOMAS ADAMS

How measured?

Life is to be measured by action, not by time; a man may die old at thirty, and young at eighty; nay, the one lives after death, and the other perished before he died.

THOMAS FULLER

To live well is to live twice.

SAMUEL WARD

A musician is commended not that he played so long, but that he played so well. And thus it is not the days of our life, but the goodness of our life. . . . that is acceptable unto God Almighty.

JOSIAS SHUTE

Those that die young?

Long life and length of days is the blessing and gift of God, that which He promises to all those who fear Him and walk in His ways.

Objection: But many of the children of God die untimely, and live not long; how, then, is this true?

Answer: This is not simply a blessing, as if he were happy that lives long, but as a symbol or sign of God's good favour and love. If, then, He shows His love to some rather by taking them out of this life, than by prolonging their days, He doth the rather perform His promise than break it. A man promises ten acres of ground in one field, and gives him a hundred in another, he has not broken his promise. So if God have promised long life, that is, a hundred years here, and after not give it him, but gives him eternity in the heavens, He has not broken His promise.

RICHARD STOCK

Youth and age:

If youth be sick of the *will-nots*, old age is in danger of the *shall-nots*.

WILLIAM SECKER

The old *cannot* live long, the young *may* die very quickly.

JOHN RAINOLDS

None can be too young to amend, that is old enough to die.

THOMAS ADAMS

LORD'S DAY, THE

God sanctifies it by *consecration*, we sanctify it by *devotion*.

EZEKIEL HOPKINS

For notwithstanding this rest and cessation from labour which is required on the Lord's day, yet three sorts of works may and ought to be performed. . . . these are works of *piety*, works of *necessity*, and works of *charity*.

EZEKIEL HOPKINS

A thanksgiving-day hath a double precedency of a fast-day. On a fast-day we eye God's anger; on a thanksgiving-day we look to God's favour. In the former we specially mind our corruptions; in the latter, God's compassions; therefore a fast-day calls for sorrow, a thanksgiving-day for joy. But the Lord's day is the highest thanksgiving day.

GEORGE SWINNOCK

What fitter day to ascend to heaven, than that on which He arose from earth, and fully triumphed over death and hell. Use your Sabbaths as steps to glory, till you have passed them all, and are there arrived.

RICHARD BAXTER

LORD'S SUPPER, THE

Its importance:

The Lord's supper is memorative, and so it has the nature and use of a pledge or token of love, left by a dying to a dear surviving friend. It is like a ring plucked off from Christ's finger, or a bracelet from His arm, or rather His picture from His breast, delivered to us with such words as these: "As oft as you look on this, remember Me; let this help to keep Me alive in your remembrance when I am gone, and out of sight.

JOHN FLAVEL

Nowhere is God so near to man as in Jesus Christ: and nowhere is Christ so familiarly represented to us as in this holy sacrament.

RICHARD BAXTER

LORD'S SUPPER

He has left us this dark glass, wherein we may see His face till He return with a full glory; and is it an affection to Him never to look upon His picture, the medal of Himself, wherein He has engraven the tracks of His dying love; all that He did, all that He purchased, all His fulness, all His treasures. . . . ? Well, but we may remember Christ other ways without this ceremony? We may, but do we?

STEPHEN CHARNOCK

As a man, looking steadfastly on a dial, cannot perceive the shadow move at all, yet viewing it after a while, he shall perceive that it hath moved: so, in hearing of the Word, but especially in the receiving of the Lord's Supper, a man may judge even his own faith, and other graces of God, to be little or nothing increased, neither can he perceive the motion of God's Spirit in him at that present, yet by the fruits and effects thereof, he shall afterward perceive that God's Spirit hath by little and little wrought greater faith and other graces in him.

DANIEL CAWDRAY

If it be a token of Divine goodness to appoint it, it is no sign of our estimation of Divine goodness to neglect it.

STEPHEN CHARNOCK

Participants?

This sacrament is a sacrament of nourishment, unrenewed men therefore are not fit for it. They are dead (Ephesians 2:1); and what has a dead man to do with a feast? Men must be alive before they be nourished.

STEPHEN CHARNOCK

We must not only examine whether we have a wedding-garment, but also whether it be well kept and brushed; whether no moths be got into it, no new spots dashed upon it. . . . Graces are to be purified, as well as sins purged out; grace, as well as metal, for want of rubbing and exercise, will gather dust.

STEPHEN CHARNOCK

LORD'S SUPPER

As to that which the generality of our people have taken most offence at, viz, our strictness about the sacrament, have we done more than our commission warrants us? Have we not often told you the danger, that to eat and drink unworthily is to eat and drink your own damnation? Can you blame us if we have at once consulted your and our own safety? Will you quarrel or censure us, because we would not give you that which, in the state you were, would have been to you a cup of poison, and would certainly have aggravated your damnation? Forgive us this wrong. But who hindered or deprived you of that ordinance? Was it not your own fault?

JOHN OLDFIELD

Is it bread only?

For the signs to be turned into the thing signified, is utterly against the nature of a sacrament, and makes it no sacrament, for there is no sign. For every sacrament doth consist of a sign, and a thing signified.

HENRY SMITH

There is more in sacramental bread than in common bread. Though the nature is not changed, the use is changed. It does not only nourish the body as it did before, but also it brings a bread with which it nourishes the soul. For as sure as we receive bread, so sure we receive Christ; not only the benefits of Christ, but Christ.

HENRY SMITH

He lies before us like a pelican, which letteth her young ones suck her blood, so that we may say, the Lord invited us to supper, and He Himself was our meat.

HENRY SMITH

LOVE

Love is the queen of the graces; it outshines all the others, as the sun the lesser planets.

THOMAS WATSON

Love is that jewel of human nature which commands a valuation wherever it is found.

JOHN OWEN

Faith deals with invisibles, but God hates that love which is invisible.

THOMAS WATSON

A man that is charitable and not pure, is better to others than to himself.

THOMAS MANTON

Love is not only full of benevolence, but beneficence. Love which enlarges the heart, never straitens the hand.

THOMAS WATSON

Charity offereth honey to a bee without wings.

JOHN TRAPP

Love and doctrine:

Love to God is armour of proof against error. For want of hearts full of love, men have heads full of error; unholy opinions are for want of holy affections.

THOMAS WATSON

Christ came not to possess our brains with some cold opinions, that send down a freezing and benumbing influence into our hearts. Christ was a master of the life, not of the school; and he is the best Christian whose heart beats with the purest pulse towards heaven, not he whose head spins the finest cobweb.

RALPH CUDWORTH

174

LOVE

What is in the Word a law of precept, is in the heart a law of love.

STEPHEN CHARNOCK

Love to God:

If my respects to my Saviour be for the loaves and fishes, my heart is carried away with those baskets of fragments; but, if I can love God for His goodness' sake, this love shall out-last time, and over-match death.

JOSEPH HALL

Love is the only thing in which we can retaliate with God. If God be angry with us, we must not be angry again; if He chide us, we must not chide Him again; but if God loves us, we must love Him again. There is nothing in which we can answer God again, but love. We must not give Him word for word, but we must give Him love for love.

THOMAS WATSON

"We love Him because He first loved us." Love is like an echo, it returneth what it receiveth.

THOMAS MANTON

We are never nearer Christ than when we find ourselves lost in a holy amazement at His unspeakable love.

JOHN OWEN

Love to the brethren:

"He that loved Him that begat, loves him also that is begotten of Him." (1 John 5:1). It is possible to love a saint, yet not to love him as a saint; we may love him for something else, for his ingenuity, or because he is affable and bountiful. A beast loves a man, but not as he is a man, but because he feeds him, and gives him provender. But to love a saint as he is a saint, this is a sign of love to God.

THOMAS WATSON

So peculiar is this blessing of the Gospel, that Christ appoints it for the badge and cognizance by which they should not only know one another, but even strangers would be able to know

LOVE

them from any other sect and sort of men in the world: "By this shall all men know that ye are My disciples, that ye love one another."

WILLIAM GURNALL

Affection without action is like Rachel, beautiful but barren.

JOHN TRAPP

Love of man necessarily arises out of the love of God. The love of the creature is but the corollary to the love of the Creator. This is what the Christian finds, as a matter of fact. His heart is overcharged with love to God. It finds its way out in love to man. His direct service of God cannot, in the nature of things, go very far. He worships God publicly in His house. He glorifies Him secretly in the constant outpourings of his heart. He gives of his substance to the maintenance of every cause which is God's cause. But here it ends. God is so mighty, so self-contained, that with all our puny efforts, much cannot be done to serve Him. So the Christian looks about to see how he is to show his love for God. He soon finds the way. Clearly, it must be by love for his fellow-men.

JOHN HOOPER

A greater hell I would not wish any man, than to live and not love the beloved of God.

THOMAS BROOKS

The saints are the walking pictures of God. If God be our Father, we shall love to see His picture of holiness in believers; shall pity them for their infirmities, but love them for their graces. . . . It may justly be suspected that God is not Father of those who love not His children. Though they retain the communion of saints in their creed, they banish the communion of saints out of their company.

THOMAS WATSON

Wicked men seem to bear great reverence to the saints departed; they canonize dead saints, but persecute living. In vain do men stand up at the creed, and tell the world they believe in God, when they abominate one of the articles of the creed, namely, the communion of saints. Surely, there is no greater sign of a man ripe for hell, than this, not only to lack grace, but to hate it.

THOMAS WATSON

Think oft of heaven, and what a thing a saint will be in glory, when he shall shine as the stars, and be equal to the angels, and then you will quickly see cause to love them.

RICHARD BAXTER

Of love there be two principal offices, one to give, another to forgive.

JOHN BOYS

Despise not thy neighbour, but think thyself as bad a sinner, and that the like defects may befall thee. If thou canst not excuse his doing, excuse his intent which may be good; or if the deed be evil, think it was done of ignorance; if thou canst no way excuse him, think some great temptation befell him, and that thou shouldst be worse if the like temptation befell thee; and give God thanks that the like as yet hath not befallen thee. Despise not a man being a sinner, for though he be evil today, he may turn tomorrow.

WILLIAM PERKINS

N.B.:

He loves but little who tells how much he loves.

JOHN BOYS

MALICE

Malice is mental murder.

THOMAS WATSON

Charity begins with itself, malice with another.

JOHN BOYS

MALICE, MARRIAGE

N.B.:

None prove worse enemies than those that have received the greatest kindnesses, when once they turn unkind. As the sharpest vinegar is made of the purest wine. . . . so the highest love bestowed upon friends, being ill digested or corrupt, turns to the most unfriendly hatred.

ABRAHAM WRIGHT

MARRIAGE

As God by creation made two of one, so again by marriage He made one of two.

THOMAS ADAMS

Marriage is both honourable and onerable.

GEORGE SWINNOCK

The wife was made of the husband's rib; not of his head, for Paul calleth the husband the wife's head; not of the foot, for he must not set her at his foot. The servant is appointed to serve, and the wife to help. If she must not match with the head, nor stoop at the foot, where shall he set her then? He must set her at his heart, and therefore she which should lie in his bosom was made in his bosom.

HENRY SMITH

Woman takes her being from man, man takes his well-being from woman.

THOMAS ADAMS

Marriage doth signify merry-age.

HENRY SMITH

MARRIAGE

Guidelines:

To direct thee to a right choice . . . the Holy Ghost gives thee two rules in the choice of a wife, godliness and fitness . . . if they be not like, they will not like.

HENRY SMITH

It is not evil to marry but good to be wary.

THOMAS GATAKER

Look not for better within than thou seest without, for every one seemeth better than she is; if the face be vanity, the heart is pride.

HENRY SMITH

First, he must choose his love, and then he must love his choice.

HENRY SMITH

A prudent wife commands her husband by obeying him.

JOHN TRAPP

A gracious wife satisfieth a good husband, and silenceth a bad one.

GEORGE SWINNOCK

If he cannot reform his wife without beating, he is worthy to be beaten for choosing no better.

HENRY SMITH

Give passions no time; for if some men's anger stand but a night, it turneth to malice, which is incurable.

HENRY SMITH

Knowing once a couple which were both choleric, and yet never fell out, I asked the man how they did order the matter that their infirmity did not make them discord? He answered me, When her fit is upon her, I yield to her, as Abraham did to Sarah; and when my fit is upon me, she yields to me; and so we never strive together, but asunder.

HENRY SMITH

MARRIAGE, MEANS OF GRACE

If thou art a man of holiness, thou must look more for a portion of grace in thy wife, than a portion of gold with a wife; thou must look more after righteousness than riches; more after piety than money; more after the inheritance she hath in heaven, than the inheritance she hath on earth; more at her being new born, than at her being high born.

THOMAS BROOKS

When Adam was away, Eve was made a prey.

HENRY SMITH

The three marriages of Christ:

We read in Scripture of three marriages of Christ. The first was when Christ and our nature met together. The second is, when Christ and our soul join together. The third is, the union of Christ and His church.

HENRY SMITH

MEANS OF GRACE

"Channels only:"

It is not enough to make use of ordinances, but we must see if we can find God there. There are many that hover about the palace, and yet do not speak with the prince.

THOMAS MANTON

It is not enough to sit under the means; woeful experience teacheth us that there are some no sun will tan; they keep their own complexion under the most shining and burning light of the Gospel.

WILLIAM GURNALL

Take heed of resting upon closet duties, take heed of trusting in closet duties. Noah's dove made use of her wings, but she did not trust in her wings, but in the ark. . . . There are many that go a round of duties. . . . and rest upon them when they have done, using the means as mediators, and so fall short of Christ and heaven at once. Closet duties rested in will as eternally undo a man as the greatest and foulest enormities; open wickedness slays her thousands, but a secret resting upon duties slays her ten thousands. . . . Open profaneness is the broad dirty road, that leads to hell, but closet duties rested in is a sure way, though cleaner way, to hell.

THOMAS BROOKS

Mistake not, I pray you: these duties must be had and used, but still a man must not stay there. Prayer says, "There is no salvation in me;" and the sacraments and fasting say, "There is no salvation in us;" all these are subservient helps, no absolute causes of salvation.

ISAAC AMBROSE

Danger of neglect:

To live above them, while we use them, is the way of a Christian; but to live above ordinances, as to live without them, is to live without the compass of the Gospel lines, and so without the government of Christ. Let such beware, lest while they would be higher than Christians, they prove in the end lower than men.

RICHARD BAXTER

What is Jordan that I should wash in it? What is the preaching that I should attend on it, while I hear nothing but what I knew before? What are these beggarly elements of water, bread and wine? Are not these the reasonings of a soul that forgets who appoints the means of grace?

WILLIAM GURNALL

If we once become listless to duty, we shall quickly become lifeless in it.

STEPHEN CHARNOCK

Neglect not private or public ordinances. Your bodies may as probably live without diet, as your souls without duties. This is God's way, by which He infuseth grace where it is wanting, and increaseth grace where it is.

GEORGE SWINNOCK

MEANS OF GRACE

The Christian's armour decays two ways: either by violent battery, when the Christian is overcome by temptation to sin; or else by neglecting to furbish and scour it with the use of those means which are as oil to keep it clean and bright.

WILLIAM GURNALL

A strange plant needs more care than a native of the soil. Wordly desires, like a nettle, breed of their own accord, but spiritual desires need a great deal of cultivating.

THOMAS MANTON

There are no men more careful of the use of means than those that are surest of a good issue and conclusion, for the one stirs up diligence in the other. Assurance of the end stirs up diligence in the means. For the soul of a believing Christian knows that God has decreed both.

RICHARD SIBBES

Use thy duties, as Noah's dove did her wings, to carry thee to the ark of the Lord Jesus Christ, where only there is rest.

ISAAC AMBROSE

The two blind men. . . . (Matthew 20:30), they could not open their own eyes; that was beyond their power, but they could get into the way where Jesus passed, and they could cry to Him for sight, who only could recover it. Those that are diligent in the use of means and ordinances they sit in the way where Jesus passes by.

DAVID CLARKSON

N.B.:

Means must be neither trusted nor neglected.

JOHN TRAPP

Neither be idle in the means, nor make an idol of the means.

WILLIAM SECKER

MEDITATION

The "what" of meditation?

Meditation is chewing the cud.

THOMAS WATSON

Meditation is like the charging of a piece, and prayer the discharging of it.

GEORGE SWINNOCK

Meditation is the best beginning of prayer, and prayer is the best conclusion of meditation.

GEORGE SWINNOCK

The "why"?

Meditation will keep your hearts and souls from sinful thoughts. When the vessel is full you can put in no more. . . . If the heart be full of sinful thoughts, there is no room for holy and heavenly thoughts: if the heart be full of holy and heavenly thoughts by meditation, there is no room for evil and sinful thoughts.

WILLIAM BRIDGE

The end of study is information, and the end of meditation is practice, or a work upon the affections. Study is like a winter sun, that shines, but warms not: but meditation is like a blowing upon the fire, where we do not mind the blaze, but the heat. The end of study is to hoard up truth; but of meditation to lay it forth in conference or holy conversation.

THOMAS MANTON

Meditation applieth, meditation healeth, meditation instructeth.

EZEKIEL CULVERWELL

183

MEDITATION

If I have observed anything by experience, it is this: a man may take the measure of his growth and decay in grace according to his thoughts and meditations upon the person of Christ, and the glory of Christ's Kingdom, and of His love.

JOHN OWEN

Singing God's praise is a work of the most meditation of any we perform in public. It keeps the heart longest upon the thing spoken. Prayer and hearing pass quick from one sentence to another; this sticks long upon it.

JOHN LIGHTFOOT

The exercising thyself to godliness in solitude, will be a probable proof of thy uprightness. Men are withheld in company from doing evil by the iron curb of fear or shame, and provoked to do good by the golden spurs of praise or profit; but in solitariness there are no such curbs in the way of lust to hinder our passage, nor such baits in the way of holiness to encourage our progress. The naked lineaments and natural thoughts of the soul are best discerned in secret.

GEORGE SWINNOCK

What is the reason there is so much preaching and so little practice? For want of meditation. . . . Constant thoughts are operative, and musing makes the fire burn. Green wood is not kindled by a flash or spark, but by constant blowing.

THOMAS MANTON

The Christian is like some heavy birds, as the bustard and others that cannot get upon the wing without a run of a furlong or two, or a great bell that takes some time to the raising of it. Now, meditation is the great instrument thou art to use in this preparatory work, allow thyself some considerable portion of time before the day of extraordinary prayer for thy retirement, wherein thou mayest converse, most privately with thy own heart.

WILLIAM GURNALL

Our design in meditation must be rather to cleanse our hearts, than to clear our heads.

GEORGE SWINNOCK

MEDITATION

We do not meditate that we may rest in contemplation, but in order to obedience.

THOMAS MANTON

The "when"?

As it is every man's work, so it is every day's work. The Sabbath day is our market day; we do not go to the market to buy meat into the house only for the market day, but for all the time until the market day comes about again. . . . David saith that his meditation was at work all the day long: "It is my meditation all the day." . . . . Yea, in Psalm 1 he takes in the night too: "He delighteth in the law of the Lord, and therein doth he meditate day and night."

WILLIAM BRIDGE

Accustom yourself to a serious meditation every morning. Fresh airing our souls in heaven will engender in us a purer spirit and nobler thoughts. A morning seasoning will secure us for all the day. . . . The thoughts of God were the first visitors David had in the morning (Psalm 139:17-18). God and his heart met together as soon as he was awake, and kept company all the day after.

STEPHEN CHARNOCK

The "how"?

Continued meditation brings great profit to the soul. Passant and transient thoughts are more pleasant, but not so profitable. Deliberate meditation is of most use because it secures the return of the thoughts.

THOMAS MANTON

There is abundant matter for our meditation; as the nature and attributes of God, the states and offices of Christ, the threefold state of man, the four last things. . . . out of these we may choose sometimes one thing, sometimes another, to be the particular object of our thoughts. To undertake more than one at a time will deprive us of the benefit of all. Too much food will rather

185

MEDITATION

destroy rather than increase the natural heat: a little wood may help that fire to burn, which a great quantity would smother.

GEORGE SWINNOCK

Do not overdo in point of violence or length; but carry on the work sincerely according to the abilities of your minds and bodies; lest going beyond your strength, you craze your brains, and discompose your minds, and disable yourselves, to do anything at all. Though we cannot estimatively love God too much, yet it is possible to think of Him with too much passion, or too long at once, because it may be more than the spirits and brain can bear. . . . You little know how lamentable and distressed a case you will be in, or how great an advantage the tempter hath, if once he do but tire you by overdoing.

RICHARD BAXTER

There are two things that make meditation hard. The one is, because men are not used thereunto. . . . and another is, because they do not love God enough. Everything is hard at the first: writing is hard at the first, painting hard at the first. . . . meditation will be hard at the first. There is nothing not hard to those that are unwilling. There is nothing hard to those that love, love makes all things easy. Is it a hard thing for a lover to think or meditate on the person loved?

WILLIAM BRIDGE

A true Christian must endeavour himself to deliver, not in gross, but by retail, the millions of God's mercy to his soul; in secret thought chewing the cud of every circumstance with continual contemplation.

EZEKIEL CULVERWELL

The only cause why you forget so fast as you hear. . . . is because you went from sermon to dinner, and never thought any more of the matter; as though it were enough to hear; like sieves, which hold water no longer than they are in a river.

HENRY SMITH

The sweet spices of divine works must be beaten to powder by meditation, and then laid up in the cabinet of our memories.

ABRAHAM WRIGHT

186

N.B.:

Meditate on our making, that we may fall in love with our Maker.

DAVID DICKSON

I will conclude with that excellent saying of Bernard: "Lord, I will never come away from Thee without Thee." Let this be a Christian's resolution, not to leave off his meditations of God till he find something of God in him.

THOMAS WATSON

MERCY

Can mercy miscarry?

The mercies of God make a sinner proud, but a saint humble.

THOMAS WATSON

Hezekiah was a holy man, yet he swells big under mercy. (2 Chronicles 32). No sooner doth God lift his house higher than others, but he lifts up his heart in pride higher than others. When God hath made him high in honours, riches, victories, ay, and in spiritual experiences, then his heart flies high, and he forgets God, and forgets himself, and forgets that all his mercies were from free mercy, that all his mercies were but borrowed mercies. Surely, it is better to lack any mercy than an humble heart, it is better to have no mercy than lack an humble heart.

THOMAS BROOKS

There are two sorts of mercies that are seldom eclipsed by the darkest affliction that befalls the saints in their temporal concerns, that is, sparing mercy in this world, and saving mercy in that to come.

JOHN FLAVEL

MERCY

Few can bear great and sudden mercies without pride and wantonness, till they are hampered and humbled to carry it moderately.

SAMUEL LEE

Irresistible:

Thy sorrows outbid thy heart, thy fears outbid thy sorrows, and thy thoughts go beyond thy fears; and yet here is the comfort of a poor soul: in all his misery and wretchedness, the mercy of the Lord outbids all these, whatsoever may, can, or shall befall thee.

THOMAS HOOKER

Innumerable:

Mercies are either ordinary or extraordinary—our common necessaries, or the remarkable supplies which we receive now and then at the hand of God. Thou must not only praise Him for some extraordinary mercy, that comes with such pomp and observation that all thy neighbours take notice of it with thee. . . . . but also for ordinary every-day mercies. . . . these common every-day mercies are many. Thus David enhanceth the mercies of this kind,—"O God, how great is the sum of them! If I should count them, they are more in number than the sand." . . . . What is lighter than a grain of sand, yet what is heavier than the sand upon the sea-shore? . . . . Who will not say that a man shows greater kindness in maintaining one at his table with ordinary fare all the year than in entertaining him at a great feast twice or thrice in the same time?

WILLIAM GURNALL

Its abuse:

Take heed of abusing this mercy of God. . . . To sin because mercy abounds, is the devil's logic. . . . he that sins because of God's mercy, shall have judgement without mercy.

THOMAS WATSON

Mercy is not for them that sin and fear not, but for them that fear and sin not.

THOMAS WATSON

Without faith we are not fit to desire mercy, without humility we are not fit to receive it, without affection we are not fit to value it, without sincerity we are not fit to improve it.

STEPHEN CHARNOCK

N.B.:

Take notice not only of the mercies of God, but of God in the mercies. Mercies are never so savoury as when they savour of a Saviour.

RALPH VENNING

Delayed mercies:

The delay of your mercies is really to your advantage. . . . The foolish child would pluck the apple whilst it is green, but when it is ripe, it drops of its own accord, and is more pleasant and wholesome.

JOHN FLAVEL

It is a greater mercy to have a heart willing to refer all to God, and be at His disposal, than to enjoy presently the mercy we are most eager and impatient for; for in that God pleases you, in this you please God.

JOHN FLAVEL

N.B.:

A visitor (seeking to console the dying Thomas Hooker): Sir, you are going to receive the reward of your labour.
Thomas Hooker: Brother, I am going to receive mercy!

MINISTRY, THE

A minister . . . a merchant of invaluable jewels.

ABRAHAM WRIGHT

Concern:

In our prayers for our people, God will teach us what we shall preach unto them. We cannot pray for them, but we must think on what it is we pray for, and that is the consideration of their condition. . . . The apostles "gave themselves to prayer and the word." Prayer is in the first place.

JOHN OWEN

Men whose calling and work it is to study the Scripture, or the things revealed therein, and to preach them to others, cannot but have many thoughts about spiritual things, and yet may be, and oftentimes are, most remote from being spiritually minded. They may be forced by their work and calling to think of them early and late, evening and morning, yet their minds be no way rendered or proved spiritual thereby. . . . And the reasons of it are manifest. It requires as much if not more watchfulness, more care, more humility, for a minister to be spiritually minded in the discharge of his calling, than for any other sort of men in theirs. . . . because the commonness of the exercise of such thoughts, with their design upon others in their expression, will take off their power and efficacy. And he will have little benefit by his own ministry who endeavours not in the first place an experience in his own heart of the power of the truths which he doth teach unto others.

JOHN OWEN

The word *work* forbids loitering and the word *ministry* lording.

JOHN BOYS

Ministers are not cooks, but physicians and therefore should not study to delight the palate, but to recover the patient.

JEAN DAILLE

He that is more frequent in his pulpit to his people than he is in his closet for his people, is but a sorry watchman.

JOHN OWEN

The labours of the ministry are fitly compared to the toil of men in harvest, to the labours of a woman in travail and to the agonies of soldiers in the extremity of a battle.

JOHN FLAVEL

Consecration:

Though Noah's servants built the ark, yet themselves were drowned. God will not accept of the tongue where the devil has the soul. Jesus did "do and teach." If a man teach uprightly and walk crookedly, more will fall down in the night of his life than he built in the day of his doctrine.

JOHN OWEN

The doctrine of a minister must credit his life, and his life adorn his doctrine.

JEAN DAILLE

In the Law God appointed that the lip of the leper should be covered, Leviticus 13:45. Neither should he be permitted to speak the oracles of God, who though he is by office an angel, yet by life is a leper.

THOMAS WATSON

Brethren, it is easier to declaim against a thousand sins of others, than to mortify one sin in ourselves.

JOHN FLAVEL

A traitorous commander, that shooteth nothing against the enemy but powder, may cause his guns to make as great a sound as some that are laden with bullets; but he doth not hurt to the enemy by it. So one of these men may speak loud and mouth it with an affected fervency, but he seldom doth any great execution against sin and Satan. . . Is that man likely to do much good, or fit to be a minister of Christ, that will speak for him an hour, and by his life will preach against Him all the week beside? . . . . If you stand at the door of the Kingdom of grace, to

MINISTRY

light others in, and will not go in yourselves, when you are burnt to the snuff you will go out with a stink, and shall knock in vain at the gates of glory that would not enter at the door of grace.

RICHARD BAXTER

Three things make a preacher—reading, prayer and temptation.

JOHN TRAPP

He doth preach most that doth live best.

JOHN BOYS

The minister should prepare himself inwardly and outwardly. The inward preparation is if his mind and soul be instructed and furnished with godly doctrine and a fervent spirit and zeal to teach his audience, to establish them in the truth, and to exhort them to perpend and mark well the merits and deservings of Christ. The outward preparation, the more simple it is, the better it is.

JOHN HOOPER

Unholiness in a preacher's life will either stop his mouth from reproving, or the people's ears from receiving.

WILLIAM GURNALL

A minister may fill his pews, his communion roll, the mouths of the public, but what *that* minister is on his knees in secret before God Almighty, that he is and no more.

JOHN OWEN

N.B.:

The ministry will not grace the man; the man may disgrace the ministry.

JOSEPH HALL

Concentration:

I have known some good men who have been so addicted to their study, that they have thought the last day of the week sufficient to prepare for their ministry, they then employ all the rest of the week in other studies. But your great business is to trade with your spiritual abilities. . . . A man may preach a very good sermon, who is otherwise himself; but he will never make a good minister of Jesus Christ, whose mind and heart is not always in the work. Spiritual gifts will require continual ruminating on the things of the Gospel in our minds.

JOHN OWEN

A faithful minister must see before he say.

EDWARD MARBURY

An ignorant minister is none of God's making, for God gives gifts where He gives a calling.

HENRY WILKINSON

He that knows nothing will believe anything.

THOMAS FULLER

It is not with us, as with other labourers: they find their work as they leave it, so do not we. Sin and Satan unravel almost all we do, the impressions we make on our people's souls in one sermon, vanish before the next.

JOHN FLAVEL

The minister's work debilitates nature; like the candle, he wastes while he shines.

WILLIAM GURNALL

The call into the ministry:

The inward call is not enough; to preserve order in the church, an outward call is necessary. As Peter, Acts 10, was called of God to go to Cornelius; and then, besides that, he had a call from Cornelius himself.

THOMAS MANTON

MINISTRY

God's Law hath not commanded me to hear everyone that speaketh a good discourse or reads a chapter, he must be specially authorized to preach, or I shall not be specially obliged to hear.

JOHN COLLINGES

A minister's self-examination:

(1) You have heaven to win or lose yourselves. . . . A holy calling will not save an unholy man.
(2) You have sinful inclinations as well as others.
(3) (You) have greater temptations than most men.
(4) The tempter will make his first and sharpest onset upon you. If you will be leaders against him, he will spare you no further than God restrains him.
(5) Many eyes are upon you, and therefore there will be many to observe your falls.
(6) Your sins are more aggravated than those of other men. They have more of hypocrisy in them.
(7) The honour of your Lord and Master, and of His holy truth, doth lie more on you than other men.
(8) The souls of your hearers and the success of your labours, do very much depend upon your self-examination.

RICHARD BAXTER

What if the minister be unworthy?

As a famished man, who doth never refuse any wholesome food prepared for him by his host, though his host himself will not taste thereof; and, likewise, a very sick patient, who never rejecteth healthful medicine, though his physician doth minister the same with a leprous hand. . . . Notwithstanding, the preacher himself be careless, be leprous. . . . yet the godly hearer will not forsake this heavenly food, or make light account of this wholesome medicine. . . . but feed hungrily upon it, apply it in time, lay it up in his heart, yield all reverence to it, and delight only therein, as in the very joy of his soul.

DANIEL CAWDRAY

194

N.B.:

The Christian's life should put his minister's sermon in print.
WILLIAM GURNALL

MIRACLES

Their true significance:

We call those miracles which are wrought out of the track of nature, and contrary to the usual stream and current of it, which men wonder at because they seldom see them and hear of them, as things rarely brought forth in the world; when, the truth is, there is more of power expressed in the ordinary station and motion of natural causes, than in those extraordinary exertings of power.... That fire should continually ravage and consume, and greedily swallow up everything that is offered to it, seems to be the effect of as admirable a power as the stopping of its appetite a few moments as in the case of the Three Children. Is not the raising of some small seeds from the ground, with a multiplication of their numerous posterity, an effect of as great a power as our Saviour's feeding many thousands with a few loaves by a secret augmentation of them? Is not the chemical producing so pleasant and delicious a fruit the grape from a dry earth, insipid rain, and a sour vine, as admirable a token of Divine power as our Saviour's turning the water into wine?
STEPHEN CHARNOCK

Why don't they happen today, as in the days of the apostles?

We have the full use and benefit of the Holy Ghost which was given then, that seal that was then set to the Christian doctrine and Scriptures stands there still. When Christ hath fully proved to the world the truth of His mediatorship, office, and doctrine, must He still continue the same actions? Is it not enough that He sealed it up once, but must He set a new seal for every man that requireth it in every age? Then miracles would be no miracles. Must your landlord seal your lease anew every time you will causelessly question his former seal? Then, if Christ had done miracles among a thousand, every man that was not present

195

should come and say, "Do the like before me also, or I will not believe." Will you put God to this, that either He must work constant miracles in every age, and before every man, or else He must not be believed?

RICHARD BAXTER

N.B.:

The raising a dead body to life would astonish us, but we are unaffected that every day so many living men are born.

OWEN BATES

MODESTY

In apparel:

They that borrow the fashions of the Egyptians may get their boils and their blotches. Certainly such as fear the Lord should go in no apparel but first, such as they are willing to die in; secondly, to appear before the Ancient of Days in; thirdly, to stand before the judgement seat in.

THOMAS BROOKS

MORALISTS, THE

Good but not good enough:

The want of a renewed heart is a hair on the moral man's pen, that blurs and blots his copy when he writes fairest. His uprightness does others more good in this world than himself in the next.

WILLIAM GURNALL

MORALISTS

God can love nothing but Himself and what He finds of Himself in the creature. All services without something of God's image and Spirit in them are nothing. As the product of a million of cyphers: though you still add to them, signifies nothing; but add one figure, an unit, the Spirit, grace, it will make the product to be many millions of high account with God. All the significancy depends upon the figure without which, if absent, the rest would be nothing. All moral perfections, without a new nature, are but cyphers in God's account: "Without faith it is impossible to please Him."

STEPHEN CHARNOCK

The archer may lose his game by shooting short as well as shooting wide. The hypocrite shoots wide, the moralist shoots short, of the mark.

WILLIAM GURNALL

Dost thou not think that thou needest Christ as much as any other? There is a generation of men in the world. . . . who because their corruptions have not left such a brand of ignominy upon their name, as some others lie under, but their conversations have been strewed with some flowers of morality, whereby their names have kept sweet among their neighbours, therefore they do not at all listen to the offers of Christ, neither do their consciences much check them for this neglect. . . . Oh remember, proud man, who thou art, and cease thy vain attempt. Art not thou of Adam's seed? Hast thou not traitor's blood in thy veins? If "every mouth be stopped" how darest thou open thine? If "all the world become guilty before God, that by the deeds of the law, no flesh can be justified in His sight;" where then shalt thou stand to plead thy innocency before Him who sees thy black skin under thy white feathers, thy foul heart through thy fair carriage? It is faith in Christ that alone can purify thy heart, without which thy washed face and hands will never commend thee to God.

WILLIAM GURNALL

Works make not the heart good, but a good heart makes the works good.

STEPHEN CHARNOCK

MORALISTS

Morality and Christianity differ specifically: the moralist works from nature, a little refined by education; the Christian from nature, thoroughly renewed by the Holy Ghost.

GEORGE SWINNOCK

Here is the difference between profane and civil men, that though these last have something that when grace is wrought will be more serviceable to grace than a profane man has, and is in itself, comparing things with things, higher; yet, compare it with the working of grace, this man is farther off the working of it, because a profane man will sooner see himself wicked. The publicans and sinners went faster to heaven than the Pharisees; yea, I say, there may be a greater nighness between the things, when yet there is a greater distance between the working of them and bringing them together. Thus, brother and sister are nigher in blood, but farther off marrying each other than two strangers; and thus two men upon the tops of two houses, opposite to each other in one of your narrow streets—they are nearer to each other in distance than those below are, yet in regard of coming each to the other they may be said to be farther off, for the one must come down, and then climb up again. Thus now a moral man, though he seems nearer to a state of grace, yet is really farther off; for he must be convinced of his false righteousness, and then climb up to the state of grace, to see himself as low and vile as the profanest man in the world, as every man when he is humbled does.

THOMAS GOODWIN

Civility is a good staff to walk with among men, but it is a bad ladder to climb up to heaven.

THOMAS WATSON

N.B.:

The young man in the Gospel might have been a better man if he had not been so good.

WILLIAM GURNALL

OBEDIENCE

God commands nothing but what is beneficial. "O Israel, what doth the Lord require of thee, but to fear the Lord thy God, and to keep His statutes, which I command thee this day, for thy good?" To obey God, is not so much our duty as our privilege.

THOMAS WATSON

Some will obey partially, obey some commandments, not others; like a plough which, when it comes to a still piece of earth, makes a baulk. But God that spake all the words of the moral law, will have all obeyed.

THOMAS WATSON

As the saint is described sometimes by a "clean heart," so also sometimes by "clean hands," because he has both; the holiness of his heart is seen at his fingers' ends.

GEORGE SWINNOCK

This is the true obedience, whether to God or man, when we look not so much to the letter of the law, as to the mind of the law-maker.

JOHN TRAPP

True obedience hath no lead at its heels.

THOMAS ADAMS

Sacrifice without obedience is sacrilege.

WILLIAM GURNALL

It is our bounden duty to live in obedience, but it would prove our utter ruin to live on obedience.

WILLIAM SECKER

I had also this consideration, that if I should now venture all for God, I engaged God to take care of my concernments; but if I forsook Him and His ways for fear of any trouble that should come to me or mine, then I should not only falsify my profes-

OBEDIENCE

sion, but should count also that my concernments were not so sure. . . . This was a smarting consideration, and was as spurs unto my flesh.

JOHN BUNYAN

After thou hast prayed, observe what God doth towards thee; especially how He doth guide thy feet and heart after prayer; there is much in that. That which was the spirit of supplication in a man when he prayed, rests upon him as the spirit of obedience in his course.

THOMAS GOODWIN

Judas heard all Christ's sermons.

THOMAS GOODWIN

Civil obedience?

If it be asked of the obedience due unto the prince and unto the magistrate, it answereth that all obedience in the Lord is to be rendered. And if it come to pass that any other be asked, it so refuseth that it disobeyeth not in preferring obedience to the great God before that which is to be given to mortal man.

THOMAS CARTWRIGHT

It is a sure sign of hypocrisy to be unrighteous and careless in civil dealings, how conscientious soever thou mayest seem to be in sacred duties. He that seems righteous towards men, and is irreligious towards God, is but an honest heathen; and he that seems religious towards God, and is unrighteous towards men, is but a dissembling Christian.

GEORGE SWINNOCK

200

ORDINANCES

Their limitations:

Till the Kingdom of grace be in our hearts, ordinances do not purify us, but we pollute them. Even the prayer of an ungracious person becomes sin, Proverbs 15:8. In what a sad condition is a man before God's Kingdom of grace is set up in his heart! Whether he comes or comes not to the ordinance, he sins. If he does not come to the ordinance, he is a contemnor of it; if he does come, he is a polluter of it.

THOMAS WATSON

A man may go to hell with baptismal water upon his face.

JOHN TRAPP

Spiritual appetizers:

The more a saint tastes of God in an ordinance, the more are his desires raised and whetted, and the more are his teeth set on edge for more and more of God. . . . A little mercy may save the soul, but it must be a great deal of mercy that must satisfy the soul.

THOMAS BROOKS

The manna of the Spirit doth usually fall down in the dews of ordinances.

GEORGE SWINNOCK

I do not say that ever a dead soul hath been enlivened in this ordinance, this being an ordinance appointed by Christ, not to beget spiritual life where there was none, but to increase it where the Spirit hath formerly begun it. In this ordinance, weak hands and feeble knees have been strengthened, and fainting hearts have been comforted, and questioning souls have been resolved, and staggering souls have been settled, and falling souls have been supported.

THOMAS BROOKS

ORDINANCES, PARENTS

The ordinances of God are the marts and fairs whereat Christians must trade for grace.

GEORGE SWINNOCK

Sacrament, not sacrifice:

In a sacrifice we give, and in a sacrament we receive; and therefore we say our sacrifice, and Christ's sacrament.

HENRY SMITH

Who may partake?

Take care that these holy things be administered only to those who are meet and worthy, according unto the rule of the gospel. Those who impose on pastors the promiscuous administration of these divine ordinances, or the application of the seals unto all without difference, do deprive them of their ministerial office and duty.

JOHN OWEN

N.B.:

To live above ordinances is to live below a saint.

GEORGE SWINNOCK

PARENTS

A corrupted legacy:

If it be the usual method of Divine Providence to visit the iniquity of the fathers upon the children, see then what great reason parents have to beware that they do not lay up a stock of plagues and curses for their posterity; nor clog the estate which they leave them, with so many debts to be paid to the justice of God as will certainly undo them.

EZEKIEL HOPKINS

PARENTS

You are instrumental causes of all their spiritual misery; and that, (1) By *generation*, (2) *Imitation*.

JOHN FLAVEL

If parents would have their children blessed at church and at school, let them beware they give their children no corrupt examples at home by any carelessness, profaneness, or ungodliness. Otherwise, parents will do them more harm at home than both pastors and schoolmasters can do them good abroad. For the corrupt example of the one fighteth with the good instruction of the other, which is so much the more dangerous because that corrupt walking is armed with nature, and therefore more forcibly inclineth the affections of the children to that side.

RICHARD GREENHAM

Let them (children) . . . go untaught and they will grow so headstrong that they will sooner be broken than bended.

RICHARD GREENHAM

N.B.:

Let me take heed therefore that I do not over-love him, that I do not cocker him, and as it were mar and kill his soul by over-cherishing his body.

WILLIAM WHATELY

The revenge of the cradle:

O how many parents have complained with the tree in the fable, that their very hearts have been riven asunder with those wedges that were cut out of their own bodies! What a grief was Esau to Isaac and Rebecca! What scourges were Absalom and Amnon to David!

JOHN FLAVEL

As for those parents who will not use the rod upon their children, I pray God He useth not their children as a rod for them.

THOMAS FULLER

203

PARENTS, PATIENCE

Some parents, like Eli, bring up their children to bring down their house.

GEORGE SWINNOCK

Let parents remember that therefore oftentimes they have disordered and disobedient children to themselves because they have been disobedient children to the Lord and disordered to their parents when they were young; wherefore because they have not repented, the Lord punisheth their sins committed against others with the like sin in others against themselves.

RICHARD GREENHAM

Well doth David call children "arrows"; for if they be well bred, they shoot at their parents' enemies; and if they be evil bred, they shoot at their parents.

HENRY SMITH

N.B.:

If you neglect to instruct them in the way of holiness, will the devil neglect to instruct them in the way of wickedness? No; if you will not teach them to pray, he will to curse, swear, and lie; if ground be uncultivated, weeds will spring.

JOHN FLAVEL

PATIENCE

Companion to all virtues:

Patience to the soul is as bread to the body.... we eat bread with all our meats, both for health and relish; bread with flesh, bread with fish, bread with broths and fruits. Such is patience to every virtue; we must hope with patience, and pray in patience, and love with patience, and whatsoever good thing we do, let it be done in patience.

THOMAS ADAMS

PATIENCE

The blissful position of the patient man:

The patient man is merry indeed. . . . The jailers that watch him are but his pages of honour, and his very dungeon but the lower side of the vault of heaven. He kisseth the wheel that must kill him; and thinks the stairs of the scaffold of his martyrdom but so many degrees of his ascent to glory. The tormentors are weary of him, the beholders have pity on him, all men wonder at him; and while he seems below all men, below himself, he is above nature. He hath so overcome himself, that nothing can conquer him.

THOMAS ADAMS

They who are wicked, although they cannot see the goodness of other virtues, yet can see the goodness of patience, and perceive when they see a patient man and an impatient man both sick of one disease; yet both are not troubled alike, but that he who has most patience has most ease, and he who is most impatient is most tormented, like a fish which strives with the hook.

HENRY SMITH

Part of the cure:

Our physician makes these outward blisters in our bodies, to draw out the poisonous corruption that is in our souls: and therefore let us endure what He imposes with patience, and never murmur against Him for effecting His cure; knowing that it is but childish folly to abhor the medicine more than the disease. . . .

GEORGE DOWNAME

To lengthen my patience is the best way to shorten my troubles.

GEORGE SWINNOCK

N.B.:

Patience must not be an inch shorter than affliction.

THOMAS ADAMS

PATIENCE, PEACE

The perfect example:

Who cares for Caesar when he is dead? But what more effica-
cious than Christ when He died? He was most practical when
He seemed to do nothing. In patience He reigned and triumphed; He subjected the greatest enemies to Himself, Satan,
and death, and the wrath of God, and all. In the same manner
all things are ours, the worst things that befall God's children,
death, and afflictions, and persecutions. There is a kingdom of
patience set up in them. The Spirit of God subdues all base fears
in us, and a child of God never more triumphs than in his greatest troubles.

RICHARD SIBBES

N.B.:

Mercy hath a heaven, and justice a hell, to display itself to
eternity, but long-suffering hath only a short-lived earth.

HENRY SMITH

PEACE

God the Father is called the "God of peace" (Hebrews 13:20).
God the Son, the "Prince of peace" (Isaiah 9:6). God the Holy
Ghost, the "Spirit . . . of peace" (Ephesians 4:3).

THOMAS WATSON

The godly man, when he dies, "enters into peace" (Isaiah 57:2);
but while he lives, peace must enter into him.

THOMAS WATSON

When a man's ways please God, the stones of the street shall be
at peace with him.

WALTER CRADOCK

And therefore you who think so basely of the Gospel and the
professors of it, because at present their peace and comfort are

not come, should know that it is on the way to them, and comes
to stay everlastingly with them; whereas your peace is going
from you every moment, and is sure to leave you without any
hope of returning to you again. Look not how the Christian
begins, but ends.

WILLIAM GURNALL

PERFECTION

Distinctive of God:

God is perfectly good. All the perfection we can arrive at in this
life is sincerity. We may resemble God a little, but not equal
Him; He is infinitely perfect.

THOMAS WATSON

Goal of the saints:

This is the sum of all; for he which can abstain not only from
evil, but from the appearance of evil, is so perfect as a man can
be in this sinful life.

HENRY SMITH

This life was not intended to be the place of our perfection, but
the preparation for it.

RICHARD BAXTER

A prayer of the saints:

O good God, guide me by Thy holy hand, that I may keep myself
within the lists of Christianity, being modest in apparel, moderate (in) diet, chaste and temperate in speech, sober in fashion
and my ordinary deportment, respective to my superiors, amiable to my equals, without pride and insolency towards these
that are below me, courteous and affable and yet without vanity
and popularity towards all.

SAMUEL HIERON

207

PERSECUTION

God examineth with trials, the devil examineth with temptations, the world examineth with persecutions.

HENRY SMITH

Much grace exercised, brings persecution: for the sweeter and better the fruit is, the more slinging there will be at the tree.

VAVASOR POWELL

It much more concerned us, to be sure that we deserved not suffering, than that we be delivered from it.

RICHARD BAXTER

N.B.:

He that liveth the life of the persecutor dieth also the death of the bloody man.

JOHN PENRY

PIETY

Piety hath a wondrous virtue to change all things into matter of consolation and joy. No condition in effect can be evil or sad to a pious man: his very sorrows are pleasant, his infirmities are wholesome, his wants enrich him, his disgraces adorn him, his burdens ease him; his duties are privileges, his falls are the grounds of advancement, his very sins (as breeding contrition, humility, circumspection, and vigilance), do better and profit him: whereas impiety doth spoil every condition, doth corrupt and embase all good things, doth embitter all the conveniences and comforts of life.

ISAAC BARROW

PRAISE

Praise is a soul in flower.

THOMAS WATSON

Praise shall conclude that work which prayer began.

WILLIAM JENKYN

Alas, for that capital crime of the Lord's people—barrenness in praises! Oh, how fully I am persuaded that a line of praises is worth a leaf of prayer, and an hour of praises is worth a day of fasting and mourning.

JOHN LIVINGSTONE

The servants of the Lord are to sing His praises in this life to the world's end; and in the next life, world without end.

JOHN BOYS

Praising God is one of the highest and purest acts of religion. In prayer we act like men; in praise we act like angels.

THOMAS WATSON

Self-love may lead us to prayers, but love to God excites us to praises.

THOMAS MANTON

PRAYER

Prayer is the soul's breathing itself into the bosom of its heavenly Father.

THOMAS WATSON

Praying is the same to the new creature as crying is to the natural. The child is not learned by art or example to cry, but

PRAYER

instructed by nature; it comes into the world crying. Praying is not a lesson got by forms and rules of art, but flowing from principles of new life itself.

WILLIAM GURNALL

You can do more than pray, after you have prayed, but you cannot do more than pray until you have prayed.

JOHN BUNYAN

Prayer is nothing but the promise reversed, or God's Word formed into an argument, and retorted by faith upon God again.

WILLIAM GURNALL

Key to character:

I had rather learn what some men really judge about their own justification from their *prayers* than their *writings*.

JOHN OWEN

Deeper than words:

Words are but the body, the garment, the outside of prayer; sighs are nearer the heart work. A dumb beggar getteth an alms at Christ's gates, even by making signs, when his tongue cannot plead for him; and the rather, because he is dumb.... Tears have a tongue, and grammar, and language, that our Father knoweth. Babes have no prayer for the breast, but weeping: the mother can read hunger in weeping.

SAMUEL RUTHERFORD

Many dumb beggars have been relieved at Christ's gate by making signs.

WILLIAM SECKER

Its efficacy:

I had rather stand against the cannons of the wicked than against the prayers of the righteous.

THOMAS LYE

PRAYER

Good prayers never come weeping home. I am sure I shall receive, either what I ask or what I should ask.

JOSEPH HALL

The angel fetched Peter out of prison, but it was prayer fetched the angel.

THOMAS WATSON

Prayer is putting the promises into suit.

JOHN TRAPP

God never denied that soul anything that went as far as heaven to ask it.

JOHN TRAPP

Prayer will make a man cease from sin, or sin will entice a man to cease from prayer.

JOHN BUNYAN

God may deny your wantonness, but not your wants.

JOHN FLAVEL

Bernard never went from God without God.

JOHN TRAPP

Pray often; for prayer is a shield to the soul, a sacrifice to God, and a scourge for Satan.

JOHN BUNYAN

That which begins not with prayer, seldom winds up with comfort.

JOHN FLAVEL

Israel prevailed with God in wrestling with Him, and therefore it is that he prevails with men also. If so be that we will wrestle with God for a blessing, and prevail with Him, then we need not to fear but we shall wrestle the enemies out of it also.

ALEXANDER HENDERSON

PRAYER

Misbelief doth seek many ways for delivery from trouble; but faith hath but one way—to go to God, to wit, by prayer, for whatsoever is needful.

DAVID DICKSON

Why prayers are ineffective?

When people do not mind what God speaks to them in His word, God doth as little mind what they say to Him in prayer.

WILLIAM GURNALL

Christ went more readily ad crucem, than we to the throne of grace.

THOMAS WATSON

God looks not at the elegancy of your prayers, to see how neat they are; nor yet at the geometry of your prayers, to see how long they are; nor yet at the arithmetic of your prayers, to see how many they are; nor yet at the music of your prayers, nor yet at the sweetness of your voice, nor yet at the logic of your prayers; but at the sincerity of your prayers, how hearty they are. There is no prayer acknowledged, approved, accepted, recorded, or rewarded by God, but that wherein the heart is sincerely and wholly. The true mother would not have the child divided. God loves a broken and a contrite heart, so He loathes a divided heart. God neither loves halting nor halving.

THOMAS BROOKS

Be very particular in secret prayer, both as to sins, wants and mercies.... Be not ashamed to open out all thy necessities.... Before God we may speak out our minds fully, and name the persons that afflict, affront, and trouble us; and woe to them that a child of God upon a mature judgement names in prayer! I find not that such a prayer in Scripture ever returned empty. A great reason why we reap so little benefit in prayer is, because we rest too much in generals.

SAMUEL LEE

(The hypocrite) When he hath got what he hath a mind to in prayer, he hath no more mind to pray.

JOSEPH CARYL

Prayer that is faithless is fruitless.

THOMAS WATSON

It is a sweet saying of one, "O Lord; I have come to Thee; but by Thee, I will never go from Thee, without Thee."

THOMAS BROOKS

Steps to efficacy:

"Ask...." (Matthew 7:7). If we don't receive by asking, then let us seek; if we don't receive by seeking, then let us knock.

THOMAS MANTON

A Christian should shut both the door of his closet and the door of his lips so close, that none should hear without what he says within.

THOMAS BROOKS

The speech of the mouth must not go before, but always follow after the conception of the mind. Many times as a musician's fingers will run over a song which he has been used to play, although his mind is otherwise occupied; so many in prayer will run over that form of words they have been used to utter, though their minds are roving about other matters. Oh, let the absurdity of the fault breed in us a loathing of it.

ISAAC AMBROSE

There must be delight on our parts. Joy is the tuning the soul. The command to rejoice precedes the command to pray: "Rejoice evermore; pray without ceasing." Delight makes the melody; prayer else will be but a harsh sound.

STEPHEN CHARNOCK

When thou prayest before others, observe on what thou bestowest thy chief care and zeal, whether in the externals or internals of prayer, that which is exposed to the eye and ear of

PRAYER

men, or that which should be prepared for the eye and ear of God; the devout posture of thy body, or the inward devotion of thy soul; the pomp of thy words, or the power of thy faith; the agitation of thy bodily spirits in the vehemency of thy voice, or the fervency of thy spirit in heartbreaking affections. These inward workings of the soul in prayer, are the very soul of prayer.

WILLIAM GURNALL

Furnish thyself with arguments from the promises to enforce thy prayers, and make them prevalent with God. The promises are the ground of faith, and faith, when strengthened, will make thee fervent, and such fervency ever speeds and returns with victory out of the field of prayer. . . . The mightier any is in the Word, the more mighty he will be in prayer.

WILLIAM GURNALL

Where God hath not a mouth to speak, men must not have a tongue to ask.

CHRISTOPHER NESSE

Cold prayers always freeze before they reach heaven.

THOMAS BROOKS

Observe whether thy fervency in prayer be uniform; a false heart may seem very hot in praying against one sin, but he can skip over another, and either leave it out of his confession, or handle it very gently, as a partial witness, that would fain save the prisoner's life he comes against, will not speak all he knows, but minceth his evidence; thus doth the hypocrite deal with his darling lust.

WILLIAM GURNALL

Take heed of carrying purposes of going on in sin with thee to the throne of grace! This were a horrible wickedness indeed. . . . Is it not enough to sin, but wouldst thou make God accessary to His own dishonour also?

WILLIAM GURNALL

PRAYER

To an effectual prayer there must concur the intention of the mind and the affections of the heart; else it is not praying but parrotting.

JOHN TRAPP

We must join our endeavour in the use of all means with our prayers, whether they be put up for spiritual or temporal blessings. . . . We must pray with our hand at the pump, or the ship will sink in sight of our prayers. Is it temporal subsistence thou prayest for? Pray and work, or pray and starve. Dost thou think to set God at work, while thou sittest with thy hand in thy bosom?

WILLIAM GURNALL

Do not any day, upon any pretence, omit to offer up thy morning and evening sacrifices. Remember, so often as thou neglectest morning prayer, so often thou art all the day naked, destitute of thy spiritual guard, and exposed to all manner of evils and enemies, and dost forespeak thyself an evil day; and so often as thou omittest evening prayer thou presumest upon sleep, and rest, and safety, without God's leave, and fore-speakest thyself an evil night.

GEORGE SWINNOCK

Pray in prosperity, that thou mayest speed when thou prayest in adversity; own God now, that He may acknowledge thee then. Shall that friend be welcome to us, that never gives us a visit, but when he comes to borrow? This is a right beggar's trick, but not a friend's part.

WILLIAM GURNALL

When thou prayest, rather let thy heart be without words, than thy words without a heart.

JOHN BUNYAN

Pray often rather than very long at a time. It is hard to be very long in prayer, and not slacken in our affections

WILLIAM GURNALL

215

PRAYER

I have been benefited by praying for others; for by making an errand to God for them I have gotten something for myself.

SAMUEL RUTHERFORD

When you do not hear so much and so often from God in preaching, let God hear the more and oftener from you in prayer. Ply the throne of grace. Give God no rest till He make Jerusalem a praise in the earth.

JOHN WHITLOCK

You should, in Tertullian's phrase, with a holy conspiracy, besiege heaven.

THOMAS MANTON

One way to get comfort is to plead the promise of God in prayer, show Him His handwriting; God is tender of His Word.

THOMAS MANTON

N.B.:

He that cannot pray, let him go to sea, and there he will learn.

Quoted by JOHN TRAPP

The privileges of prayer:

A praying man can never be very miserable, whatever his condition be, for he has the ear of God; the Spirit within to indite, a Friend in heaven to present, and God Himself to receive his desires as a Father. It is a mercy to pray, even though I never receive the mercy prayed for.

WILLIAM BRIDGE

Ah! How often, Christians, hath God kissed you at the beginning of prayer, and spoken peace to you in the midst of prayer, and filled you with joy and assurance upon the close of prayer!

THOMAS BROOKS

PRAYER

How can I know that my prayers are prompted by the Spirit?

When they are not only vocal, but mental; when they are not only gifts, but groans.

THOMAS WATSON

Does prayer move God?

Though God be not changed by it (prayer) in Himself, yet the real change that is made by it on ourselves, doth infer a change in God by mere relation or extrinsical denomination; He being, according to the tenor of His own covenant, engaged to punish the unbelieving, prayerless, and disobedient, and to pardon them that are faithfully desirous and obedient. So that in prayer, faith and fervency are so far from being useless, that they as much prevail for the thing desired by *qualifying ourselves for it*, as if indeed they moved the mind of God to a real change; even as he that is in a boat, and by his hook layeth hold of the bank, doth as truly by his labour get nearer the bank, as if he drew the bank to him.

RICHARD BAXTER

Should an unbeliever pray?

Though an unbeliever sin in praying, yet it is not a sin for him to pray. There is sin in the manner of his praying; but prayer, as to the act and substance of it, is his duty. He sins, not because he prays, that is required of him, but because he prays amiss, not in that manner that is required of him. There are abominations in the prayers of a wicked man, but for him to pray is not an abomination, it is the good and acceptable will of God, that which He commands.

DAVID CLARKSON

Extemporaneous prayers?

Some lay it to the charge of extemporary prayers, as if it were a diminution of God's majesty to offer them unto Him, because they cost nothing, but come without any pains or industry to provide them. A most false aspersion (2 Samuel 24:24).

PRAYER

Surely preparation of the heart (though not premeditation of every word) is required thereunto. And grant the party, praying at that very instant, forestudies not every expression, yet surely he has formerly laboured with his heart and tongue too, before he attained that dexterity of utterance, properly and readily to express himself. Many hours in the night no doubt he is waking, and was, by himself, practicing Scripture phrase and the language of Canaan, whilst such as censure him for his laziness were fast asleep in their beds.

THOMAS FULLER

God can pick sense out of a confused prayer.

RICHARD SIBBES

Written prayers?

Set prayers are prescript forms of our own or others' composing; such are lawful for any, and needful for some.

Lawful for any. Otherwise God would not have appointed the priests a form of blessing the people. Nor would the Saviour have set His prayer, which is both a prayer in itself, and a pattern or platform of prayer.

Needful for some. Namely, for such who as yet have not attained to pray extempore by the spirit. But as little children are so ambitious of going alone, that they scorn to take the guidance of a form or bench to direct them, but will venture by themselves. . . . so many confess their weakness, in denying to confess it, who, refusing to be beholden to a set form of prayer, prefer to say nonsense, rather than nothing, in their extempore expressions. More modesty, and no less piety, it had been for such men to have prayed longer with set forms that they might pray better without them.

THOMAS FULLER

Is it lawful to pray in a set form of words? Nothing but very great ignorance can make you really doubt it. Hath God anywhere forbid it? You will say that it is enough that He hath not

218

commanded it. I answer, That in general He hath commanded it you that all be done to edification; but He hath given to you no particular command or prohibition. No more hath He commanded you to pray in English, French, or Latin; nor to sing psalms in this tune or that; nor after this or that version or translation.

RICHARD BAXTER

Hath it not the show of error to say that no man may use any set prayer, seeing there be many set prayers, and psalms, and blessings in the Holy Scripture, which were used in the same form?

HENRY SMITH

Those who will never enter the water but with flags or bladders under them will scarce ever learn to swim; and it cannot be denied but that the constant and unvaried use of set forms of prayer may become a great occasion of quenching the Spirit, and hindering all progress or growth in gifts or graces.

JOHN OWEN

N.B.:

Overvalue not therefore the manner of your own worship, and overvilify not other men's of a different mode.

RICHARD BAXTER

Joint prayers?

There is a wonderful prevalency in the joint prayers of His people. When Peter was in prison, the church met and prayed him out of his enemies' hands. A prince will grant a petition subscribed by the hands of a whole city, which, may be, he would not at the request of a private subject, and yet love him well too. There is an especial promise to public prayer: "Where two or three are gathered together in My name, there am I in the midst of them."

WILLIAM GURNALL

PRAYER

Delayed answers to prayer?

You must distinguish between delays and denials.

THOMAS BROOKS

A saint is to put forth his faith in prayer, and afterwards follow his prayer with faith.

VAVASOR POWELL

He hath engaged to answer the prayers of His people, and "fulfil the desires of those that fear Him." But it proves a long voyage sometimes before the praying saint hath the return of his adventure. There comes oft a long and sharp winter between the sowing-time of prayer, and the reaping. He hears us indeed as soon as we pray, but we oft do not hear of Him so soon. Prayers are not long in their journey to heaven, but long a coming thence in a full answer.

WILLIAM GURNALL

Objection: Where is omnipotence so long when I cry with a dry throat and pained breast, and am not heard?
Answer: Omnipotence is in God, and no elsewhere. Be sure not always at a call to claw your scabbed back. Neither is it omnipotence's part to flatter you, or, as a pick-thank servant ready waiting on, to say "aye" and "nay" to your "yeas" and "nays". In a word, omnipotence is at hand to save you when God will, not to humour your impatience as you will.

SAMUEL RUTHERFORD

Set no time to the Lord the creator of time, for His time is always best.

SAMUEL RUTHERFORD

N.B.:

Yea, but we have waited a long time. Well, but yet know that you are at the right door.

JEREMIAH BURROUGHS

(Referring to the Saviour's delay in responding to the request of the Syrophenician woman) It is said that "He *answered* not a word," but it is not said, He *heard* not a word. These two differ much. Christ often heareth when He doth not answer—His not answering is an answer. . . .

SAMUEL RUTHERFORD

PREACHING

Divinely decreed:

A public interpretation or dividing the Word, performed by an ambassador or minister who speaks to the people instead of God, in the name of Christ.

JOHN PRESTON

It was by the ear, by our first parents listening to the serpent, that we lost paradise; and it is by the ear, by hearing of the Word, that we get to heaven. "Hear, and your souls shall live." (Isaiah 55:3).

THOMAS WATSON

A jealous mistress:

Those who sweat in worldly employments, are commonly but cold in the pulpit.

WILLIAM JENKYN

The preacher, after a sort, is more to be honoured than the ruler, for Aaron was the elder brother, but Moses was the younger brother; and therefore, if there be any appendix, the magistrate is the appendix, for if Aaron's Urim and Thummim would have served (Exodus 28:30), Moses' rod and staff should not have been needed; but when the tongue could not persuade, the rod did compel, and so came in the magistrate.

HENRY SMITH

PREACHING

Once we had golden ministers and wooden vessels, now we have wooden ministers and golden vessels.

JOHN TRAPP

Perfecting the method:

Screw the truth into men's minds.

RICHARD BAXTER

It must needs be that every sentence of the Holy Scripture containeth in it at least one general doctrine.

JOHN UDALL

When the fire is stirred up and discovered it giveth more heat than when it is not, so the Word of God by preaching and interpreting maketh a greater flame in the hearts of the hearers than when it is read.

THOMAS CARTWRIGHT

We are not sent to get galley-slaves to the oars, or a bear to the stake: but He sends us to woo you as spouses, to marry you to Christ.

WALTER CRADOCK

If a hardened heart be to be broken, it is not stroking but striking that must do it.

RICHARD BAXTER

An hot iron, though blunt, will pierce sooner than a cold one, though sharper.

JOHN FLAVEL

Solomon confessed that he studied for his doctrines, Eccles. 12:10. . . . Daniel was a prophet, and yet he desired respite to interpret Nebuchadnezzar's dream, Daniel 2:16. . . . It seems that Solomon and Daniel would not count them sermons which come forth, like untimely births, from uncircumcised lips, and unwashed hands, as though they had the Spirit at command-ment. . . . For if Jesus would have us consider what we ask before we come to pray, much more should we consider before we come to preach; for it is harder to speak God's Word, than to speak to God.

HENRY SMITH

Rhetorical flowers and flourishes, expressions without impressions in praying or preaching, are not true bread, but a tinkling cymbal to it.

CHRISTOPHER NESSE

N.B.:

I preached as never sure to preach again, and as a dying man to dying men.

RICHARD BAXTER

PRIDE

Pride loves to climb up, not as Zaccheus to see Christ, but to be seen.

WILLIAM GURNALL

This is certainly pride, for it is a lifting up of the heart above God and against God and without God.

THOMAS MANTON

A proud faith is as much a contradiction as a humble devil.

STEPHEN CHARNOCK

The more godly a man is, and the more graces and blessings of God are upon him, the more need he hath to pray, because Satan is busiest against him, and because he is readiest to be puffed up with a conceited holiness.

RICHARD GREENHAM

The ultimate sin:

I may say of pride, many sins have done wickedly, but thou surmountest them all; for the wrathful man, the prodigal man,

PRIDE

the lascivious man, the surfeiting man, the slothful man, is
rather an enemy to himself than to God; the envious man, the
covetous man, the deceitful man, the ungrateful man, is rather
an enemy to men than to God; but the proud man sets himself
against God (because he doth against His laws), he maketh
himself equal with God (because he doth all without God and
craves no help of Him); he exalteth himself above God (because
he will have his own will).

HENRY SMITH

As death is the last enemy; so pride the last sin that shall be
destroyed in us.

JOHN BOYS

Pride is the shirt of the soul, put on first and put off last.

GEORGE SWINNOCK

And if God spared not the angels, whom He placed in the
highest heavens, but for their pride threw them down headlong
to the nethermost hell, how much less shall He spare the proud
dust and ashes of the sons of men, but shall cast them from the
height of their earthly altitude to the bottom of that infernal
dungeon! "Humility makes men angels; pride makes angels
devils;" as that Father said .... Oh let us be humbled by our
repentance, that we may not be brought down to everlasting
confusion: let us be cast down upon our knees, that we may not
be cast down upon our faces. For God will make good His own
Word, one way; "A man's pride shall bring him low."

JOSEPH HALL

Many facets:

This is their work as soon as they rise, to put a pedlar's shop
upon their backs, and colour their faces, and prick their ruffs,
and frizzle their hair, and then their day's work is done, as
though their office were to paint a fair image every morning,
and at night to blot it out again.

HENRY SMITH

PRIDE

They which will be strutters shall not want flatterers, which will praise everything that they do, and everything that they speak, and everything that they wear, and say it becomes them well to wear long hair; that it becomes them well to wear bellied doublets; that it becomes them well to jet in their going; that it becomes them well to swear in their talking.

HENRY SMITH

When the devil cannot stay us from a good work, then he laboureth by all means to make us proud of it.

HENRY SMITH

It is the light head and the aspiring mind which through pride and ambition flieth into the prince's palace.

LAURENCE CHADERTON

Men are more unwilling to part with their righteousness than with their sins.

STEPHEN CHARNOCK

The cure:

Our father was Adam, our grandfather dust, our great-grand-father nothing.

WILLIAM JENKYN

Only a Christian of strong grace can bear the strong wine of commendation without the spiritual intoxication.

WILLIAM JENKYN

To crucify this corruption, Providence takes off the bridle of restraint from ungodly men, and sometimes permits them to traduce the names of God's servants, as Shimei did David's. Yea, they shall fall into disesteem among their friends, as Paul did among the Corinthians; and all this to keep down the swelling of their spirits at the sense of those excellencies that are in them.

JOHN FLAVEL

N.B.:

For the avoiding of this vice (pride), God suffereth men to fall into other vices, which men abhor and punish, as theft and fornication, and drunkenness, to make them ashamed by these vices, which were not ashamed of pride.

HENRY SMITH

PROMISES OF GOD

Absolute:

The being of God may as well fail as the promise of God.

TIMOTHY CRUSO

Promises, though they be for a time seemingly delayed, cannot be finally frustrated. . . . the heart of God is not turned though His face be hid; and prayers are not flung back, though they be not instantly answered.

TIMOTHY CRUSO

Precious:

Three things are called precious in the Scripture: the blood of Christ is called "precious blood," 1 Peter 1:19; and faith is called "precious faith," 2 Peter 1:1; and the promises are called "precious promises," 2 Peter 1:4.

THOMAS BROOKS

Christ's performances outstrip His promises.

NEHEMIAH ROGERS

Blissful:

"Peter was in prison, but prayer was made without ceasing of the church to God for him" (Acts 12:5). What greater happiness than to have God's promises and the saints' prayers!

THOMAS WATSON

PROMISES OF GOD, PROSPERITY

It is better to be as low as hell with a promise, than in Paradise without one.

JOHN FLAVEL

Their neglect:

For the most part we live upon successes, not promises:—unless we see and feel the print of victories, we will not believe.

JOHN OWEN

PROSPERITY

No proof of Divine favour:

No man knows the heart of God stands toward him by His hand. His hand of mercy may be toward a man when His heart may be against that man, as you see in the case of Saul and others. And the hand of God may be set against a man when the heart of God is dearly set upon him, as you may see in Job and Ephraim. No man knows either love or hatred by outward mercy or misery; for all things come alike to all, to the righteous and the unrighteous, to the good and to the bad, to the clean and to the unclean. The sun of prosperity shines as well upon brambles of the wilderness, as fruit-trees of the orchard; the snow and hail of adversity light upon the best garden, as well as upon the stinking dunghill or the wild waste. Ahab's and Josiah's ends concur in the very circumstances. Saul and Jonathan, though different in their natures, deserts, and deportments, yet in their deaths they were not divided. Health, wealth, honours, crosses, sicknesses, losses, are cast upon good men and bad men promiscuously. "The whole Turkish empire," says Luther, "is nothing else but a crust cast by Heaven's great Housekeeper to His dogs." Moses dies in the wilderness as well as those that murmured. Nabal is rich as well as Abraham; Ahithophel wise as well as Solomon, and Doeg is honoured as well as Saul, as well as Joseph and Pharaoh.

THOMAS BROOKS

PROSPERITY

As men cherish young plants at first, and fence them about to keep them from hurt, but when they are grown, they remove them, and then leave them to the wind and weather, so God besets His children first with props of inward comforts, but afterwards exposes them to storms and winds, because they are better able to bear it. Therefore let no man think himself the better because he is free from troubles. It is because God sees him not fit to bear greater.

RICHARD SIBBES

Full of peril:

Seldom seest thou a man make haste to be rich, and thrive in religion. Christ's message to John holds true; the poor are most forward in receiving and following the Gospel. As thou lovest thy zeal, beware of resolving to be rich, lest gain prove thy godliness; take heed of ambitious aspiring, lest courts and great places prove ill airs for zeal, whither it is as easy to go zealous as to return wise. Peter, while he warmed his hands, cooled his heart.

SIR RICHARD BAKER

Who seeth not that prosperity increaseth iniquity? and where is more want, there is less wantonness.

THOMAS ADAMS

Prosperity is no friend to a sanctified memory, and therefore we are cautioned, when we are full, lest we forget God. Noah, who had seen the whole world drowned in water, was no sooner safe on shore, and in the enjoyment of plenty, than he forgot God, and drowned himself in wine.

WILLIAM GURNALL

Where one thousand are destroyed by the world's frowns, ten thousand are destroyed by the world's smiles. The world, siren-like, sings us and sinks us.

THOMAS BROOKS

And as men's diversions increase from the world, so do their entanglements from Satan. When they have more to do in the world than they can well manage, they shall have more to do from Satan than they can well withstand.

JOHN OWEN

Afflictions, like bills and pikes, make a terrible show when they cannot reach us; but the temptations of prosperity, like unseen bullets, wound and kill us before they are discerned.

GEORGE DOWNAME

David could bear persecution without murmuring, but when he came to prosperity he could not turn away his eyes from vanity.

SIR RICHARD BAKER

Transitory:

Build your nest upon no tree here; for you see God has sold the forest to death.

SAMUEL RUTHERFORD

PROVIDENCE

There are three things in providence: God's foreknowing, God's determining, and God's directing all things to their periods and events.

THOMAS WATSON

Providence is the perpetuity and continuance of creation.

RICHARD SIBBES

Tell me, if God had never a creature to look to in all the world but thee, wouldst thou believe that He would regard thy heart, and words, and ways, or not? If He would, why not now as well as then! Is He not as sufficient for thee, and as really present with thee, as if He had no other creature else? If all men in the world were dead save one, would the sun any more illuminate that one than now it doth? Mayest thou not see as well by the light of it now, as if it had never another to enlighten? And dost thou see a creature do so much, and wilt thou not believe as much of the Creator? If thou think us worms too low for God so exactly to observe, thou mayest as well think that we are too low for Him to create, or preserve?

RICHARD BAXTER

Why God's providences are often misunderstood?

Take a straight stick, and put it into the water; then it will seem crooked. Why? Because we look upon it through two mediums, air and water: there lies the *deceptio visus;* thence it is that we cannot discern aright. Thus the proceedings of God, in His justice, which in themselves are straight, without the least obliquity, seem unto us crooked: that wicked men should prosper, and good men be afflicted; that the Israelites should make the bricks, and the Egyptians dwell in the houses; that servants should ride on horse-back, and princes go on foot: these are things that make the best Christians stagger in their judgements.

And why? Because they look upon God's proceedings through a double medium of flesh and spirit, so that all things seem to go cross, though indeed they go right enough. And hence it is that God's proceedings, in His justice, are not so well discerned, the eyes of man alone being not competent judges thereof.

THOMAS FULLER

Some providences, like Hebrew letters, must be read backwards.

JOHN FLAVEL

When it is providence versus promise?

God is to be trusted when His providences seem to run contrary to His promises. God promised David to give him the crown, to make him king; but providence turns contrary to His promise; David was pursued by Saul, was in danger of his life; but all this while it was David's duty to trust God. The Lord doth oftentimes, by cross providence, bring to pass His promise. God promised Paul the lives of all that were with him in the ship; but now the providence of God seems to run quite contrary to His promise; the winds blow, the ship splits and breaks in pieces; and thus God fulfilled His promise; upon the broken pieces of the ship, they all come safe to shore. Trust God when providences seem to run quite contrary to promises.

THOMAS WATSON

Grace makes the promise and providence the payment.

JOHN FLAVEL

Let not fortune, which hath no name in Scripture, have any in thy divinity. Let providence, not chance, have the honour of thy acknowledgements, and be thy Oedipus in contingencies. Mark well the paths and winding ways thereof; but be not too wise in the construction, or sudden in the application. The hand of providence writes often by abbreviatures, hieroglyphics, or short characters, which, like the laconism on the wall, are not to be made out but by a hint or key from that Spirit which indited them.

SIR THOMAS BROWNE

Their perfect timing:

We find a multitude of providences so timed to a minute, that had they occurred just a little sooner or later, they had mattered little in comparison with what now they do. Certainly, it cannot be chance, but counsel, that so exactly works in time. Contingencies keep to no rules. . . . The angel calls to Abraham, and shows him another sacrifice just when his hand was giving the fatal stroke to Isaac (Genesis 22:10-11). A well of water is shown to Hagar just when she had left the child, as not able to see its death (Genesis 21:16,19). Rabshakeh meets with a blasting providence, hears a rumour that frustrated his design, just when ready to make an assault upon Jerusalem. (Isaiah 37:8).

JOHN FLAVEL

Their wisdom:

The wisdom of providence in our provisions. And this is seen in proportioning the quantity, not satisfying our extravagant wishes, but answering our real needs; consulting our wants, not our wantonness. "But my God shall supply all your need."

JOHN FLAVEL

God made meat before mouths.

JOHN TRAPP

RECREATION

Circumscribed:

All lawful recreation is only in the use of things indifferent, which are in themselves neither commanded nor forbidden.

WILLIAM PERKINS

First; recreation may not be in the use of holy things, that is, in the use of the Word, sacraments, prayer, or in any act of religion. . . . Second; recreation may not be made of the sins or offenses of men. They ought to be unto us the matter of sorrow and mourning. . . . Third; we may not make recreations of God's judgements, or of the punishments of sin.

WILLIAM PERKINS

Games may be divided into three sorts: games of wit or industry, games of hazard, and a mixture of both. Games of wit or industry are such as are ordered by the skill and industry of man. Of this sort are shooting in the longbow, shooting in the caliver, running, wrestling, fencing, music, and the games of chess and draughts. . . . These, and all of this kind, wherein the industry of the mind and body hath the chiefest stroke, are very commendable, and not to be disliked. Games of hazard are those in which hazard only bears the sway and orders the game, and not wit; wherein also there is, as we say, chance, yea mere chance in regard of us. Now games that are of mere hazard, by the consent of godly divines are unlawful. The reasons are these: First, games of mere hazard are indeed lots, and the use of a lot is an act of religion, in which we refer unto God the

232

determination of things of moment that can no other way be determined. . . . Secondly, such games are not recreations, but rather matter of stirring up troublesome passions, as fear, sorrow. . . . Thirdly, covetousness is commonly the ground of them all. Whereupon it is that men usually play for money. And for these causes such plays. . . . are unlawful. The third kind of plays are mixed, which stand partly of hazard and partly of wit, and in which hazard begins the game and skill gets the victory, and that which is defective by reason of hazard is corrected by wit. . . . Now the common opinion of learned divines is that, as they are not to be commended, so they are not simply to be condemned, and if they be used they must be used very sparingly.

WILLIAM PERKINS

Guidelines:

How are we to use recreations?. . . . four special rules:

Rule 1. We are to make choice of recreations that are of least offense and of the best report.

Rule 2. Our recreations must be profitable to ourselves and others, and they must tend also to the glory of God.

Rule 3. The end of our recreation must be to refresh our bodies and minds.

Rule 4. Recreation must be moderate and sparing, even as the use of meat and drink and rest.

WILLIAM PERKINS

REGENERATION

Descriptions:

Regeneration is not a removal of the old substance or faculties of the soul. Some thought that the substance of Adam's soul was corrupted when he sinned, therefore suppose the substance of

REGENERATION

his soul to be altered when he is renewed. Sin took not away the substance, but the rectitude; the new creation therefore gives not a new faculty but a new quality. The cure of the leprosy is not a destroying of the fabric of the body, but the disease; yet in regard of the greatness of man's corruption, the soul is so much changed by these new habits, that it is as it were a new soul, a new understanding, a new will.

STEPHEN CHARNOCK

In regeneration nature is not ruined, but rectified. The convert is the same man, but new made. The faculties of his soul are not destroyed, but they are refined; the same viol, but new tuned. Christ gave not the blind man new eyes, but a new sight to the old ones. Christ did not give Lazarus a new body, but enlivened his old body. So God in conversion doth not bestow a new understanding, but a new light to the old; not a new soul, but a new life to the old one.

GEORGE SWINNOCK

There may be several things which may help to make the life fair in the eyes of men; but nothing will make it amiable in the eyes of God, unless the heart be changed and renewed. All the medicines which can be applied, without the sanctifying work of the Spirit, though they may cover, they can never cure the corruption and diseases of the soul.

GEORGE SWINNOCK

Nor is regeneration an addition to nature. Christ was not an addition to Adam, but a new Head by Himself. . . . Grace grows not upon the old stock. It is not a piece of cloth sewn to an old garment, but the one is cast aside, the other wholly taken on. . . . It is not a new varnish, nor do old things remain under a new paint, nor new plaster laid upon old; a new creature, not a mended creature.

STEPHEN CHARNOCK

Repentance is a change of the mind, and regeneration is a change of the man.

THOMAS ADAMS

REGENERATION

Adoption gives us the privilege of sons, regeneration the nature of sons.

STEPHEN CHARNOCK

Regeneration is a universal change of the whole man.... it is as large in renewing as sin was in defacing.

STEPHEN CHARNOCK

The creation of the world is a shadow of the regeneration of a Christian. First, there was an earth without form, void, and a darkness upon the face of the deep. Predestination is this great deep, which cannot be discovered or discerned. There the light was separated from the darkness; here knowledge is separated from ignorance of the soul; there is calling. Then was the sun created; so here the bright beams of grace are diffused into our hearts which fill us with spiritual joy; there is sanctification. Lastly, Adam was created after the image of God, and placed in Paradise; so the new man is confirmed to the image of Christ, and shall be reposed in the paradise of everlasting glory.

THOMAS ADAMS

In the first creation, God made man after His own image. So in the second creation or regeneration, God doth create men after His own image, in knowledge, righteousness, true holiness, and love.

VAVASOR POWELL

Reader, make sure of this inward change; otherwise, though thy conversation may be specious, it can never be gracious, nor thy profession durable. ... I wonder not that many professors disown the Lord Jesus, when they are ignorant why they at any time owned Him. He that takes up religion on trust, will lay it down when it brings him into trouble. He that follows Christ, he knoweth not why, will forsake Him, he knoweth not how.

GEORGE SWINNOCK

N.B.:

Thou must be righteous and holy, before thou canst live righteously and holily.

WILLIAM GURNALL

235

REGENERATION, RELIGION

Importance of early regeneration:

As an early regeneration makes for God's honour, so it makes for your own interest. Your new birth will be the gentler. The work of conscience will be more kindly, without the horrors they have who have lain many years soaking in the old nature. More of hell must be flashed in an old sinner's face, to awaken him from his dead sleep. Paul, who had sinned some years with an high hand, was struck to the earth. Christ, as it were, took him by the throat, and shook him: Acts 9:6. He trembling and astonished said, "Lord, what wilt Thou have me to do?" There will be more amazing aggravations of sin to reach the conscience and consequently more anguish. Putrified wounds require more lancing; and therefore are more painful in the cure than those which are but newly made. The more we are alienated from the life of God, the harder it will be to return to live that life again.

STEPHEN CHARNOCK

RELIGION

Religion is not a thing which it is possible to put off and put on like a Sunday dress.... If you think you are doing so, believe me that as yet it is not a religion, but a web of delusions.

EDWARD REYNOLDS

An heifer that is not used to the yoke struggles; the yoke pincheth the neck, but after a while she carries it more gently. ... So the way of religion is irksome at the first, but after, it gives great comfort and contentment. ... each day will bring more comfort than the other.

JOSIAS SHUTE

The abstract of religion is to imitate Him whom thou dost worship. Such an one hath done me insufferable wrong, how can I forgive him? God would. Another has gotten into my debt, and abuseth my patience, how can I forbear him? God would.

Be thou a follower of God in grace, that thou mayest ascend to
His glory.

THOMAS ADAMS

REPENTANCE

Man and God:

Repentance with man is the changing of his will; repentance
with God is the willing of a change.

JOHN TRAPP

Sine qua non:

There is no other fortification against the judgements of God
but repentance. His forces be invisible, invincible; not repelled
with sword and target; neither portcullis nor fortress can keep
them out; there is nothing in the world that can encounter them
but repentance.

THOMAS ADAMS

God will not pardon for repentance, nor yet without it.

THOMAS WATSON

Accompanying signs:

There cannot be a true sorrow of heart for a sin that is past, but
presently there doth arise a purpose not to sin for the future.

THOMAS GOODWIN

Let the quantity of thy sins be the measure of thy repentance.

ISAAC BARGRAVE

A stroke, from guilt, from wrath, broke Judas' heart into despair;
a look from love, from Christ, broke Peter's into tears.

GEORGE SWINNOCK

REPENTANCE

Other things may be the worse for breaking, yet a heart is never at the best till it be broken.

SIR RICHARD BAKER

He grieves truly that weeps without a witness.

GEORGE SWINNOCK

Wouldst thou know when thou hast been humbled enough for sin? When thou art willing to let go thy sins.

THOMAS WATSON

The wicked do but weep for their sins past, but the godly purpose to sin no more.

HENRY SMITH

The convictions of hypocrites and reprobates are usually confined to some very few gross transgressions. Saul grants no more but the *persecuting of David.* Judas grants only the *betraying of innocent blood;* but usually those convictions by which the Lord prepareth His own way in the soul, although they may begin at one or more gross particular transgressions, yet they stop not; but the man is led on to see many breaches of the law, and "innumerable evils compassing him," as David speaketh in the sight of his sin.

WILLIAM GUTHRIE

A repenting man is more angry at his own heart that consenteth to sin than he is at the devil who did tempt him to sin.

SAMUEL RUTHERFORD

Now the Lord looks upon my sins, they are now before Him; and we should never rest till we have by repentance moved Him to blot them out. Yea, to this end we should ourselves call them to remembrance. For the more we remember them, the more God forgets them; the more we forget them, the more God remembers them.

WILLIAM BRADSHAW

Amendment of life is the best repentance.

JOHN TRAPP

238

REPENTANCE

Pseudo-repentance:

If an unregenerate man should leave off sin under fear of death or hell, it would not be out of hatred to sin, but out of the fear of the punishment, as the bird is kept from the bait by the scarecrow.

THOMAS MANTON

Take heed thou prayest not with a reservation, be sure thou renouncest what thou wouldst have God remit. God will never remove the guilt as long as thou entertainest the sin. . . . It is desperate folly to desire God to forgive what thou intendest to commit. Thou hadst as good speak out, and ask leave to sin with impunity, for God knows the language of thy heart, and needs not thy tongue to be an interpreter. . . . Hypocrisy is too thin a veil to blind the eyes of the Almighty. Thou mayest put thy own eyes out, so as not to see Him; but thou canst never blind His eyes that He should not see thee.

WILLIAM GURNALL

Danger of delay:

Whoever delays his repentance does in effect pawn his soul with the devil.

THOMAS MANTON

The more we defer, the more difficult and painful our work needs prove; every day will both enlarge our task and diminish our ability to perform it. Sin is never at a stay; if we do not retreat from it, we shall advance in it, and the further on we go, the more we have to come back; every step we take forward must be repeated; all the web we spin must be unravelled.

UNKNOWN

Vice, as it groweth in age, so it improveth in stature and strength. . . . so we shall dwindle and prove more impotent, for it feedeth upon our vitals, and thriveth by our decay; it waxeth mighty by stripping us of our best forces, by enfeebling our reason, by perverting our will, by corrupting our temper, by debasing our courage, by seducing all our appetites and passions to a treacherous compliance with itself; every day our mind groweth more blind, our will more rusty, our spirit more

REPENTANCE

faint, our passions more headstrong and untamable; the power and empire of sin do strangely by degrees encroach, and continually get ground upon us, till it hath quite subdued and enthralled us. First we learn to bear it; then we come to like it; by and by we contract a friendship with it; then we dote upon it; at last we become enslaved to it in bondage.

ISAAC BARROW

By delay of repentance, sin strengthens, and the heart hardens. The longer ice freezeth, the harder it is to be broken.

THOMAS WATSON

He that resolves to be virtous, but not till some time hereafter, resolves against being virtuous in the meantime; and as virtue at such a distance is easily resolved on, so it is as easy a matter always to keep it at that distance. "The next week," says the sinner, "I will begin to be sober and temperate, serious and devout;" but the true sense of what he says is this, "I am fully bent to spend this present week in riot and excess, in sensuality and profaneness, or whatever vice it is that I indulge myself in;" and if we do it thus often, if it be our common course to put off our repentance thus from time to time, this is a most shrewd sign that indeed we never intend to repent at all.

EDMUND CALAMY

The Lord hath made a promise *to* late repentance, but where hath He made a promise *of* late repentance?

THOMAS BROOKS

The time of God's grace to sinners doth many time expire before death.

PHILIP HENRY

Many have *the space* of repentance, who have not *the grace* of repentance.

WILLIAM SECKER

If God's to-day be too soon for thy repentance, thy to-morrow may be too late for His acceptance.

WILLIAM SECKER

You cannot repent too soon, because you do not know how soon it may be too late.

THOMAS FULLER

Death-bed repentance suspect?

No man ought to flatter and deceive himself in deferring his conversion by alleging the example of the penitent thief, saved even at the last hour upon the cross, and carried to Paradise that same day with Christ, for this act was a special miracle, reserved for the manifestation of Christ's power and glory at that hour upon the cross; and, besides, this act was upon a most rare confession made by the thief at that instant when almost all the world forsook Christ.

DANIEL CAWDRAY

Though true repentance is never too late, yet late repentance is seldom true.

THOMAS BROOKS

N.B.:

It is an old saying, Repentance is never too late; but it is a true saying, Repentance is never too soon.

HENRY SMITH

REPROOF

A Christian obligation:

You would count him unworthy the name of a friend who, knowing a thief or an incendiary to lurk in your family with a design to kill, or rob, or burn your house, would conceal it from you, and not acquaint you with it in his own accord. There is no such thief, murderer, incendiary, as sin........ Silence or concealment in this case is treachery. He is the most faithful friend, and worthy of most esteem and affection, that deals most plain-

REPROOF

ly with us in reference to the discovery of our sin. He that is reserved in this case is but a false friend, a mere pretender to love, whereas, indeed, he hates his brother in his heart. (Leviticus 19:17).

DAVID CLARKSON

A foolish physician he is, and a most unfaithful friend, that will let a sick man die for fear of troubling him; and cruel wretches are we to our friends, that will rather suffer them to go quietly to hell, than we will anger them, or hazard our reputation with them.

RICHARD BAXTER

It was well done of Paul to reprove Peter to his face, and it was well done of Peter, to praise Paul in his absence.

THOMAS ADAMS

Demands rectitude in the reprover:

If my carriage be unblamable, my counsel and reproof will be the more acceptable. Wholesome meat often is distasteful, coming out of nasty hands. A bad liver cannot be a good counselor or bold reprover; such a man must speak softly for fear of awaking his own guilty conscience. If the bell be cracked, the sound must needs be jarring.

GEORGE SWINNOCK

An open reproof of our betters is little better than a libel.

THOMAS FULLER

He cannot be a bold reprover, that is not a conscientious liver; such a one must speak softly, for fear of waking his own guilty conscience.

WILLIAM GURNALL

Demands grace in the receiver:

Oh, that I might never be so void of love to my fallen brother as not to give him a serious reproof, nor so void of love to myself as not to receive a serious reproof.

GEORGE SWINNOCK

REPROOF

Grace will teach a Christian contentedly to take those potions that are wholesome, though they are not toothsome.

GEORGE SWINNOCK

It is one of the most dangerous diseases of professors, and one of the greatest scandals of this age, that persons taken for eminently religious are more impatient of plain, though just, reproof than many a drunkard, swearer, or fornicator; and when they have spent hours or days in the seeming earnest confession of their sin, and lament before God and man that they cannot do it with more grief and tears, yet they take it for a heinous injury in another that will say half so much against them, and take him for a malignant enemy of the godly who will call them as they call themselves.

RICHARD BAXTER

Care in administration:

Sometimes a sudden reproof, upon the commission of the sin, has reformed the sinner; but this is not always safe. When men's spirits are hot, and their minds drunk with passion, they are more apt to beat the Christian than to hear his counsel. Abigail would not tell Nabal of his danger till he was sober.

But if there be no probability of a better season, after some ejaculations to heaven for assistance and success, take the present opportunity. Fabius conquered by delaying, but Caesar overcame by expedition. Though it is not ordinarily so good to sow corn when the wind is high, yet the husbandman will rather do it in such weather than not at all.

GEORGE SWINNOCK

When the earth is soft, the plough will enter. Take a man when he is under affliction, or in the house of mourning, or newly stirred by some moving sermon, and then set it home, and you may do him good. Christian faithfulness doth require us, not only to do good when it falls in our way, but to watch for opportunities of doing good.

RICHARD BAXTER

REPROOF

"If thy brother offend thee, tell him his fault between him and thee." The presence of many may make him take up an unjust defence, who in private would have taken upon him a just shame. The open air makes sores to rankle—other's crimes are not to be cried at the market. Private reproof is the best grave to bury private faults.

GEORGE SWINNOCK

A man may, by a parable or an history pertinent to the purpose, convince a sinner's conscience and not openly injure his credit. Paul, in his sermon to Felix, seemed to shoot at random, not naming any, but his arrow pierced that unrighteous prince to the quick. A wise reprover in this is like a good fencer, who, though he strike one part, yet none that stand by could perceive from his eye, or the carriage of his arm, that he aimed at that more than the rest.

GEORGE SWINNOCK

It is an excellent example that Paul giveth us (Galatians 2:2). He communicateth the Gospel to them, yet privately to them of reputation, lest he should run in vain. Some men would take this to be a sinful complying with their corruption, to yield so far to their pride and bashfulness as to teach them only in private, because they would be ashamed to own the truth in public. But Paul knew how great a hindrance men's reputation is to their entertaining of the truth, and that the remedy must not only be fitted to the disease, but also to the strength of the patient, and that in so doing, the physician is not guilty of favouring the disease, but is praiseworthy for taking the right way to cure it.

RICHARD BAXTER

It is not for every fool to handle snuffers at or about the candles, lest perhaps, instead of mending the light, they put the candle out.

JOHN BUNYAN

244

REPROOF

I see iron first heated red-hot in the fire, and afterwards beaten and hardened with cold water. Thus will I deal with an offending friend; first heat him with deserved praise of his virtue, and then beat upon him with reprehension.

JOSEPH HALL

Reprove seriously. Reproof is an edged tool, and must not be jested with. Cold reproofs are like the noise of cannons a great way off, nothing affrighting us. He that reproves sin merrily, as one that takes a pride to show his wit and to make the company laugh, will destroy the sinner instead of the sin.

GEORGE SWINNOCK

To tell a man of his sins as softly as Eli did his sons, reprove him as gently as Jehosaphat did Ahab, "Let not the king say so," doth usually as much harm as good. I am persuaded the very manner of some men's reproof and exhortation hath hardened many a sinner in the way of destruction. To tell them of sin, or ، ᶜ heaven, or hell, in a dull, easy careless language, doth make men think you are not in good sadness, nor do mean as you speak; but either you scarce think yourselves such things are true, or else you take them in such a slight and indifferent manner.

UNKNOWN

Oh, sirs, deal with sin as sin, and speak of heaven and hell as they are, and not as if you were in jest.

RICHARD BAXTER

Reprove compassionately. Soft words and hard arguments do well together. Passion will heat the sinner's blood, but compassion will heal his conscience.

GEORGE SWINNOCK

The reprover should have a lion's stout heart, or he will not be faithful, and a lady's soft hand, or he is not like to be successful.

GEORGE SWINNOCK

Some men would receive more blows with more patience, if they were given them with more prudence.

GEORGE SWINNOCK

REPROOF, RESURRECTION

The minister is to reprove the sins of all, but to name none. Paul, being to preach before a lascivious and unrighteous prince, touched him to the quick, but did not name him in his sermon. Felix's conscience saved Paul that labour.

WILLIAM GURNALL

RESURRECTION

Its certainty:

We are more sure to arise out of our graves than out of our beds.

THOMAS WATSON

The body also?

The body shall be awaked out of its dead sleep, and quickened into a glorious immortal life. The soul and body are the essential parts of man; and though the inequality be great in their operations that respect holiness, yet their concourse is necessary. Good actions are designed by the counsel and resolution of the spirit, but performed by the ministry of the flesh. Every grace expresses itself in visible actions by the body. In the sorrows of repentance it supplies tears, in fastings its appetites are restrained, in thanksgivings the tongue breaks forth into the joyful praises of God. All the victories over sensible pleasure and pain are obtained by the soul in conjunction with the body. Now it is most becoming the Divine goodness not to deal so differently, that the soul should be everlastingly happy, and the body lost in forgetfulness; the one glorified in heaven, the other remain in the dust. From their first setting out in the world to the grave they ran the same race, and shall enjoy the same reward. Here the body is the consort of the soul in obedience and sufferings, hereafter in fruition. When the crown of purity or palm of martyrdom shall be given by the great Judge in the view of all, they shall both partake in the honour. Of this we have an earnest in the resurrection of Christ in His true body, who "is the first-fruits of them that sleep."

WILLIAM BATES

RESURRECTION

It is congruous to the wisdom and governing justice of God, that the same body which was partaker with the soul in sin and duty should be partaker with it in suffering or felicity.

RICHARD BAXTER

What sort of body?

If a skilful workman can turn a little earth and ashes into such curious transparent glasses as we daily see, and if a little seed that bears no show of such a thing can produce the more beautiful flowers of the earth; and if a little acorn can bring forth the greatest oak; why should we once doubt whether the seed of everlasting life and glory, which is now in the blessed souls with Christ, can by Him communicate a perfection to the flesh that is dissolved into its elements?

RICHARD BAXTER

Many blessings are promised to our outward man, here in this life; and hereafter it is to be made a glorious and incorruptible body, like unto the glorious body of our Lord Jesus Christ: it is to be clothed with light and crowned with rays, never more to suffer injuries without or diseases within.

EZEKIEL HOPKINS

The great prototype:

Christ, like the sun eclipsed by the moon, got Himself out by His resurrection; and, as the sun by the moon, He was darkened by them to whom He gave light. His death did justify us, His resurrection did justify His death. He buried the law with Himself, and both with honour; He raised up the Gospel with Himself, and both with glory. His resurrection was the first stone of the foundation, "In Christ shall all be made alive," and the last stone of the roof, for God assures us that all come to judgement by this token, that He raised Him up from the dead (Acts 17:31). Satan danced on His grave for joy; when he had Him there once, he thought Him sure enough; but He rose again and trampled on the devil's throne with triumph. This is the faith peculiar to Christians. . . . His resurrection is not only the object of our faith, but the example of our hope.

THOMAS ADAMS

247

RESURRECTION, RICHES

Him, that this day (Easter Sunday) rose from the clods, we expect from the clouds, to raise our bodies, to perform His promises, to finish our faith, to perfect our glory, and to draw us unto Himself. I do not say, Come, see the place where they laid Him, that is empty; but, Come, see the place where He is; here is the Lord. I say not with Mary, They have taken away the Lord, and I know not where they have laid Him; He is personally in heaven, He is mystically, sacramentally, yea, in a spiritual sense, He is really here. . . . As God spake to the fish, and it cast up Jonah, commanded the earth, and it delivered up Jesus; so He will speak to all creatures, and they shall not detain one dust of our bodies.

THOMAS ADAMS

N.B.:

Oh! how precious is the dust of a believer! though the world mind it not, yet it is precious unto God. The husbandman has some corn in his barn, and he has other corn in the ground; and the corn that is in the ground, is as precious to him as that which is in the barn.

THOMAS WATSON

RICHES

Transitory:

Riches may leave us while we live, we must leave them when we die.

THOMAS FULLER

Riches are long in getting with much pains, hard in keeping with much care, quick in losing with more sorrow.

THOMAS FULLER

RICHES

Danger in excess:

The heart of a Christian, like the moon, commonly suffers an eclipse when it is at the full, and that by the interposition of the earth.

JOHN FLAVEL

When a man is to travel into a far country. . . . one staff in his hand may comfortably support him, but a bundle of staves would be troublesome. Thus a competency of these outward things may happily help us in the way to heaven, whereas abundance may be hurtful.

RICHARD SIBBES

Where there is no *want*, there is usually much *wantonness*.

JOHN FLAVEL

Christ telleth us, "It is easier for a camel to go through the eye of a needle, than for a rich man to enter into the Kingdom of heaven." Our Saviour, indeed, doth not speak of an impossibility, but of the difficulty of it and the rareness of it. Job unfolded the riddle, and got through the needle's eye with three thousand camels. But it is hard to be wealthy, and not wanton.

GEORGE SWINNOCK

You desire not the biggest shoes or clothes, but the meetest; so do by your dignity and estate.

RICHARD BAXTER

As hills, the higher the barrener; so men commonly the wealthier the worse; the more honour the less holiness.

THOMAS FULLER

Solomon got more hurt by his wealth, than he got good by his wisdom.

THOMAS BROOKS

The richest crowns cast all their splendour and glory outwardly, but inwardly they are felt to be weighty upon the heads of such as bear them.

PETER DRELINCOURT

RICHES

N.B.:

Scripture speaketh in such general language, as if salvation had been almost appropriated to the poor, and the rich had been excluded, because of the rarity of their salvation.

RICHARD BAXTER

Avarice not confined to the affluent:

As sick men used to love health better than those that never felt the want of it; so it is too common with poor men to love riches better than the rich that never needed. And yet, poor souls, they deceive themselves, and cry out against the rich, as if they were the only lovers of the world, when they love it more themselves though they cannot get it.

RICHARD BAXTER

The Christian perspective:

All our pieces of gold are but current to the grave; none of them will pass in the future world. Therefore as merchants when they travel make over their monies here, to receive them by bills of exchange in another country; let us do good with our goods while we live, that when we die, by a blessed bill of exchange, we may receive them again in the Kingdom of heaven (Luke 16:9). To part with what we cannot keep, that we may get that we cannot lose, is a good bargain. Wealth can do us no good, unless it help us toward heaven.

THOMAS ADAMS

It is hard to carry a full cup without spilling, and a full estate without sinning.

THOMAS WATSON

As the remedy to quench his thirst that is vexed with a hot fever cometh not of giving him drink, but of taking away his fever which causeth his thirst: even so the way to grow rich is not by heaping of riches, but by diminishing the covetousness and unlawful desire of the same.

DANIEL CAWDRAY

Let us make the poor our friends by our alms, not our enemies by our scorns. We had better have the ears of God full of their prayers, than heaps of money in our own coffers with their curses.

THOMAS ADAMS

N.B.:

Poverty hath slain a thousand, but riches have slain ten thousand. They are very uncertain, they promise that which they cannot perform, neither can they afford a contented mind.

RICHARD GREENHAM

RUMOR

Rumour is a loud liar, like a snowball that gathereth as it goeth.

JOHN TRAPP

The thief doth send one only to the devil; the adulterer two; but the slanderer hurteth three; himself, the party to whom, and the party of whom he telleth his tale.

JOHN BOYS

Fame creates something of nothing.

THOMAS FULLER

The first tale is good till the second be heard.

JOHN TRAPP

SALVATION

The way:

Now believing is nothing else but the accepting of Christ for thy Lord and Saviour as He is offered to thee in the gospel; and this

251

SALVATION

accepting is principally, if not only, the act of thy will; so that if thou art sincerely and cordially willing to have Christ upon His own terms, upon gospel terms, that is, to save thee and rule thee, to redeem thee and to reign over thee, then thou art a believer.

THOMAS BROOKS

We are not saved *for* believing but *by* believing.

THOMAS TAYLOR

But the Lord God of His infinite and great goodness towards man exceeding His favour unto the lost angels had before all beginning of His great love towards (the) elect appointed of His free gift the means whereby His wrath should be satisfied, man's sin and guilt done away, and he brought into a far more blessed state than he was created in Adam.

JOHN PENRY

The Lord does not tie Himself to a particular way, or use the same order with all. He comes sometimes in a still small voice. Such as have had godly parents, and have sat under the warm sunshine of religious education, often do not know how or when they were called. . . . They know by the heavenly effects that they are called, but the time or manner they know not. Thus God deals with some. Others are more stubborn and knotty sinners, and God comes to them in a rough wind. He uses more wedges of the law to break their hearts. . . . This call, though it is more visible than the other, yet is no more real.

THOMAS WATSON

It is in vain for us to rise early and to lie down late, and to eat the bread of sorrow all the day, if the Lord give not the assistance of His Spirit to the means that we use.

SAMUEL RUTHERFORD

The Trinity involved:

In election we behold God the Father choosing; in vocation, God the Son teaching; in justification, God the Holy Ghost sealing; in salvation, the whole Deity crowning.

THOMAS ADAMS

SALVATION

Difficult?

'Tis no easy matter to be saved. 'Twas difficult work to Jesus Christ to work redemption for us. 'Tis difficult work to the Spirit to work grace in us, and to carry it on against corruptions, temptations, distractions.

PHILIP HENRY

A pragmatic test:

By this thou shalt know whether thou hast given it (thy heart) to Him or no; if the heart be gone, all will follow. As the sun riseth first, and then the beasts arise from their dens, the fowls from their nests, and men from their beds; so when the heart sets forward to God all the members will follow after it, the tongue will praise Him, the foot will follow Him, the ear will attend Him, the eye will watch Him, the hand will serve Him, nothing will stay after the heart, but every one goes.

HENRY SMITH

It more pleaseth the saints that they enjoy God, than that they enjoy salvation. False and carnal spirits will express a great deal of desire after salvation, for they like salvation, heaven, and glory well; but they never express any longing desire after God and Jesus Christ. They love salvation, but they care not for a Saviour. Now that which faith pitcheth most upon is God Himself; He shall be my salvation, let me have Him, and that is salvation enough.

JOSEPH CARYL

Urgent:

It is the duty of all the sons and daughters of Adam, who hear the Gospel preached, and Christ offered to them, to believe in, or receive, Christ, whether they be prepared or not prepared.

GILES FIRMIN

N.B.:

As the Lord lives, I durst promise it in His name, if we would seek Him we should see the salvation of the Lord.

SAMUEL RUTHERFORD

SELF-EXAMINATION

Self-examination is a spiritual inquisition set up in the soul.
THOMAS WATSON

Its inestimable value:

Examination will help the Christian that has fallen and bruised himself to heal the wound whilst it is fresh, before it is festered.
GEORGE SWINNOCK

The bird is easily killed in the egg, but when once hatched and fledged, we may kill it when we can catch it. A frequent reckoning with ourselves will pluck sin up before it is rooted in the soul.
GEORGE SWINNOCK

Make up your spiritual accounts daily; see how matters stand between God and your souls (Psalm 77:6). Often reckonings keep God and conscience friends. Do with your hearts as you do with your watches, wind them up every morning by prayer, and at night examine whether your hearts have gone true all that day, whether the wheels of your affections have moved swiftly toward heaven.
THOMAS WATSON

Self-examination is the beaten path to perfection.
WILLIAM SECKER

The right standard:

Men compare themselves with men, and readily with the worst, and flatter themselves with that comparative betterness. This is not the way to see spots, to look into the muddy streams of profane men's lives; but look into the clear fountain of the Word, and there we may both discern and wash them; and consider the infinite holiness of God, and this will humble us to the dust.
ROBERT LEIGHTON

SELF-EXAMINATION

Let us not commend our graces to the eye of our deluded judgements, as shopkeepers do their coarse wares, by setting coarser by them, or by setting in our sight the examples of others who come short of us; but let us compare our little sparks of grace with those bright flames which have shone in the patriarchs, prophets, and apostles, yea, in our Saviour, Christ Himself. And so we shall not be proud of our progress, but ashamed rather of our small proficiency; and with the apostle, "forgetting those things which are behind, and reaching forth to those things that are before," we shall "press towards the mark for the prize of the high calling of God in Christ Jesus."

GEORGE DOWNAME

Let no soul examine itself by any lower marks than this, participation of the Divine nature, conformity to the Divine image. Examine what alliance your soul has to God; "whose is the image and superscription."

JOHN SHAW

"The heart is a grand imposter." It is like a cheating tradesman, which will put one off with bad wares; the heart will put a man off with seeming grace, instead of saving.

THOMAS WATSON

This duty of examining and proving presupposes that there is some sure standard. . . . Now that rule is the Word of God; but as in matters of doctrine men have left the Scriptures, the sure rule, and taken up antiquity, universality, tradition, and the like. . . . so in matters of godliness, when we should try ourselves according to the characters and signs that the Scripture deciphers, we take up principles in the world, the applause of others, the conversation of most in the world. And thus it is with us as men in an hospital, because every one is either wounded or lame, or some way diseased, therefore none are offensive to each other.

CORNELIUS BURGESS

SELF-EXAMINATION

The right procedure:

It especially concerns thee to search out the pollutions of thy spirit, of thy understanding, judgement, and will. . . . For as the sins of princes are greater than those of other men, because they are their rulers, so are the sins of these of a higher guilt, because it is their duty, and they are placed to guide the rest. And it concerns thee to be the more strictly inquisitive into these sins, because of all others they most conceal themselves, and as their operations are more strong, so with less noise, as poison works more strongly in the head than in the stomach, though it be perceived more there than in the head. Inquire thou into the sins of these ringleaders in thee; and as in case of treason, the government inquires most after the contrivers of it, so look not thou so much to the members of the body, and the lusts which war in them, as unto that corrupted judgement and will in thee that devised the means to satisfy those lusts, which fed them with thoughts and fancies, which were privy to the first contrivance of the treason, and gave way, and consented to it. The lusts which war in the members are but weapons, instruments (Romans 6:19). You must therefore look to the higher powers of sin in the soul, to the throne of unrighteousness there, whose agents those lusts are.

THOMAS GOODWIN

There is a vanity which I have observed in many pretenders to nobility and learning, when men seek to demonstrate the one by their coat of arms, and the records of their family, and the other by a gown, or a title, or their names standing in the register of the university, rather than by the accomplishments and behaviour of gentlemen or scholars. A like vanity, I doubt, may be observed in many pretenders to religion. Some are searching God's decretals to find their names written in the Book of Life, when they should be studying to find God's name written upon their hearts, "Holiness to the Lord" engraven upon their souls.

JOHN SHAW

What a deal of sorrow and after-complaining might this small labour prevent! How many miles travel, besides the vexation, may a traveller save by inquiring of the way!

RICHARD BAXTER

SELF-EXAMINATION

There be many things that move, and yet their motion is not an argument of life. A windmill when the wind serveth, moveth, and moveth very nimbly too; yet this cannot be said to be a living creature. No; it moveth only by an external cause, by an artificial contrivance. So it is also if a man see another man move, and move very fast, in those things which of themselves are the ways of God: you shall see him move as fast to hear a sermon as his neighbour doth; is as forward and hasty to thrust himself and bid himself a guest to the Lord's table (when God hath not bid him) as any. Now, the question is, what principle sets him a-work? If it be an inward principle of life, out of a sincere affection and love to God and His ordinances, it argueth that man hath some life of grace; but if it be some wind that bloweth on him—the wind of state, the wind of law, the wind of danger, of penalty, the wind of fashion or custom—to do as his neighbours do; if these or the like be the things that draw him thither, this is no argument of life at all: it is a cheap thing, it is a counterfeit and dead piece of service.

MARTIN DAY

Holy men have kept the sessions at home, and made their hearts the foremen of the jury, and examined themselves as we examine others. The fear of the Lord stood at the door of their souls, to examine every thought before it went in, and at the door of their lips, to examine every word before it went out, whereby they escaped a thousand sins which we commit, as though we had no other work.

HENRY SMITH

An example:

1. Can I choose to undergo the greatest suffering rather than commit the least sin?
2. Can I embrace Christ with His cross?
3. Can I work for God, though there were no wages?
4. Can I swim against the stream, be good in bad times and places?
5. Can I pull out right eyes for Christ and cut off right hands, etc?

PHILIP HENRY

257

SERVICE, CHRISTIAN

Underscored in God's plan:

God hath work to do in this world; and to desert it because of its difficulties and entanglements, is to cast off His authority. It is not enough that we be just, that we be righteous, and walk with God in holiness; but we must also serve our generation as David did before he fell asleep.

JOHN OWEN

Christ keeps no servants only to wear a livery.

WILLIAM JENKYN

For God requiring the first-born for His offering, and the first-fruits for His service, requireth the first labours of His servants.

HENRY SMITH

The sinner's shame:

It can be written on the tomb of an unrepentant sinner.... "Here lies a man who in all his life never worked one hour for God."

WILLIAM GURNALL

The saint's shame:

Oh, then be ashamed, Christians, that worldlings are more studious and industrious to make sure of pebbles, than you are to make sure of pearls.

THOMAS BROOKS

God hath many servants, but little service in the world.

THOMAS ADAMS

We should not serve God by fits, as we used to pray when the night comes, to hear when the Sabbath comes, to fast when Lent comes, to repent when death comes; but the service of the heart is a continual service.

HENRY SMITH

Social action?

It is then, an error, though it is but few, I think, that are guilty of it, to think that all religion lieth in minding only the life to come, and disregarding all things in this present life; all true Christians must seriously mind both the end and the means or way. If they mind not, believingly, the end, they will never be faithful in the use of means. If they mind not, and use not, diligently, the means, they will never obtain the end. None can use earth well that prefer not heaven, and none come to heaven, at age, that are not prepared by well using earth.

RICHARD BAXTER

To be conversant in holy duties is indeed more sweet to a man's self, and is a heaven upon earth; but to be conversant in our calling is more profitable to others—to the Church, the commonwealth, or the family—and so may glorify God more. "More fruit" is brought forth when both are joined and wisely subordinated, so as the one is not a hindrance to the other.

THOMAS GOODWIN

Is it nothing for a man to be employed in comforting, relieving, and supporting others? This is so great a service that the very angels are employed therein.

WILLIAM BRIDGE

Is hardship involved?

Our journey is up-hill, with a dead body upon our backs, the devil doing what he can to pull us down.

PHILIP HENRY

Health comes not from the clouds without seeking, nor wealth from the clods without digging.

JOHN KING

Spiritual rest maketh no man idle, spiritual walking maketh no man weary.

NATHANIEL HARDY

SERVICE, SIN

If the tongue, or the hand, or the ear, think to serve God without the heart, it is the irksomest occupation in the world, the hour of tediousness, like a long sickness; he is tired before he begin, and thinketh himself in the stocks until the sermon be ended, and until his prayer be done.

HENRY SMITH

Certainty of reward:

We may be losers for Him, we shall never be losers by Him.

THOMAS WATSON

Degrees of reward?

And let me tell you, the more labour you have put forth for the Kingdom of heaven, the more degrees of glory you shall have. As there are degrees of torment in hell, so of glory in heaven (Matthew 23:14). As one star differeth from another in glory, so shall one saint (1 Corinthians 15:41). Though every vessel of mercy shall be full, yet one may hold more than another.

THOMAS WATSON

SIN

Definitions:

Sin hath the devil for its father, shame for its companion, and death for its wages.

THOMAS WATSON

Sin is the dare of God's justice, the rape of His mercy, the jeer of His patience, the slight of His power, and the contempt of His love.

JOHN BUNYAN

A holy man knows that all sin strikes at the holiness of God, the glory of God, the nature of God, the being of God, and the law of

God: and therefore his heart rises against all; he looks upon
every sin as the Scribes and Pharisees that accused Christ; and
as that Judas that betrayed Christ; and as that Pilate that condemned Christ; and as those soldiers that scourged Christ; and
as those spears that pierced Christ.

THOMAS BROOKS

Sin is the strength of death and the death of strength.

THOMAS ADAMS

Original sin:

Let original sin make us walk with continual jealousy and
watchfulness over our hearts. The sin of our nature is like a
sleeping lion, the least thing that awakens it makes it rage. The
sin of our nature, though it seems quiet, and lies as fire hid
under the embers, yet if it be a little stirred and blown up by a
temptation, how quickly may it flame forth into scandalous
evils? Therefore we had need always to walk watchfully. . . . A
wandering heart needs a watchful eye.

THOMAS WATSON

Man lost not his faculties but the rectitude of them.

THOMAS GOODWIN

We deceive ourselves if we say, we are without original sin, or
without actual sin, in external conversation, in internal inclination. . . . the fairest printed books have their errata.

PHILIP HENRY

Not only the worst of my sins, but the best of my duties speak
me a child of Adam.

WILLIAM BEVERIDGE

Some talk that the devil hath a cloven foot; but whatever the
devil's foot be, to be sure his sons have a cloven heart.

RICHARD ALLEINE

Iniquity can plead antiquity.

THOMAS ADAMS

SIN

Universal sin:

As long as there are spots in the moon, it is vain to expect anything spotless under it.

THOMAS FULLER

National sin:

Let me persuade you to believe that the Gospel is not entailed upon England; England has no letters patent of the Gospel; the Gospel is removable. God took away the ark and forsook Shiloh, and He not only took away the ark, but the temple also. He unchurched the Jews, He unchurched the seven churches of Asia, and we know not how soon He may unchurch us.

EDMUND CALAMY

A boat rows against the stream; the current punishes it. So is a nation violating a law of God; it is subject to a judgement. The boat turns and goes with the stream; the current assists it. So is a nation which has repented and put itself into harmony with God's law; it is subject to a blessing. But the current is the same; it has not changed, only the boat has changed its relationship to the current. Neither does God change—we change; and the same law which executed itself in punishment now expresses itself in reward.

THOMAS BROOKS

Presumptuous sins:

Despair is hope stark dead, presumption is hope stark mad.

THOMAS ADAMS

Better to bear than to swear, and to die than to lie.

THOMAS BROOKS

To commit that sin, but two things are required—light in the mind, and malice in the heart.

THOMAS GOODWIN

A sin of infirmity may admit apology; a sin of ignorance may find out excuse; but a sin of defiance can find no defence.

SIR RICHARD BAKER

Secret sins:

Take heed of secret sins. They will undo thee if loved and maintained: one moth may spoil the garment; one leak drown the ship; a penknife stab and kill a man as well as a sword; so one sin may damn the soul; nay, there is more danger of a secret sin causing the miscarrying of the soul than open profaneness, because not so obvious to the reproofs of the world; therefore take heed that secret sinnings eat not out good beginnings.

JEREMIAH BURROUGHS

Secret sins are more dangerous to the person in some respects than open sins. For a man doth, by his art of sinning, deprive himself of the help of his sinfulness. Like him who will carry his wound covered, or who bleeds inwardly, help comes not in because the danger is not descried nor known. If a man's sin breaks out there is a minister at hand, a friend near, and others to reprove, to warn, to direct; but when he is the artificer of his lusts, he bars himself of all public remedy.

OBADIAH SEDGWICK

We can never sin but there will be two witnesses present to observe and register it, our own selves and God Himself.

RALPH VENNING

Go down into your hearts and take the keys of them and ransack your private cupboards, and narrowly observe what junkets your souls have hitherto lived upon, and gone behind the door and there secretly and stoutly made a meal of them. As dogs have bones they hide and secretly steal forth to gnaw upon, so men have sins they hide under their tongues as sweet bits.

THOMAS GOODWIN

Every clout will cover our sores, but the finest silk will not cover our sins.

HENRY SMITH

263

SIN

Besetting sins?

Many being reproved, answer, Alas! you must bear with me in this, it is my fault; as if every man were allowed his own fault. There is a private Sodom within us; we are loth to part with that. Men say of their sins as Jacob said of his sons, "Go, all but Benjamin." Other vices we will not so much stick for, but, "Oh, that Ishmael might live!" There is still some worm in the root of the tree that will spoil the fruit. We extenuate it; is it not a little one? But a little hair makes a great blot in the paper.

THOMAS ADAMS

Exchanged sins:

Some think themselves improved in piety, because they have left prodigality and reel into covetousness.

THOMAS FULLER

Progressive sins:

First we practice sin, then defend it, then boast of it.

THOMAS MANTON

We commonly say, it is not the last blow of the axe that fells the oak; perhaps the last may be a weaker blow than any of the former, but the other blows made way for the felling of it, and at length a little blow comes and completes it. So our former sins may be the things that make way for our ruin, and then at length some lesser sins may accomplish it.

JEREMIAH BURROUGHS

Sins are like circles in the water when a stone is thrown into it; one produces another. When anger was in Cain's heart, murder was not far off.

PHILIP HENRY

It is Satan's custom by small sins to draw us to greater, as the little sticks set the great ones on fire, and a wisp of straw kindles a block of wood.

THOMAS MANTON

There be three degrees, as it were so many ages, in sin. First —secret sin; an ulcer lying in the bones, but skinned over with hypocrisy. Secondly—open sin, bursting forth into manifest villany. The former is corruption, the second is eruption. One sin is a step to another more heinous; for *not observing*, is followed with *not remembering*—and *forgetfulness* of duty draweth on *disobedience and rebellion*. Thirdly—frequented and confirmed sin, and that is rank poison, envenoming soul and body.

DAVID DICKSON

Sins of commission and omission:

As sinful commissions will stab the soul; so sinful omissions will starve the soul.

THOMAS BROOKS

Sins of omission are aggravated by knowledge.

THOMAS MANTON

Some sins of omission are like great men, that never go without many followers.

GEORGE SWINNOCK

Make it your business to avoid *known omissions*, and God will keep you from feared commissions.

SAMUEL ANNESLEY

Its degradation:

Sin has degraded man and made him a beast. It is true, he has the shape of a man, but, alas! he is degenerated into a bestial and beastly nature.... It would be better to be a beast than to be like a beast, living and dying like one. It would be better to be Balaam's ass than such an ass as Balaam himself was.... But to set this degeneration and degradation of man by sin before you more clearly and fully, I shall deal with it under three headings: Sin has made man (a) like a beast, (b) like the worst of beasts, (c) worse than the beasts.

RALPH VENNING

SIN

O miserable man, what a deformed monster has sin made you! God made you "little lower than the angels"; sin has made you little better than the devils.

JOSEPH ALLEINE

It has degraded man, by defiling him, and has almost unmanned him; for, as our text speaks of sin as a man, the Holy Scripture speaks of man as if he were sin, and every man were a man of sin.

RALPH VENNING

Sin never ruins but where it reigns.

WILLIAM SECKER

For if the guilt of sin be so great that nothing can satisfy it but the blood of Jesus; and the filth of sin be so great that nothing can fetch out the stain thereof but the blood of Jesus, how great, how heinous, how sinful must the evil of sin be!

WILLIAM BRIDGE

Pollution is the forerunner of perdition.

JOHN TRAPP

Its burden:

And they are as mighty as they are many. The sands are many, but then they are not great; the mountains great but then they are not many. But woe is man, my sins are as many as the sands, and as mighty as the mountains. Their weight is greater than their number.

JOSEPH ALLEINE

I think this should be a terror to an unconverted soul, to think he is a burden to the creation. "Cut it down; why cumbereth it the ground" (Luke 13:7). If inanimate creatures could but speak, your food would say, "Lord, must I nourish such a wretch as this, and yield forth my strength for him, to dishonour Thee? No, I will choke him rather, if Thou wilt give commission." The very air would say, "Lord, must I give this man breath, to set his tongue against heaven, and scorn Thy people, and vent his pride and wrath, and filthy talk, and belch out oaths and blasphemy against Thee? No, if thou wilt but say the word, he shall be breathless for me." His poor beast would say, "Lord, must I carry him upon his wicked designs? No, I will break his bones, I will end his days rather, if I may have but leave from Thee." A wicked man; the earth groans under him, and hell groans for him, till death satisfies both. While the Lord of hosts is against you, be sure the host of the Lord is against you.

JOSEPH ALLEINE

Every creature has a quarrel with a sinner.

THOMAS WATSON

Its shame:

Take heed an hour produce not that which may shame us for ever.

GEORGE HUTCHESON

If the best man's faults were written in his forehead, it would make him pull his hat over his eyes.

JOHN TRAPP

Sin may be the occasion of great sorrow, when there is no sorrow for sin.

JOHN OWEN

Its deceitfulness:

There are three false notions whereby the deceitfulness of sin deludes the souls of men:

1. That it is *one sin alone* wherein alone they would be indulged. Let them be spared in this *one thing*, and in all others they will be exact enough.... One sin willingly lived in is as able to destroy a man's soul as a thousand.

2. They judge that although they cannot *shake off their sin*, yet they will continue still to love God and abound in the duties of His worship.... Where God is not loved above all, He is not loved at all.

3. They determine that at *such or such a season* or time, after such satisfaction given unto their lusts or pleasures, they will utterly give over, so as that iniquity shall not be their ruin. . . . He that will not now give over, say what he will and pretend what he will, never intends to give over, nor is it probable, in an ordinary way, that ever he will do so.

JOHN OWEN

But sin goeth in a disguise, and thence is welcome; like Judas, it kisseth and kills; like Joab, it salutes and slays.

GEORGE SWINNOCK

The arts that sin uses to disguise itself. If sin were not an ugly thing, would it wear a mask? If it did not have evil designs, would it walk in disguise and change its name? Truth is not ashamed of its name or nakedness; it can walk openly and boldly. Sin, on the contrary, is a cheat, a lie, and therefore lurks privily and puts on false names and colours; for if it were to appear like itself—as it sooner or later will do to all, either for conversion or confusion—it would frighten men into dying fits, as it did the Apostle, and when they come to themselves they would abhor and hate it, as Paul and the Prodigal did. Men would never be so hardy in sinning but that sin hardens them by deceiving them; so the Apostle says, "Take heed lest any be hardened through the deceitfulness of sin" (Hebrews 3:13).

RALPH VENNING

Its anesthesia:

Custom of sinning takes away the sense of it; the course of the world takes away the shame of it.

JOHN OWEN

Its cosmic repercussions:

But how are things altered since sin came into the world! The angels He has charged with folly (Job 4:18). The heavens are not clean in His sight (Job 15:15). Man in his best estate is altogether vanity (Psalm 39:5). The earth is under a curse (Genesis 3:17-18). Indeed the whole creation groans (Romans 8:21-22).

JOSEPH HALL

Its retribution:

Joseph's brethren had done heinously ill: what becomes of their sin? It makes no noise, but follows them slyly and silently in the wilderness; it follows them home to their father's house; it follows them into Egypt. All this while there is no news of it; but when it found them cooped up three days in Pharaoh's ward, now it bays at them, and flies in their faces. . . . where wickedness hath led the way, there punishment must follow.

JOSEPH HALL

Oh, better were it for you to die in a jail, in a ditch, in a dungeon, than die in your sins. If death, as it will take away all your comforts, would take away all your sins too, it were some mitigation; but your sins will follow you when your friends leave you, and all worldly enjoyments shake hands with you. Your sins will not die with you as a prisoner's other debts will; but they will go to judgement with you there to be your accusers; and they will go to hell with you there to be your tormentors.

JOSEPH ALLEINE

What does Satan at the sinner's elbows? He helps him to contrive sin. He tempts him to commit sin. He terrifies him for sin. He that has Satan standing at his right hand, is sure to be set at God's left hand. Here is the misery of such as oppose God's royal sceptre, that He will set everything in the world against them. If there be either justice in heaven or fire in hell, sinners shall not be unpunished.

THOMAS WATSON

The Lord has a golden sceptre and an iron rod. Psalm 2:9. Those who will not bow to the one, shall be broken by the other.

THOMAS WATSON

SIN

It is said of a prisoner, that standing at the bar, indicted for felony, he was asked by the judge what he could say for himself. "Truly, my lord," says he, "I did mean no hurt when I stole; it is an evil custom that I have gotten; I have been used to it ever since I knew anything." "Why, then," says the judge, "if it be thy custom to steal, it is my custom to hang up thieves."

GEORGE SWINNOCK

This is the triumph that virtue hath over vice, that wheresoever she is most hated, there she is often wished for. And this is the great punishment that God bringeth upon the wicked (even as the poet Persius said)—that though they love not virtue, nor cannot like to follow her, yet they should pine away with a longing desire after her. And this I am sure, it striketh deep and woundeth the conscience of the wicked, though they have set their heart as an adamant stone, and made their face like flint, yet grace pierceth throughout their concupiscence and they say sometime, "The way of virtue is better." There was never so impure and dissolute an adulterer but he hath said sometime, "The chaste body is best." There never was so blasphemous nor vile a swearer but sometime he hath trembled at God's majesty. There was never man so proud and ambitious but sometime he remembereth he is but earth and ashes. There was never such a usurer nor covetous wretch, but sometime he thinketh his gold and silver shall canker and the rust of it shall be a witness against him.... There was never so high-minded nor vainglorious a king but he hath sometime thought his crown would fall from his head, and the crown of righteousness was better.

EDWARD DERING

Woe to that sinner that gets that which falls (to) him and is his due, for that is hell!

SAMUEL RUTHERFORD

Sin unto death?

What is this sin unto death? Two things concur in it; illumination in the mind and malice in the heart.

JOHN COTTON

Sin against the Holy Ghost?

If any say "My sin was worse than Adam's, for I have sinned against the Holy Ghost," I answer, if thou hast sinned against the Holy Ghost, repent and thou shalt be pardoned, for the cause why that sin cannot be forgiven is not want of mercy in God or merits in Christ, but such abundance of hardness in them, that they will not seek to God for pardon or for grace to repent.

WILLIAM WHATELY

Sins of saints and sins of sinners?

Sins therefore are thus distinguished: the sins of the people of God are said to be sins that men commit; the others are those which are counted sins of devils.

JOHN BUNYAN

A sheep may fall into a ditch, but it is the swine that wallows in it.

WILLIAM GURNALL

A man is known by his custom, and the course of his endeavours, what is his business. If a man be constantly easily, frequently carried away to sin, it discovers a habit of soul, and the temper of his heart. Meadows may be overflown, but marsh-ground is drowned with the return of every tide. A child of God may be carried away, and act contrary to the bent of the new nature; but when men are overcome with every temptation, it argues a habit of sin.

THOMAS MANTON

There is a wide difference between a child under wrath and a child of wrath.

THOMAS GOODWIN

Sins in the saints are but wasps without their stings; and if the wasps without their stings be so troublesome, how troublesome are the wasps that have their stings in them; how troublesome is sin in itself.

WILLIAM BRIDGE

SIN

The eclipses of the sun are seldom without witnesses. If you take yourselves to be the light of the church, you may well expect that men's eyes should be upon you. If other men may sin without observation, so cannot you.

RICHARD BAXTER

It is not one or two good actions, but a good conversation, which will speak a man to be a right Christian. A true believer, like the heavenly orbs, is constant and unwearied in his motion and actings. Enoch *"walked* with God," it is not taking a step or two in a way which denominates a man a *walker,* but a continued motion. No man is judged healthy by a flushing colour in his face, but by a good complexion. God esteems none holy for a particular carriage, but for a general course. A sinner in some few acts may be very good: Judas repents, Cain sacrifices, the Scribes pray and fast; and yet all were very false. . . . A saint in some few acts may be very bad: Noah is drunk, David defiles his neighbour's wife, and Peter denies his best friend; yet these persons were heaven's favourites. The best gold must have some grains of allowance. Sheep may fall into the mire, but swine love day and night to wallow in it. A Christian may stumble, nay, he may fall, but he gets up and walks on in the way of God's commandments; the bent of his heart is right, and the scope of his life is straight, and thence he is deemed sincere.

GEORGE SWINNOCK

Carnal and unregenerate men. . . . for fear or some other reasons, they shake hands with their sins, yet they have many a longing heart after them; they part, and yet they are loth to part asunder. Hence it is, that as the merchant throws away his goods in a storm because he cannot keep them, so they, in the times of sickness and distress, when the sea grows high and the tempest rageth, when they begin to apprehend what death is and what hell is, and know, unless the vessel be lighted, they cannot be safe, then they are hard at work, heave overboard their usury, their drunkenness, their swearing, and such like stuff, not out of hatred to them, but love to themselves; for if they could but continue in their sins and be saved when they have done, they would never part with them at all.

JAMES STILE

None can hate it (sin) but those that love the law of God; for all hatred comes from love. A natural man may be angry with his sin, but hate it he cannot; nay, he may leave it, but not loathe it; if he did, he would loathe all sin as well as any one sin.

ABRAHAM WRIGHT

N.B.:

The best duties of unbelievers are but white lies.

JOHN OWEN

Sins of the saints?

I will not judge a person to be spiritually dead whom I have judged formerly to have had spiritual life, though I see him at present in a swoon as to all evidences of the spiritual life. And the reason why I will not judge him so is this—because if you judge a person dead, you neglect him, you leave him; but if you judge him in a swoon, though never so dangerous, you use all means for the retrieving of his life.

JOHN OWEN

The more the Spirit shines in the heart, the more evil it discovers. A Christian thinks it worse with him that it was, whereas his grace may not grow less, but his light greater.

THOMAS WATSON

(David) His heart was more often out of tune than his harp.

THOMAS BROOKS

It is in many places a lost labour to seek for Christianity among Christians.

JOHN OWEN

"Are there not with you, even with you, sins against the Lord your God?" (2 Chronicles 28:10). . . . If your discourse be not profane, is it not vain? Have you not your self-seekings, rash censures, indecent dresses? If the wicked of the land swear, do you not sometimes slander? If they are drunk with wine, are you not drunk sometimes with passion? If their sin be blas-

pheming, is not your sin murmuring? . . . The sins of God's
children go nearer to His heart than the sins of others. . . . The
sins of the wicked anger God, the sins of His own people grieve
Him.

THOMAS WATSON

A sin acted in the temple was greater than if the same had
been by a Jew committed in his private dwelling, because the
temple was a consecrated place. The saint is a consecrated
person, and by acts of unrighteousness he profanes God's
temple; the sin of another is theft, because he robs God of the
glory due to Him; but the sin of a saint is sacrilege, because he
robs God of that which is devoted to Him in an especial manner.

WILLIAM GURNALL

The sins of the godly are worse than others, because they bring a
greater reproach upon religion. For the wicked to sin, there is
no other expected from them; swine will wallow in the mire;
but when sheep do so, when the godly sin, that redounds to the
dishonour of the Gospel: "By this deed thou hast given great
occasion to the enemies of the Lord to blaspheme."

THOMAS WATSON

A fault in a stranger is not so much taken notice of as a fault in a
child: a spot in black cloth is not so much observed; but a spot in
scarlet every one's eye is upon it.

THOMAS WATSON

If once a man commence a professor, the eyes of all are upon
him; and well they may, for his profession in the world is a
separation from the world. Believers condemn those by their
lives who condemn them by their lips. Righteous David saw
many who were waiting to triumph in his mistakes. Hence the
more they watched, the more he prayed: "Teach me Thy way, O
Lord, and lead me in a plain path, because of mine enemies."
. . . they make use of your weakness as a plea for their wickedness. Men are merciless in their censures of Christians; they
have no sympathy for their infirmity: while God weighs them in
more equal scales, and says, "The spirit is willing, but the flesh
is weak."

WILLIAM SECKER

An eminently holy man puts life into a whole community; on the contrary, a loose professor endangers the entire body. A scab on the wolf's back is not so infectious to the sheep, because they will not be drawn away by such company; but when it gets into the flock that read, hear, and pray together, then there is fear it will spread.

WILLIAM GURNALL

Religion is the same that ever it was, only it suffers by them that make profession of it. Whatever disadvantage it falls under in the world, they must at length answer for in whose misbelief and practice it is corrupted.

JOHN OWEN

Corruption is, though dejected from its regency, yet not ejected from its inherency; it intermingleth with our best works.

JOHN TRAPP

Sins of the saints: Example - lack of patience:

There are no sins God's people are more subject to than unbelief and impatience. They are ready either to faint through unbelief, or to fret through impatience.

THOMAS WATSON

Example - lack of love:

Some suspect all men, and some none: both are in fault; the former in the most sinful fault, the latter in the most honest, but more dangerous to themselves. . . . Howsoever things fall out, it is best to keep our bias always on the right side; and to incline still to a better, rather than to a worse opinion of men, than they deserve. For though it be best of all, to judge of others just as they are: yet seeing that is always hard and sometimes impossible, we shall less offend God in judging of men too well, though sometimes to our own damage, than too ill, with certain injury to them, and sin in ourselves, in the violation of the law of charity, which "is not suspicious."

JOHN ROBINSON

SIN

Example - lack of gratitude:

As the Lord loveth a cheerful giver, so likewise a cheerful thanksgiver.

JOHN BOYS

What the sin against the Holy Ghost is in Divinity, that ingratitude is in morality, an offence unpardonable.

THOMAS FULLER

Thankless men are like swine feeding on acorns, which, though they fall upon their heads, never make them look up to the tree from which they come.

JEAN DAILLE

When he hath all things, he is unthankful; and when he hath nothing, he beginneth to be thankful. (Nebuchadnezzar).

HENRY SMITH

What unthankfulness is it to forget our consolations, and to look upon matters of grievance; to think so much upon two or three crosses as to forget an hundred blessings.

RICHARD SIBBES

Example - lack of submission:

"Thy will be done." (Some) have only said it, but not learned it. If things be not according to their mind. . . . they are discontented and querrulous. . . . Rachel cried, "Give me children, or I die." (Genesis 30:1). God let her have a child, but it cost her her life. (Genesis 35:18). Israel was not content with manna, but they must have quails, and God punished them by letting them have their will. "And while the flesh was yet between their teeth, the wrath of the Lord was kindled against them, and the Lord smote them with a great plague" (Numbers 11:31, 33) . . . many have importunately desired the life of a child, and could not bring their will to God's to be content to part with it; and the Lord has punished them by letting them have their will; for the child has lived and been a burden to them. Seeing their wills crossed God, their child shall cross them.

THOMAS WATSON

Five words cost Zachariah forty weeks' silence.

THOMAS FULLER

Example - a complaining spirit:

As it is with a vessel that is full of liquor, if you strike upon it, it will make no great noise; but if it be empty, then it makes a great noise: so it is with the heart. A heart that is full of grace and goodness within, will bear a great many strokes and never make any noise; but an empty heart, if that be struck, will make a noise.

JEREMIAH BURROUGHS

Why dost thou complain of thy troubles? It is not trouble that troubles but discontent. It is not the water without the ship, but the water that gets within the leak, which drowns it. It is not outward affliction that can make the life of a Christian sad: a contented mind would sail above these waters; but when there is a leak of discontent open, and trouble gets into the heart, then it is disquieted and sinks. Do therefore as the mariners, pump the water out and stop this spiritual leak in thy soul, and no trouble can hurt thee.

THOMAS WATSON

Injuries are registered in marble to all posterity, whilst benefits are written on the sand.

THOMAS FULLER

Complain to God you may, but to complain *of* God, you must not.

JOHN FLAVEL

Complain without cause, and thou shalt have cause to complain.

THOMAS TAYLOR

While I live in the world, my condition is to be but a pilgrim, a stranger, a traveller, and a soldier. . . . When a man is at home, if he has not things according to his desire, he will be finding fault. But if a man travels abroad, perhaps he meets not with

277

convenience as he desires; yet this very thought may moderate a man's spirit, "I am a traveller, and I must not be finding fault, though things be not so in my own family." If a man meets with ill weather, he must be content. "It is a traveller's fare," we used to say, both fair weather and foul weather; and we must be content with it. If a man were at home and it should begin to drop in his house, he cannot bear it; but when he is travelling abroad, though he meets with rains and storms, he is not so much troubled.

JEREMIAH BURROUGHS

The frog and the murmurer, both of them are bred of the mud.

THOMAS ADAMS

Example - a censuring spirit:

Do not then spend the strength of your zeal for your religion in censuring others. The man that is most busy in censuring others is always least employed in examining himself.

THOMAS LYE

Rudeness hath no respect either to sex or condition.

JOHN TRAPP

Some men's churlishness entirely swallows up their charitableness.

WILLIAM SECKER

For that judging, or condeming of others, wherewith they are so provoked, there is but one way whereby it may be done. . . . and this is in our lives. The practice of holiness judgeth all unholy persons in their own breasts.

JOHN OWEN

N.B.:

How severe justicers we can be to our own crimes in others' persons.

NEHEMIAH ROGERS

Example - stumbling at the suffering of the godly:

Men are loth to undergo hardships themselves, and therefore take up hard thoughts and sinister opinions of those that do. The flesh shrinks at sufferings, and therefore they shrink from those that suffer, lest they should be necessitated to suffer with them. . . . It is hard to drag the carcass to the prison, to the rack, to the flames; therefore men (though otherwise good) are willing to think those in error, or else too heady and rash in owning the truth, who expose themselves to sufferings, especially upon the account of some smaller truth. If they should conclude such to be in the right, they must needs voyage in the same ship, and run the same hazard. Hence the flesh, for its own security, finds some fault in those forward sufferers with which to cloak its own backwardness.

JOHN OLDFIELD

Example - unworthy motives:

Few follow Him for love, but for loaves, John 6:26; few follow Him for His inward excellencies, but many follow Him for their outward advantages; few follow Him that they may be made good by Him, but many follow Him that they may be great by Him.

THOMAS BROOKS

Example - loose living:

You must beware of being loose Christians. . . . a loose Protestant is one of the fittest persons in the world to make a strict Papist. . . . If ungodliness is in the heart, it is no difficult thing for error to get into the head. A loose heart can best comply with loose principles.

THOMAS LYE

Consequence - exacts a high price:

Saul, by casting an amorous eye upon Agag, lost his crown and kingdom; Samson, by dallying with his Delilah, lost his strength, sight, light, liberty, and life. But what are these losses to thy loss of spiritual strength, to thy loss of communion with God, to thy loss of the Spirit of light, life, liberty, and glory; to thy loss of joy unspeakable, and peace that passeth understanding?

THOMAS BROOKS

The sinful courses of God's children occasion bitterness enough; they never venture upon sin, but with great loss. If Paul give way to a little pride, God will humble him. If any give way to sin, their pilgrimage will be made uncomfortable. Eli falls into negligence and indulgence, then is the ark of God taken, his two sons are slain in battle, his daughter-in-law dies, he himself breaks his neck. Oh, the wonderful tragedies that sin works in the houses of the children of God! David, when he intermeddled with forbidden fruit, was driven from his palace, his concubines defiled, his own son slain; a great many calamities did light upon him. Therefore the children of God have cause to fear; for the Lord is a just God, and they will find it so.

THOMAS MANTON

Aids to victory:

If he cannot keep sin out, he will keep sin under.

THOMAS WATSON

When a man has judged himself, Satan is put out of office. When he lays anything to a saint's charge, he is able to retort and say, "It is true, Satan, I am guilty of these sins, but I have judged myself already for them; and having condemned myself in the lower court of conscience, God will acquit me in the upper court of heaven."

THOMAS WATSON

It is good to find out our sins, lest they find us out.

THOMAS WATSON

To provoke you to be the death of your darling sins. . . . consider, that the conquest and effectual mortifying of one bosom sin, will yield a Christian more glorious joy, comfort, and peace, than ever he hath found in the gratifying and committing of all other sins. The pleasure and sweetness that follows victory over sin is a thousand times beyond that seeming sweetness that is in the gratifying of sin.

THOMAS BROOKS

It is your duty and glory to do that every day that you would willingly do upon a dying day. Ah, how would you live and love upon a dying day? How would you admire God, rest upon God, delight in God, long for God, and walk with God, upon a dying day? How would you hate, loathe, and abhor your bosom sins upon a dying day?. . . . Thrice happy is that soul that labours with all his might to do that at first that he would give a thousand worlds to do on a dying day.

THOMAS BROOKS

To forsake sin, is to leave it without any thought reserved of returning to it again.

WILLIAM GURNALL

Beloved, it is a great thing to stand in near relations to God; and then it is a good thing to plead by them with God, forsomuch as nearer relations have strongest force with all. The servant can do more than a stranger, and the child than a servant, and the wife than a child.

OBADIAH SEDGWICK

Use sin as it will use you; spare it not, for it will not spare you; it is your murderer, and the murderer of the world: use it, therefore, as a murderer should be used. Kill it before it kills you; and though it bring you to the grave, as it did your Head, it shall not be able to keep you there.

RICHARD BAXTER

Observe, before pardon can be sealed, he must forsake not this sin, or that, but the whole law of sin. "*Let the wicked forsake his way.*" A traveller may step from one path to another, and still go on the same way, leave a dirty, deep, rugged path, for one more smooth and even; so many finding some gross sins uneasy, and too toilsome to their awakened consciences, step into a more cleanly path of civility; but alas! poor creatures, all they get is to

SIN

go a little more easily and cleanly to hell, than their beastly neighbours.

WILLIAM GURNALL

God's sovereign strategy:

Sin is worse than hell, but yet God, by His mighty over-ruling power, makes sin in the issue turn to the good of His people. Hence that golden saying of Augustine, "God would never permit evil, if He could not bring good out of evil."

THOMAS WATSON

God makes the saints' maladies their medicines.

THOMAS WATSON

God. . . . will not lightly or easily lose His people. He has provided well for us: blood to wash us in; a Priest to pray for us, that we may be made to persevere; and, in case we foully fall, an Advocate to plead our cause.

JOHN BUNYAN

Since God's strategy can overrule sin to our good, does it not lead to carelessness and unconcern on our part?

I do not say that sin works for good to an impenitent person. No, it works for his damnation, but it works for good to them that love God. . . . I know you will not draw a wrong conclusion from this, either to make light of sin, or to make bold with sin. . . . If any of God's people should be tampering with sin, because God can turn it to good; though the Lord does not damn them, He may send them to hell in this life. He may put them into such bitter agonies and soul-convulsions, as may fill them full of horror, and make them draw nigh to despair. Let this be a flaming sword to keep them from coming near the forbidden tree.

THOMAS WATSON

Because God maketh use of thy sins, art thou excused? Is not thine evil evil, because He picketh good out of it? Deceive not thyself therein. When thou hast done such service to thy Master and Maker, though seven and seven years, as Jacob did service to Laban, thou shalt lose thy wages and thy thanks also. . . . Babylon shall be the hammer of the Lord a long time to bruise the nations, himself afterwards bruised; Asshur His rod to scourge His people, but Asshur shall be more scourged. These hammers, rods, axes, saws, other instruments, when they have done their offices, which they never meant, shall be thrown themselves into the fire, and burnt to ashes. Satan did service to God, it cannot be denied, in the afflicting of Job, winnowing of Peter, buffeting of Paul, executing of Judas, and God did a work in all these either to prove patience, or to confirm faith, or to try strength, or to commend justice; yet is Satan "reserved in chains, under darkness, to the retribution of the great day." Judas did service to God, in getting honour to His blessed name for the redemption of mankind, whilst the world endureth, yet was his wages an alder-tree to hang himself upon, and, which is worse, he hangeth in hell for eternal generations. He had his wages, and lost his wages.

JOHN KING

SLANDER

David, upon sad experience, compareth a wicked, reviling tongue to three fatal weapons—a razor, a sword, and an arrow. To a razor, such a one as will take off every little hair: so a reviling tongue will not only take advantage of every gross sin committed by others, but those peccadilloes. . . . secondly, to a sword that wounds: so the tongues of reproaching men cut deeply into the credits and reputations of their brethren, but a sword doth mischief only near hand, not afar off; and, therefore, it is in the third place compared to an arrow, that can hit at a distance: and so revilers do not ill offices to those only in the parish or town where they live, but to others far remote. How much, then, doth it concern every man to walk circumspectly.

JEREMIAH BURROUGHS

SLANDER, SOLITUDE, SORROW

Should I retaliate?

In removal of it, it is best to deal with God about it; for God is the great witness of our sincerity, as knowing all things; and so to be appealed to in the case. Again, God is the most powerful asserter of our innocency; He has the hearts and tongues of men in His own hands, and can either prevent the slanderer from uttering reproach, or the hearer from the entertainment of the reproach. He that hath such power over the consciences of men can clear up our innocency; therefore it is best to deal with God about it; and prayer many times proves a better vindication than an apology.

THOMAS MANTON

The godly may sometimes be so overclouded with calumnies and reproaches as not to be able to find a way to clear themselves before men, but must content and comfort themselves with the testimony of a good conscience and with God's approbation of their integrity.

DAVID DICKSON

I will rather suffer a thousand wrongs, than offer one. . . . I will suffer many, ere I will complain of one, and endeavour to right it by contending. I have ever found, that to strive with my superior is furious; with my equal, doubtful; with my inferior sordid and base; with any, full of unquietness.

JOSEPH HALL

SOLITUDE

Solitude is a release to the soul that was imprisoned in company.

GEORGE SWINNOCK

SORROW

Sorrow commonly comes on horseback, but goes away on foot.

THOMAS ADAMS

The Christian perspective:

Ye have lost a child; nay, she is not lost to you, who is found in Christ; she is not sent away, but only sent before; like unto a star which, going out of sight, does not die and vanish, but shines in another hemisphere.

SAMUEL RUTHERFORD

Sorrows, because they are lingering guests, I will entertain but moderately, knowing that the more they are made of the longer they will continue: and for pleasures, because they stay not, and do but call to drink at my door, I will use them as passengers with slight respect. He is his own best friend that makes the least of both of them.

JOSEPH HALL

There are some things good but not pleasant, as sorrow and affliction. Sin is pleasant, but unprofitable; and sorrow is profitable, but unpleasant. As waters are purest when they are in motion, so saints are generally holiest when in affliction.

WILLIAM SECKER

SOUL, THE

Real although invisible:

I wonder whether these men believe that they breathe in summer as well as in winter. In summer they cannot see their own breath; but as cold grows on, it begins to appear. God's providence, and their own souls, are things of so subtle a nature that they cannot see them during the summer of their pleasures. But when the winter of judgement comes, this will show them a God in their just sufferings; and in that soul of theirs, which they would not believe they had, they shall feel an unspeakable torment. Then shall their pained sense supply the want of their faith.

THOMAS ADAMS

SOUL

Only satisfied in God:

The soul of man bears the image of God; so nothing can satisfy it but He whose image it bears. Our soul, says Augustine, was created as by God, so for God, and is therefore never quiet till it rest in God.

THOMAS GATAKER

The fulness of the earth can never satisfy the soul. All satisfaction and contentment arise from the conjunction of a convenient with a convenient; the conjunction of suitables. If a man have never so great an estate, if his heart be not suited to it, he hath no content. If a man have never so small an estate, if his heart be suited to it, he is content. What suitableness is there between the fulness of the earth and the better part of man, the soul! A thing is never said to be full till it be full of that for which it is made: a chest or trunk is not said to be full of air, though it be full of air. So take one of these meeting-houses; though the place be full of stools, or full of air, yet we say the church is empty; because though it be full, yet it is not full of that for which it is made, full of people.

So now, take a man that hath all the fulness of the earth; because that his soul was never made for the fulness of the earth, therefore he is said to be empty; in the midst of all his fulness, the man is an empty man, because his heart is not full of that for which he was made, and that is Christ.

WILLIAM BRIDGE

Its priority:

I do not approve the sullenness of that soul which wrongs the body; but I worse like to have the body wrong the soul. . . . If the painted popinjay, that so dotes on her own beauty, had an eye to see how her soul is used, she would think her practice more ill-favoured and unhandsome than perfuming a putrefied coffin, or putting mud into a glass of crystal. For shame, let us put the soul foremost again, and not set heaven lowest and earth uppermost.

THOMAS ADAMS

SOUL

If the soul be lost, the man is lost.

JOHN FLAVEL

The real value of an object is that which one who knows its worth will give for it. He who made the soul, knew its worth, and gave His life for it.

ARTHUR JACKSON

Its immortality?

That it hath much use of or dependence on the body in its present operations is no proof at all that when it is out of the body it cannot otherwise act or operate.

If the candle shine in the lantern, it can shine out of it, though with some difference. . . . Though the egg would die if the shell were broken, or the hen did not sit upon it, it doth not follow that therefore the chicken cannot live without a shell, or sitting on. . . . And when there is full proof that souls have a future life to live, it is folly to doubt of it, merely because we cannot conceive of the manner of their acting without a body.

RICHARD BAXTER

When the Spaniards came first among the poor Indians, they thought the horse and his rider to be one creature, as many ignorant ones think the soul and body of man to be nothing but breath and body. Whereas indeed they are two distinct creatures, as vastly different in their natures as the rider and his horse, or the bird and his cage. While the man is on horseback he moves according to the motion of the horse; and while the bird is encaged, he eats and drinks, and sleeps, and hops and sings in his cage. But if the horse fail and die under his rider, or the cage be broken, the man can go on his own feet, and the bird enjoy itself as well, yea, better, in the open fields and woods than in the cage; neither depend, as to being or action, on the horse or cage.

JOHN FLAVEL

SUFFERING

A vocation?

We are called servants, to shew how we should obey, Luke 12:38; and we are called soldiers, to shew how we should suffer, 2 Timothy 2:3.

HENRY SMITH

Christians should not be to learn their duties, when they should be doing them; nor doing them, when they should be *suffering* for them.

VAVASOR POWELL

It is, and should be the care of a Christian, not to suffer for sin, nor sin in suffering.

VAVASOR POWELL

Sufferings are but as little chips of the cross.

JOSEPH CHURCH

Resultant glory:

Look, as our greatest good comes through the sufferings of Christ, so God's greatest glory that He hath from His saints comes through their sufferings.

THOMAS BROOKS

The Gospel gets really more advantage by the holy, humble sufferings of one saint, simply for the Word of righteousness, than by ten thousand arguments used against heretics and false worship.

JOHN COLLINS

Shortest cut to heaven.

VAVASOR POWELL

Saints should fear every sin, but no sufferings.

VAVASOR POWELL

288

SUFFERING, SUICIDE, TEMPTATION

Of sinners and saints:

There is as much difference between the sufferings of the saints and those of the ungodly as there is between the cords with which an executioner pinions a condemned malefactor and the bandages wherewith a tender surgeon binds his patient.

JOHN ARROWSMITH

SUICIDE

No man must let the tenant out of the tenement, till God the landlord call for it.

THOMAS ADAMS

He that would not die when he must, and he that would die when he must not, are both of them cowards alike.

GEORGE SWINNOCK

As we cannot live without a *permittis*, so we must not die without a *dimittis*.

THOMAS ADAMS

TEMPTATION

Satan's strategies:

Satan tempts to sin under a pretence of religion. He is most to be feared when he transforms himself into an angel of light. He came to Christ with Scripture in his mouth: "It is written." The devil baits his hook with religion. He tempts many a man to covetousness and extortion under a pretence of providing for his family; he tempts some to do away with themselves, that they may live no longer to sin against God; and so he draws them into sin, under a pretence of avoiding sin.

THOMAS WATSON

TEMPTATION

When Satan assaults any poor soul, he suffers nothing to appear to the eye but pleasure, profit, a sweet satisfaction of our desires, and a phantasma of happiness. There is also wrath, and judgement, and torment, and sting of conscience belonging to it! These must be, but these shall not be seen. All the way is white snow, that hides the pit. Green grass tempts us to walk; the serpent is unseen. If temptations, like plaises, might be turned on both sides, the kingdom of darkness would not be so populous. If David could have foreseen the grief of his broken bones ere he fell upon Bathsheba, those aspersions of blood and lust had not befallen him. If Achan could have foreseen the stones about his ears before he filched those accursed things, he would never have fingered them. But as it is said of Adam and Eve after their fall, "Then their eyes were opened;" then, not before. Judas was blind till he had done the deed, then his eyes were opened, and he saw it in its true horror.

THOMAS ADAMS

If thou dost not stumble at this stone, the devil hath another at hand to throw in the way. He is not so unskilful a fowler as to go with one single shot into the field; and therefore expect him, as soon as he hath discharged one, and missed thee, to let fly at thee with a second.

WILLIAM GURNALL

Satan, like a fisher, baits his hook according to the appetite of the fish.

THOMAS ADAMS

Satan would seem to be mannerly and reasonable; making as if he would be content with one-half of the heart, whereas God challengeth all or none: as, indeed, He hath most reason to claim all that made all. But this is nothing but a crafty fetch of Satan; for he knows that if he have any part, God will have none: so the whole falleth to his share alone.

JOSEPH HALL

If you yield to Satan in the least, he will carry you further and further, till he has left you under a stupefied or terrified conscience: stupefied, till thou hast lost all thy tenderness. A stone at the top of a hill, when it begins to roll down, ceases not till it comes to the bottom. Thou thinkest it is but yielding a little, and so by degrees are carried on, till thou hast sinned away all thy profession, and all principles of conscience, by the secret witchery of his temptations.

THOMAS MANTON

N.B.:

We must also pray that the Lord give not out that measure of leave to the devil which we give out to sin.... but that He would rather make Satan a surgeon to show us our sins than a sergeant to confound us for them.

RICHARD GREENHAM

Satan's timing:

Satan's time of tempting is usually after an ordinance; and the reason is, because then he thinks he shall find us most secure.

When we have been at solemn duties, we are apt to think all is done, and we grow remiss, and leave off that zeal and strictness as before; just as a soldier, who after a battle leaves off his armour, not once dreaming of an enemy. Satan watches his time, and when we least suspect, then he throws in a temptation.

THOMAS WATSON

Satan's ally within:

We may have leaders into temptation, but it is our fault if we follow them. Nay, to come closer home, do not we tempt ourselves? Satan is not the sole cause of evil. The fowler sets his glass, spreads his net, whistles like the bird; yet cannot all this make the fowl come into his net whether she will or no. If we had not pliable ears and flexible affections, the syrans might sing in vain.

THOMAS ADAMS

TEMPTATION

Satan can never undo a man without himself; but a man may easily undo himself without Satan.

THOMAS BROOKS

There is a secret disposition in the heart of all, to all sin. . . . Mark! 'Tis Satan *tempts*, but our own lust *draws us*.

WILLIAM GURNALL

Temptations and occasions put nothing into a man, but only draw out what was in him before.

JOHN OWEN

There is no way to kill a man's righteousness but by his own consent.

JOHN BUNYAN

To want temptations is the greatest temptation of all.

SAMUEL RUTHERFORD

How to foil the tempter:

Our great Pattern hath showed us what our deportment ought to be in all suggestions and temptations. When the devil showed Him "all the kingdoms of the world and the glory of them," to tempt Him withal, He did not stand and look upon them, viewing their glory, and pondering their empire. . . . but instantly, without stay, He cries, "Get thee hence, Satan." Meet thy temptation in its entrance with thoughts of faith concerning Christ on the cross; this will make it sink before thee. Entertain no parley, no dispute with it, if thou wouldst not enter into it.

JOHN OWEN

If thou hast fallen into sin through violent temptations, seek speedily for repentance for it, recovery out of it, and reformation from it.

VAVASOR POWELL

TEMPTATION

He does not say, Watch and pray, that you be not tempted; but "Watch and pray, that ye *enter* not into temptation." It is one thing for temptation to knock at the door, and another thing to come in, when temptation enters you, you enter into temptation: take heed of that.

WILLIAM BRIDGE

The Christian's safety lies in resisting. All the armour here provided is to defend the Christian fighting, none to secure him flying.

WILLIAM GURNALL

Satan gives Adam an apple, and takes away Paradise. Therefore in all temptations let us consider not what he offers, but what we shall lose.

RICHARD SIBBES

Think of the *guilt of sin*, that you may be humbled. Think of the *power of sin*, that you may seek strength against it. Think not of the *matter of sin.* . . . lest you be more and more entangled.

JOHN OWEN

Temptations, when we meet them at first, are as the lion that reared upon Samson; but if we overcome them, the next time we see them we shall find a nest of honey within them.

JOHN BUNYAN

The way to avoid temptation is not always to apply a salve directly pertinent to the temptation; but turn off your mind and your thoughts to some other good object, and by that time your mind is settled upon other objects, you will be easily able to meet with the temptation.

WILLIAM BRIDGE

In time of war, when the great cannon fly off, the only way to avoid them is to lie down in a furrow, and so the bullets fly over. So in all temptations of Satan lie low, and be contented to be at God's disposing, and all these fiery temptations shall not be able to hurt you.

ISAAC AMBROSE

TEMPTATION

I would counsel every Christian to answer all temptations with this short saying, "The Lord is my portion.". . . . O, sir, if Satan should come to thee with an apple, as once he did to Eve, tell him that "the Lord is your portion"; or with a grape, as once he did to Noah, tell him that "the Lord is your portion"; or with a change of raiment, as once he did to Gehazi, tell him that "the Lord is your portion"; or with a wedge of gold, as once he did to Achan, tell him that "the Lord is your portion"; or with a bag of money, as once he did to Judas, tell him that "the Lord is your portion"; or with a crown, a kingdom, as once he did to Moses, tell him that "the Lord is your portion."

THOMAS BROOKS

There can be no victory where there is no combat. The victory lieth not upon us but upon Christ, who hath taken upon Him, as to conquer for us, so to conquer in us. Let us not look so much who are our enemies, as who is our Judge and Captain; not what they threaten, but what He promiseth.

RICHARD SIBBES

The cause why our oppressors prevail oft against us is, because we trust too much in our own wits, and lean too much upon our own inventions; opposing subtility to subtility, one evil device to another, matching and maintaining policy by policy, and not committing our cause to God.

ABRAHAM WRIGHT

Why the saints are the devil's special targets?

The devil desires to winnow Peter, not Judas. The more faithful servants of God we be, the more doth Satan bruise us with the flail, or grate us with the fan. The thief does not break into an empty cottage, but into some furnished house or full granary, where the fatness of the booty is a fitness to his desires. The unclean spirit finds no rest in an atheist, usurer, drunkard, swearer, etc. He knows a canker has overrun their consciences already; and that they are as sure as temptation can make them. . . . What need he tempt them that tempt themselves?

THOMAS ADAMS

294

TEMPTATION

Satan doth not tempt God's children because they have sin in them, but because they have grace in them. Had they no grace, the devil would not disturb them. . . . Though to be tempted is a trouble, yet to think why you are tempted is a comfort.

THOMAS WATSON

If God were not my friend, Satan would not be so much my enemy.

THOMAS BROOKS

Why God allows His people to be tempted?

God sometimes permits Satan to assail His dear children, the more to strengthen them in His spiritual graces, and to confirm them more fully in the assurance of His love and their salvation.

For as a city which has been once besieged and not sacked will ever after be more strong to hold out if it be assaulted by the like danger. . . . so those who are besieged and assaulted by their spiritual enemies will ever after more carefully arm themselves against them with the graces of God's Spirit, that they may not be overcome nor foiled by them.

GEORGE DOWNAME

The devil tempts, that he may deceive; but God suffers us to be tempted, to try us. Temptation is a trial of our sincerity.

THOMAS WATSON

Temptations are rather hopeful evidences that thy estate is good, that thou art dear to God, and that it shall go well with thee for ever, than otherwise. God had but one Son without corruption, but He had none without temptation.

THOMAS BROOKS

None can better discover Satan's sleights and policies, than those who have been long in the fencing-school of temptation.

THOMAS WATSON

Reading maketh a full man, prayer a holy man, temptation an experienced man.

JOHN TRAPP

Since temptation can be beneficial to the saint, will it not produce carelessness and unconcern?

There is a great deal of difference between falling into a temptation, and running into a temptation. The falling into a temptation shall work for good, not the running into it.

He that falls into a river is capable of help and pity, but he that desperately turns into it is guilty of his own death.

THOMAS WATSON

Temptation is like a knife, that may either cut the meat or the throat of a man; it may be his food or poison.

JOHN OWEN

TONGUE, THE

We know metals by their tinkling, and men by their talking.

THOMAS BROOKS

He may not be accounted an honest man of life that is an evil man in tongue.

NICHOLAS BYFIELD

An unbridled tongue is the chariot of the devil, wherein he rides in triumph. . . . The course of an unruly tongue is to proceed from evil to worse, to begin with foolishness, and go on with bitterness, and to end in mischief and madness (Ecclesiastes 10:13). The Jew's conference with our Saviour began with arguments: "We be Abraham's seed," saith they, etc.; but proceded to blasphemies: "Say we not well that thou art a Samaritan, and hast a devil?"

EDWARD REYNER

Some care not what they say in their passion; they will censure, slander, and wish evil to others. How can Christ be in the heart, when the devil has taken possession of the tongue?.... Passion disturbs reason, it is *brevis insania*, a short frenzy.... Let them whose tongues are set on fire, take heed that they do not one day in hell desire a drop of water to cool them.

THOMAS WATSON

TRINITY, THE

"Baptizing them in the name of the Father, of the Son, and of the Holy Ghost." The Father, Son, and Holy Ghost: there are three distinct persons: in the Name, not names; there is one essence.

THOMAS ADAMS

Known by faith:

The Trinity is purely an object of faith, the plumbline of reason is too short to fathom this mystery; but where reason cannot wade, there faith must swim.... This sacred doctrine, though it be not against reason, yet it is above reason.

THOMAS WATSON

As to the point of Divine *subsistence, Jehovah Elohim*, Father, Son, and Holy Ghost: three persons, but one God; or in Lee's expression—*one God without division in a Trinity of persons, and three persons without confusion in an unity of essence*—it is a discovery altogether supernatural.

JOHN ARROWSMITH

It is rashness to search, godliness to believe, safeness to preach, and eternal blessedness to know the Trinity.

THOMAS ADAMS

A mystery which my faith embraces as revealed in the Word, but my reason cannot fathom.

JOHN ARROWSMITH

TRINITY

An allegory helps:

Like as the sun in the firmament hath three distinct and sundry things, of which every one differeth from the other—as the globe, the light, and the heat; and although every one of these keep severally their properties, yet it is but one sun, and is not divided into three suns: so, in the Deity, the unity of essence is not taken away by the distinction of persons, and yet for all that there is no confounding of persons or changing of one into another. For as there is but one sun in and through the whole world, no more is there but one God. And as the sun showeth himself by his beams; even so God, as Father, doth show Himself by His Son Jesus Christ, who is His Word and eternal wisdom. And as the sun by his heat doth make us feel his force; even so God maketh us feel His virtue by His Holy Spirit, which is His infinite power.

DANIEL CAWDRAY

The ultimate failure of allegory:

Of the similitudes usually brought for its illustration that which Hilary said is most true. "They may gratify the understanding of man, but none of them exactly suit with the nature of God." For example. . . . that of a crystal ball held in a river on a sunshiny day, in which case there would be a sun in the firmament, begetting another sun upon the crystal ball, and a third sun proceeding from both the former, appearing in the surface of the water, yet but one sun in all; for in this comparison two of the suns are but imaginary, none real save that in heaven; whereas the Father, Word, and Spirit are distinct persons indeed, but each of them truly and really God.

JOHN ARROWSMITH

TRUTH

Sublimely immutable:

Such is the immutability of truth, the patrons of it make it not greater, the opposers make it not less; as the splendour of the sun is not enlarged by them that bless it, nor eclipsed by them that hate it.

THOMAS ADAMS

Should (we) think ourselves obliged to throw away gold or diamonds, because an impure hand has touched them, or to deny Christ, because the devils confessed Him?

JOHN HOWE

N.B.:

News may come that Truth is sick, but never that it is dead.

WILLIAM GURNALL

Fellow-traveler of godliness:

The apostle joins the spirit of power and a sound mind together (2 Timothy 1:7).

Holiness in practice depends much on a sound judgement. Godliness is the child of truth, and it must be nursed by its own mother. "Desire the sincere milk of the Word, that ye may grow thereby."

WILLIAM GURNALL

When men have orthodox judgements and heterodox hearts, there must needs be little love to truth.

WILLIAM GURNALL

Truth reforms as well as informs.

WILLIAM JENKYN

TRUTH

Our vindicator:

If I speak what is false, I must answer for it; if truth, it will answer for me.

THOMAS FULLER

How is it found?

We stand at better advantage to find truth, and keep it also, when devoutly praying for it, than fiercely wrangling and contending about it. Disputes roil the soul, and raise the dust of passion; prayer sweetly composeth the mind, and lays the passions which disputes draw forth; for I am sure a man may see further in a still clear day, than in a windy and cloudy.

WILLIAM GURNALL

The demands of truth?

Truth must be spoken however it be taken.

JOHN TRAPP

There is a due in a penny, as well as in a pound; therefore we must be faithful in the least truth, when season calleth for it.

RICHARD SIBBES

Truth seldom goes without a scratched face.

JOHN TRAPP

Serve Christ; back Him; let His cause be your cause; give not an hairbreadth of truth away, for it is not yours but God's.

SAMUEL RUTHERFORD

How communicated?

Some truths are wholly revealed and have no footsteps in the creatures, no prints in the creation, or in the works of God, to discern them by; and such are all the mysteries of the Gospel and of the Trinity. Other truths there are that have some *vestigia*, some characters stamped upon the creature, whereby we may discern them, and such is this. . . . that there is a God.

JOHN PRESTON

New truths?

Pray, friends, why should we be afraid of new lights? For why should there not be new lights found out in the firmament of the Scripture, as well as the astrologers find out new stars in heaven? Be not afraid to set open your windows, for any light that God shall make known unto you.

WILLIAM BRIDGE

Take no truths upon trust, but all upon trial—see 1 Thessalonians 5:21, 1 John 4:1, Acts 17:11, etc. It was the glory of that church, that they would not trust Paul himself—Paul, that had the advantage above all for external qualifications—no, not Paul himself. Take no truth upon trust; bring them to the balance of the sanctuary.

THOMAS BROOKS

N.B.:

God hath but three things dear unto Him in this world, His saints, His worship, and His truth; and it is hard to say which of these is dearest unto Him.

THOMAS GOODWIN

UNBELIEF

Greatest sin of all?

For no sin whereof men can be guilty in this world is of so horrible a nature, and so dreadful an aspect, as is this unbelief, where a clear view of it is obtained in evangelical light.

JOHN OWEN

Unbelief is the shield of every sin.

WILLIAM JENKYN

UNBELIEF, UNITY

It is common for men to make doubts when they have the mind to desert the truth.

SAMUEL RUTHERFORD

Its damning power:

Generally, it is taken for granted by all that Christ is able to save us if He will; yea, who shall question His ability to save us, though we live in sin and unbelief? And many expect that He will do so because they believe He can if He will. But indeed Christ hath no such power, no such ability: He cannot save unbelieving, impenitent sinners; for this cannot be done without denying Himself, acting contrary to His Word and destroying His own glory. . . . Christ is able to save all those, and only those, who come to God by Him. While you live in sin and unbelief, Christ Himself cannot save you.

JOHN OWEN

What faith can do to a prophecy of judgement, the same can unbelief to a promise of mercy; overthrow it.

JOSEPH CARYL

UNITY

When?

I do verily believe that when God shall accomplish it (unity), it will be the effect of love, and not the cause of love. It will proceed from love, before it brings forth love.

JOHN OWEN

But never shall all the saints unite, and come to one in love, till wrath be poured forth on all their forms and flesh. Then the Spirit shall come from on high, and gather up all the saints and men in God.

WILLIAM ERBERY

302

How?

And if ever we intend to take one step towards any agreement or unity, it must be by fixing this principle in the minds of all men—that it is of no advantage to any man whatever church or way in Christian religion he be of, unless he personally believe the promises, and live in obedience unto all the precepts of Christ; and that for him who doth so, it is a trampling of the whole Gospel under foot to say that his salvation could be endangered by his not being of this or that church or way, especially considering how much of the world hath immixed itself into all the known ways that are in it. Were this once well fixed on the minds of men, and did they practically believe that men shall not be dealt withal at the last day *by gross*, as of this or that party or church, but that every *individual* must stand upon his own bottom, *live by his own faith, or perish for want of it.*... we should quickly find their keenness in promoting and contending for their several parties taken off.

JOHN OWEN

Articles or rules for doctrine or practice in matters of religion to be imposed upon men, should be as few as may be; there is very great danger in the unnecessary multiplying them. This in all ages has caused division and exceeding disturbances in the churches of Christ.

JEREMIAH BURROUGHS

Ah, were their souls fully assured that God had loved them freely, and received them graciously, and justified them perfectly, and pardoned them absolutely, and would glorify them everlastingly, they could not but love where God loves, and own where God owns, and embrace where God embraces, and be one with every one that is one with Jesus.

THOMAS BROOKS

When I have communion with a saint, I must not look so much whether he be of such an opinion, or whether he have taken the covenant, or to have been baptized once or twice or ten times, but see if he have fellowship with the Father, and with Jesus Christ.

WALTER CRADOCK

UNITY

Why?

Labour mightily for a healing spirit. Away with all discriminating names whatever that may hinder the applying of balm to heal your wounds. . . . Discord and division become no Christian. For wolves to worry the lambs is no wonder, but for one lamb to worry another, this is unnatural and monstrous.

THOMAS BROOKS

Take away union and there can be no communion.

JOHN FLAVEL

What cannot warrant a breach where there is union, that cannot warrantably be the ground to keep up a division.

JAMES DURHAM

There may and ought to be uniting when the evils that follow division or schism, are greater and more hurtful to the church than the evils that may be supposed to follow on union.

JAMES DURHAM

There is but one God, and they that serve Him should be one. There is nothing that would render the true religion more lovely, or make more proselytes to it, than to see the professors of it tied together with the heart-strings of love.

THOMAS WATSON

N.B.:

Unity without verity is no better than conspiracy.

JOHN TRAPP

UNIVERSE, THE

Life on other planets?

I know it is a thing uncertain and unrevealed to us, whether all these globes be inhabited or not. But he that considereth, that there is scarce any uninhabitable place on earth, or in the water, or air; but men, or beasts, or birds, or fishes, or flies, or worms, and moles, do take up almost all; will think it a probability so near a certainty as not to be much doubted of, that the vaster and more glorious parts of the creation are not uninhabited; but that they have inhabitants answerable to their magnitude and glory.

RICHARD BAXTER

WAR

Sin, Satan and war have all one name; evil is the best of them. The best of sin is deformity, of Satan enmity, of war misery.

JOHN TRAPP

War makes both less meat and fewer mouths.

THOMAS FULLER

The noise of wars drowns the voice of laws.

JOHN TRAPP

In war, none are permitted to err twice.

JOHN TRAPP

305

WATCHFULNESS

Its necessity:

The Christian soldier must avoid two evils—he must not faint or yield in the time of fight, and after a victory he must not wax insolent and secure. When he has overcome, he is so to behave himself as though he were presently again to be assaulted. For Satan's temptations, like the waves of the sea, do follow one in the neck of the other.

GEORGE DOWNAME

When the soul puts her danger furthest off, and lies most secure, then 'tis nearest; therefore labour to be constant in thy holy care—the want of this spoils all. Some you shall have, that after a great fall into a sin that hath bruised them sorely, will seem very careful for a time where they set their foot, how they walk, and what company they come in, but as soon as the soreness of their consciences wears off, their watch breaks up, and they are as careless as ever; like one that is very careful to shut up his shop strongly, and maybe sit up late to watch it also, for two or three nights after it hath been robbed, but then minds it no more.

WILLIAM GURNALL

N.B.:

The Christian's work is too curious to be done well between sleeping and waking, and too important to be done ill, and slubbered over, no matter how.

WILLIAM GURNALL

Special precautions:

Set a strong guard about thy outward senses: these are Satan's landing places, especially the eye and the ear.

WILLIAM GURNALL

Be as careful, Christian, after extraordinary prayer, as a man would be after taking strong physic; a little disorder in thy walking may be of sad consequence.

WILLIAM GURNALL

Satan tempts after some discoveries of God's love. As a pirate sets on a ship that is richly laden, so when a soul hath been laden with spiritual comforts the devil will be shooting at him, to rob him of all. The devil envies to see a soul feasted with spiritual joy.

THOMAS WATSON

WICKED, THE

Their success - transitory:

No marvel if the worldling escape earthly afflictions. God corrects him not. He is base born and begot. God will not do him the favour to whip him. The world afflicts him not, because it loves him: for each man is indulgent to his own. God uses not the rod where He means to use the Word. The pillory or scourge is for those malefactors that shall escape execution.

JOSEPH HALL

They have the earth in their hands (Job 9:24), who have nothing of heaven in their hearts; they bear sway in the world who are slaves to the world; they govern and order others at their will who are led captive by Satan at his will. Be not offended and troubled to see the reins of government in their hands who know not how to govern themselves, or to see them rule the world who are unworthy to live in the world.

JOSEPH CARYL

When a soldier was to die for taking a bunch of grapes against the general's command, and going to execution he went eating his grapes, one of his fellows rebuked him, saying; "What! Are you eating your grapes now?" The poor man answers, "I

WICKED

prithee, friend, do not envy me these grapes, for they do cost me dear;" so they did indeed, for they cost him his life. Thus, let no man envy the prosperity of the wicked, nor fret at the men of this world who live in pleasure and wallow in the sensual delights of this life; they know no better, they seek after no better things. There is little cause why any man should grudge what they have, for they must give a sad account of what they have received, and pay dear at the last—even without God's preventing mercy—the loss of their immortal souls to all eternity.

JEREMIAH BURROUGHS

You think Providence does not deal righteously because the unworthy are exalted, and the worthy depressed. Do but tarry awhile, and you will have no cause to complain, or to grow weary of godliness, or to cry up a confederacy with evil men; they are never nearer their own ruin than when they come to the height of their exaltation. . . . Who would envy those that climb up a ladder for execution?

THOMAS MANTON

Their joy - illusory:

Many sinners who seem so jocund in our eyes, have not such merry lives as you think for. A book may be fairly bound and gilded, yet have but sad stories writ within it. Sinners will not tell us all the secret rebukes that conscience from the Word gives them. If you will judge of Herod by the jollity of his feast, you may think he wanted no joy; but at another time we see that John's ghost walked in his conscience: and so doth the Word haunt many a one, who to us appear to lay nothing to heart; in the midst of their laughter their heart is sad; you see the lightning in their face, but hear not the thunder that rumbles in their conscience.

WILLIAM GURNALL

In all their jollity in this world, they are but as a book fairly bound, which when it is opened is full of nothing but tragedies. So when the book of their consciences shall be once opened, there is nothing to be read but lamentations and woes.

RICHARD SIBBES

Their punishment - compounded:

An unbeliever shall have a double condemnation; one from the law which he hath transgressed, and another from the gospel, which he hath despised: as a malefactor, that being condemned and dead in law, rejecteth his prince's pardon. But it is otherwise with these that are in Christ Jesus. The law cannot condemn them, because they have appealed; the gospel cannot because they have believed.

JOHN TRAPP

N.B.:

It is no miracle if he that lives like a beast dies like a beast.

FRANCIS CHEYNELL

WILL, THE

Man's will:

In the state of innocence the will was the weakest, but in regeneration God has made it the firmest and best. God has provided that the hedge should be stronger where it was broken.

JOHN COTTON

God's will:

As to the will of God, it falls under a twofold consideration of His secret and revealed will. The distinction is found in that Scripture: "The secret things belong unto the Lord our God: but these things which are revealed belong unto us" (Deuteronomy 29:29). The first is the rule of His own actions: the latter of ours.

JOHN FLAVEL

This revealed will of God is either manifested to us in His Word, or in His works. The former is His *commanding* will, the latter His *affecting* or *permitting* will.

JOHN FLAVEL

WITNESS

The saints are to bear a threefold testimony to, and for Christ and His truths: Breath-testimony, Life-testimony, and Blood-testimony.

VAVASOR POWELL

One eye-witness is better than ten ear-witnesses.

THOMAS ADAMS

The upright soul is constant in his profession, and changes not his behaviour according to his companions. Oh, that I might never through shame or fear disown Him who has already acknowledged me!

GEORGE SWINNOCK

WORLD, THE

Pleasure, profit, preferment are the worldling's trinity.

JOHN TRAPP

A sea of glass, a pageant of fond delights, a theatre of variety, a labyrinth of error, a gulf of grief, a sty of filthiness, a vale of misery, a state of deceit, a cage full of owls, a den of scorpions, a wilderness of wolves, a cabin of bears, a whirlwind of passions, a feigned comedy, a detestable frenzy.

ARTHUR DENT

No fulfillment:

Let us not foolishly imagine that our minds can be satisfied and filled with worldly vanities, nor greedily affect and seek after a greater measure, when we are not satisfied with a less, supposing that the access of quantity may bring contentment; seeing the hunger which we feel in our hearts proceeds not from want of earthly abundance, but because it is unnatural nourishment for the mind of man, so that it can no more satisfy our souls' hunger, than it can satisfy our bodies to feed upon the wind.

GEORGE DOWNAME

Men that are in the valley think, if they were at the top of such a hill, they should touch the heavens. Men that are in the bottom of poverty, or disgrace, or pain, think if they could get up to such a mountain, such a measure of riches, and honours, and delights, they could reach happiness. Now Solomon had got to the top of this hill, and seeing so many scrambling and labouring so hard, nay, riding on one another's necks, and pressing one another to death to get foremost, doth seem thus to bespeak them: "Sirs, ye are all deceived in your expectations! I see the pains ye take to get up to this place, thinking that when you come hither, ye shall touch the heavens, and reach happiness: but I am before you at the top of the hill—I have treasures, and honours, and pleasures in variety and abundance (Ecclesiastes 2:11-12), and I find the hill full of quagmires instead of delights, and so far from giving me satisfaction, that it causeth much vexation; therefore be advised to spare your pains, and spend your strength for that which will turn to more profit; for, believe it, you do but work at the labour in vain." "Vanity of vanities, all is vanity," saith the Preacher.

GEORGE SWINNOCK

A godly man preferreth grace before goods, and wisdom before the world.

RICHARD BERNARD

(Pleasures) Prisoners' pittance, which neither keeps alive nor suffers to die.

JOHN TRAPP

WORLD

When the race is ended, and the play is either won or lost, and ye are in the utmost circle and border of time, and shall put your foot within the march of eternity, all the good things of your short nightdream shall seem to you like ashes of a blaze of thorns or straw.

SAMUEL RUTHERFORD

The world is therefore a purgatory, that it might not be our paradise.

GEORGE SWINNOCK

The Christian and the carnal man are most wonderful to each other. The one wonders to see the other walk so strictly, and deny himself to those carnal liberties that the most take. . . . And the Christian thinks it strange that men should be so bewitched, and still remain children in the vanity of their turmoil, wearying and humouring themselves from morning to night, running after stories and fancies, and ever busy doing nothing; wonders that the delights of earth and sin can so long entertain and please men, and persuade them to give Jesus Christ so many refusals—to turn from their life and happiness, and choose to be miserable, yea, and take much pains to make themselves miserable.

ROBERT LEIGHTON

Satiated they were, but not satisfied.

JOHN TRAPP

No permanency:

We do not hold worldly things during our life, nor as long as we shall behave ourselves well in our places; but only as long as God pleases.

THOMAS MANTON

Outward things happen alike to good and bad. "There is one event to the clean and to the unclean." They are both travellers in the thoroughfare of this world, both lodge in one inn, both have the same provision; perhaps the wicked have the better cheer—but in the morning their ways part!

THOMAS ADAMS

WORLD

I cannot but look upon all the glory and dignity of this world, lands and lordships, crowns and kingdoms, even as on some brain-sick, beggarly fellow, that borrows fine clothes, and plays the part of a king or lord for an hour on a stage, and then comes down, and the sport is ended, and they are beggars again.

RICHARD BAXTER

He gives often more of the world to those that shall have no more hereafter.

ROBERT LEIGHTON

Pleasures come like oxen, slow and heavily, and go away like post-horses, upon the spur.

JOSEPH HALL

Its misuse:

Thorns will not prick of themselves, but when they are grasped in a man's hand they prick deep. So this world and the things thereof are all good, and were all made of God for the benefit of His creatures, did not our immoderate affection make them hurtful.

RICHARD SIBBES

All the danger is when the world gets into the heart. The water is useful for the sailing of the ship; all the danger is when the water gets into the ship; so the fear is when the world gets into the heart. "Thou shalt not covet."

THOMAS WATSON

Let us use worldly things as wise pilgrims do their staves and other necessaries convenient for their journey. So long as they help us forward in our way, let us make use of them, and accordingly esteem them. But if they become troublesome hindrances and cumbersome burdens, let us leave them behind us, or cast them away.

GEORGE DOWNAME

313

WORLD

Some are not made better by God's gifts; yea, many are made worse. Give Saul a kingdom, and he will tyrannize; give Nabal good cheer, and he will be drunk; give Judas an apostleship, and he will sell his Master for money.

THOMAS ADAMS

Temporal good things are not the Christian's freight, but his ballast, and therefore are to be desired to poise, not load the vessel.

WILLIAM GURNALL

Let us use the world, but enjoy the Lord.

THOMAS ADAMS

Seek not great things for yourselves in this world, for if your garments be too long, they will make you stumble; and one staff helps a man in his journey, when many in his hands at once hinders him.

WILLIAM BRIDGE

Little do they think that worldliness is a most guiltful sin in respect of God, and most hurtful in respect of men. Hark what the Word of God saith of it (Ephesians 5:5)—it is *idolatry*, and idolatry is the first sin of the first table.

RICHARD CAPEL

N.B.:

Times are bad, God is good.

RICHARD SIBBES

The true fortune of the saints:

The Gospel mentions not riches, honours, beauty, pleasures; it passes these over in silence, which yet the Old Testament everywhere makes promise of. They were then children, and God pleased them with the promise of these toys and rattles, as taking with them. But in the Gospel He has shown us He has provided some better things for us; things spiritual and heavenly.

THOMAS GOODWIN

314

WORSHIP

Asleep in church:

Take heed of drowsiness in hearing; drowsiness shows much irreverance. How lively are many when they are about the world, but in the worship of God how drowsy. . . . In the preaching of the Word, is not the bread of life broken to you; and will a man fall asleep at his food? Which is worse, to stay from a sermon, or sleep at a sermon?

THOMAS WATSON

I deny not but that a child of God may sometimes through weakness and indisposition of body drop asleep at a sermon, but it is not voluntary or ordinary. The sun may be in an eclipse, but not often; if sleeping be customary and allowed, it is a very bad sign and a profaning of the ordinance. A good remedy against drowsiness is to use a spare diet upon this day. Such as indulge their appetite too much on a Sabbath, are fitter to sleep on a couch than pray in the temple.

THOMAS WATSON

Thou must be an attentive hearer; he that is awake, but wanders with his eye or heart, what doth he but sleep with his eyes open?

WILLIAM GURNALL

Hear and. . . .

Be not only attentive in hearing, but retentive after hearing.

THOMAS WATSON

Many come to the Word only to feast their ears; they like the melody of the voice, the mellifluous sweetness of the expression, the newness of the notion (Acts 17:21). This is to love the garnishing of the dish more than the food; this is to desire to be pleased rather than edified. Like a woman that paints her face, but neglects her health.

THOMAS WATSON

315

WORSHIP

Even when the Christian through weakness of memory cannot remember the very words he hears, to repeat them; yet then he keeps the power and savour of them in his spirit, as when sugar is dissolved in wine, you cannot see it, but you may taste it. . . . so you may taste the truths the Christian heard, in his spirit, see them in his life.

WILLIAM GURNALL

The man in the pulpit?

Let not Satan persuade us to think the worse of the pure Word of God because of his corruption who delivers it. For what were this but to refuse a comfortable embassage from a gracious prince, because we dislike the qualities of the ambassadors?. . . . Yea, what is it but to cross our Saviour Christ's express commandment, who commanded all to hear even the Scribes and Pharisees who sat on Moses' chair, and to do after their words though not after their works?

GEORGE DOWNAME

The faithful hearer accuses not his minister for particularizing him. It does not follow that he aimed, because the arrow hit. Rather, our parishioner reasons thus: "If my sin be notorious, how could the minister miss it? If secret, how could he hit without God's direction?"

THOMAS FULLER

External posture?

If He be "our Lord", let us do Him reverence. It hath ever been the manner and posture of God's servants, when either they offer anything to Him (Matthew 2:11) or pray to receive anything from Him (Psalm 96:6), to do it on their knees. When the king gives us a pardon for our life, forfeited to the law, we receive it on our knees. When he bestows favour or honour, be it but a knighthood, men kneel for it. In that holy place, where men receive the forgiveness of sins, the honour of saints, so gracious a pardon, so glorious a blessing, there be some that refuse so humble a gesture to the Lord Himself. Never tell me of a humble heart, where I see a stubborn knee.

THOMAS ADAMS

God is Lord of my body also: and therefore challengeth as well reverent gesture as inward devotion. I will ever, in my prayers, either stand, as a servant, before my Master; or kneel, as a subject, to my Prince.

JOSEPH HALL

Posture in worship is too often imposture.

THOMAS WATSON

Internal requisites:

It is a poor worship to move our hats, not our hearts.

THOMAS ADAMS

You think you serve God by coming to church; but if you refuse to let the Word convert you, how should God be pleased with such a service as this?.... Every time you hear, or pray, or praise God, or receive the sacrament, while you deny God in your heart and remain unconverted, you do but despise Him, and show more of your rebellion than your obedience. . . . God biddeth you come to church and hear the Word, and so far you do well; but withal, He chargeth you to suffer the Word to work upon your hearts, and to take it home and consider it, and obey it.

RICHARD BAXTER

We may be truly said to worship God, though we want perfection; but we cannot be said to worship Him if we want sincerity.

STEPHEN CHARNOCK

In public worship all should join. The little strings go to make up a concert, as well as the great.

THOMAS GOODWIN

All in the church may hear the Word of Christ, but few hear Christ in the Word.

GEORGE SWINNOCK

N.B.:

Attention of body, intention of mind, and retention of memory, are indispensably desired of all wisdom's scholars.

JOHN TRAPP

INDEX OF AUTHORS

INDEX OF AUTHORS